Symbolic
and Mythological
Animals

This book is due for return on or before the last date shown
above; it may, subject to the book not being reserved by
another reader, be renewed by personal application, post, or
telephone, quoting this date and details of the book.

Symbolic and Mythological Animals

J. C. Cooper

Aquarian/Thorsons

An Imprint of HarperCollins*Publishers*

The Aquarian Press
An Imprint of HarperCollins*Publishers*
77–85 Fulham Palace Road,
Hammersmith, London W6 8JB

Published by The Aquarian Press 1992
3 5 7 9 10 8 6 4 2

© J. C. Cooper 1992

J. C. Cooper asserts the moral right to
be identified as the author of this work

A catalogue record for this book
is available from the British Library

ISBN 1 85538 118 4

Typeset by Harper Phototypesetters Limited
Northampton, England
Printed in Great Britain by
Mackays of Chatham, Kent

For Ben and Sally Milton

But ask now the Beasts
And they shall teach thee;
And the Fowls of the air,
And they shall teach thee;
Or speak to the Earth,
And it shall teach thee.
Job 12: 7–8

Contents

Introduction

The word 'animal' is derived from the Latin *anima*, breath, the state of possessing life or spirit and the power of movement, the quality which is possessed by, and binds together, all animate creatures, whether human or non-human. It is this unity which plays so important a part in animal mythology and symbolism. In fact it is basic, for early civilizations made little distinction between the species: what signified for the one also held for the other; the essential qualities of all were their powers of adapting to their environment and their ability to develop faculties for survival. Humans and 'animals' faced the same world, lived in close proximity and observed every movement made by each other as hunters or hunted, or as domesticated 'workers', first by pastoral tribes and later by agricultural communities. Human and animal strength and strategy had to be pitted against each other, and close bonds existed between them. Thus, in myth and folklore there is no sharp distinction made between the different branches of the animal kingdom.

The same unity is seen in the great folkloric or religious traditions. The Bible says: 'The sons of men might see that they themselves are beasts. For that which befalleth the sons of men befalleth the beasts . . . as the one dieth so the other dieth; yea they have all one breath; so that man hath no preference above a beast' (Ecclesiastes 3: 19). The Jaina, most caring of all religions, say that 'all breathing, existing, living, sentient creatures should not be slain nor treated with violence, nor abused, nor tortured, nor driven away. This is the pure and unchangeable law . . . Indifferent to worldly objects, a man should wander about treating all creatures in the world as he himself would be treated.' The notoriously callous treatment of animals among some Arabs is in direct opposition to the statement of the Prophet that 'there are rewards from benefiting every animal', and the Qu'ran which says 'there is no beast on earth nor bird which flieth with its wings but the same is a people like unto you . . . then unto their Lord they shall return.' For Pythagoreans 'the spirit wanders, comes now here now there, and occupies whatsoever frame it pleases. From beasts it passes into human bodies and from our bodies into beasts, but never perishes', while Plotinus, Porphyry and others maintained that the animal-soul must be the same as the soul of man, since the soul essence could not be different.

Celsus opposed the idea that reason was an exclusively human faculty and objected even more strongly to the notion that the universe was created for man rather than other animals. He said that only absurd pride could engender such a supposition; in this he merely confirmed the beliefs of other earlier intellectuals such as Aristotle and Cicero – Men, he said, catch and devour animals, animals catch and devour men, therefore which was created for which? Who, looking down from heaven would see the difference between men building cities and the buildings of bees and ants? Things were not created in the interest of something else but to form a harmonious whole, and, on the other side of the world, the Algonquins say: 'In the beginning of things men were animals and animals men.' They also believe in the exchange of souls from one form to the other and in the tradition, which occurs world-wide, of descent from animals.

Also appearing universally are animal deities, or those with both human and animal features; these go back to pre-history as depicted in the cave drawings and in shamanistic cultures, and gods often manifested in the forms of animals to descend to earth. It is suggested, and widely accepted, that animals were first venerated in their own rights. What Anne Ross writes of the Celts is appropriate to other traditions – that divine animals began their cult history as prized and venerated, but that later the zoomorphic gradually changed to the anthropomorphic until the latter predominated and 'finally the humanized god stands clear of the animal . . . but linked with it in cult and legend and having it as his specific and most typical attribute.' Or, as Joseph Campbell said of the early hunting people – 'the great human problem was to become linked psychologically to the task of sharing the wilderness with these beings. An unconscious identification took place and this was finally rendered conscious in the half-human, half-animal figures of the mythological totem-ancestors. The animals became the tutors of humanity.'

The animal-helper-guide theme runs through myth, legend and fairy tale, but emerges from the mythological into ordinary life in symbolism, in the power of companionship and co-operation, in codes of conduct and compassion for their own kind – and often for humanity also – from which humans could not only learn practically but could also rediscover lost powers and values of the instinctual and intuitive side of nature which have been lost by the distorted, over-rational and analytical mind. Talking animals also symbolize and express feelings and values suppressed by humans.

Animals conform to the laws of nature, they do not attempt to alter, bend or 'conquer' her – that folly is left to humanity – hence the fact that the myths and legends of all tribal people in close touch with nature, such as the Amerindians, Australian Aboriginals, Bushmen and Ainu, predominantly involve animals. The cult of animals was at its height in hunting and nomadic societies and declined with agriculture, though the spirits of vegetation were often represented in animal form.

Much of animal symbolism and mythology not only stresses the similarities shared by the entire animal kingdom, but also exposes the vulnerability and limitations of the human branch, which, although it may regard itself as dominant, cannot claim overall supremacy. It has been pointed out that in a world-Olympiad the human competitor would not win a single event but be surpassed by other animals in speed, strength, vision and endurance, also that animals display an instinctual knowledge and sixth sense either lost or not yet understood by humanity.

Another recurring theme is the triumph of the weak over the strong and the victory of nimble mind over physical prowess, the latter symbolized by the Trickster cycles and the former by such fables as that of Panopus, the great hunter of lions and leopards, being killed by a scorpion, the lowest and meanest of creatures, or the mighty lion caught in a net being liberated by the humble mouse.

It was in the Orient, as E. P. Evans points out, 'that mystical and symbolical zoology, as the natural outgrowth of the doctrine of metempsychosis, attained its most exuberant development. The monsters of Indian, Assyrian, Egyptian and archaic Greek art, sphinxes, minotaurs, human-headed bulls, lion-headed kings, horse-headed goddesses and sparrow-headed gods, are all plastic embodiments of this metaphysical tenet.' Later, much of this symbolism passed into early Christianity from the Graeco-Judaic schools of Alexandria and with contact with Greek and Middle Eastern cultures, though it shed the tenet of metempsychosis. Early Christians, such as Basil the Great and his brother Gregory of Nyesa, developed an elaborate symbolism of animals and used their characteristics and attributes as a source of moral and theological instruction, giving a mystical interpretation to all natural objects. These teachings were also enshrined and made visible in art and architecture.

The 11th and 12th centuries saw the height of animal symbolism in ecclesiastical art. Almost every utensil, ornament, embroidered vestment, architectural work and piece of furniture was decorated with some symbolic animal, real or fictitious: lions, pelicans, ostriches, cranes, dolphins and doves were depicted together with unicorns, griffins and dragons. They also ran riot in monastic cloisters. There were protests from such as Bernard of Clairvaux, who asked: 'What business have those ridiculous monstrosities, those creatures of wonderfully deformed beauty and beautiful deformity, before the eyes of studious friars, in the courts of cloisters? What mean those filthy apes, those fierce lions, those monstrous centaurs, those half-men, those spotted tigers? . . .' He objected to the coarseness of much of the symbolism and recognized its pagan ancestry. But, it must be remembered, there was a large, totally illiterate population which depended on these visible symbols for its religious instruction. The symbols are also valuable records of the beliefs and imagination of their age, for as St Bernard himself said, 'pictures are the books of the laity and unlearned'.

The symbol has a power of its own to release meanings and evoke both intellectual and emotional responses; it is also a means of integrating the conscious and unconscious, the rational and the intuitive. There is, today, a realization of the need for this balance; the purely rationalistic age has passed and the instinctual is being rediscovered through the revived interest in and understanding of symbols and myths. People in the West have been living on the dry bread of the material and are now looking for the vitalizing wine of the psyche, the spirit. Also, in an almost totally urbanized society contact is lost with nature, and as symbolism and myth are concerned essentially with nature they help to redress the imbalance and reconcile the opposites. Hence, too, the importance of animals in symbolism and myth, since they comprise so large a proportion of nature and are closely linked with all her other manifestations. They provide a union of the higher and lower elements, of heaven and earth, the sacred and the profane. Again, in this symbolism old forms are adapted to new conditions and beliefs, places and deities, as witness the Christian use of the old myths of the *Physiologus* and the early Bestiaries.

Myths are always explanatory, they are the basis of understanding the relationship between people and their natural environment, they reflect the local conditions, climate, celestial phenomena, seasonal variations, the birth-death-rebirth experience and the need for humanity to establish a working relationship with these experiences – but, as Robert Graves said: 'myths are seldom simple and never irresponsible'. The same may be said of symbols. Both, paradoxically, conceal and reveal deeper meaning.

Note: Cross references in this book are denoted in **Bold**.

A

Aardvark. One of the vessels of supernatural power, or *Ntum*, among the Kung Bushmen in Africa. As a burrowing animal it is in touch with underworld powers.

Acanthis. According to Aristotle, Pliny and Aelian, this is a bird which feeds on thistles when they are young and tender and is thus the enemy of the ass. It has been identified as the modern-day goldfinch or linnet.

Adder. In the Old Testament the 'adder' is used to cover four Hebrew names for serpents.
See **Serpent**

Ahuizol. A Mexican dog-monkey. Its long tail had a hand at its end which was used to catch men; it preyed on human eyes, teeth and nails.

Albatross. Said to brood its eggs on a floating raft and to sleep on the wing without movement. To kill one brings a curse on the killer. It is a sacred bird among the Ainu of Japan, who consider it the servant of the Chief God of the Sea and a lucky omen. Its head is worshipped by the sick, and the beak and skull, powdered and taken in hot water, provides a powerful medicine. The head is kept as a fetish against disease.

Alerion. An heraldic bird represented as an eagle 'displayed', but without beak or claws.

Alligator. A North Amerindian cult animal; appears on blackstone carvings on the north-west Coast and is the totem animal of a clan of the Cree Indians.

Amarok. A giant wolf of the Innuits (Eskimos).
See **Wolf**

Ammut or Am-mit. An ancient Egyptian underworld female monster, Eater of the Dead, who ate the hearts of those who failed to pass the test when weighed on the scales of the Judgement Hall of Osiris. She has the head of a crocodile, body of a lion and hippopotamus hindquarters.

Amphisbena or Amphivena. According to Pliny this is a serpent with two heads, the second at the end of its tail so that it 'hunteth both ways'.

Amulets. Parts of animals are frequently used as amulets, and as such confer the qualities of those animals. For example, the claw of a lion gives protection; part of an elephant, strength; a gazelle agility and so on. All amulets are apotropaic.

Anaconda. Called *Jacumama*, 'The Mother of the Waters' or 'The Water Mistress' by the Americans of Maynae; said to attract victims by its breath; it is born of the Sun and is Sister to the Moon. In Amazonian regions the anaconda represents the most powerful of reptiles (the **eagle** being the most powerful bird and the **jaguar** most powerful animal). In South America it is 'The Father of Witchcraft', greatly feared as a demon, and a large one must not even be touched for fear of transmitting the evil force, though a small one can be used in various ways, especially the skin. By using the skin the anaconda can be controlled magically, otherwise it is the embodiment of evil. Images of snakes as amulets are apotropaic.

Anka. An Arctic mythical bird of great size, being able to carry off an elephant as a cat carries a mouse. It lived 1700 years and had the phoenix's quality of burning and renewing itself. Muhammad is reported to have said that God created the Anka at the time of Moses, but the original two multiplied to such an extent that they devoured all the wild beasts and then carried off children so that the people complained to Khaled, who invoked God, who prevented them from multiplying so that they became extinct. The bird appears to be associated with the **Roc** and the Persian **Simurgh**.

Ant. A universal symbol of industry, thrift, providence and forethought, and, in the Old Testament, also of wisdom – 'Go to the ant thou sluggard; consider her ways and be wise' (Proverbs 6: 6); 'There be four things which are little upon the earth, but they are exceeding wise: the ants are a people not strong, yet they provide their meat in the summer . . .' (Proverbs 30: 24–5).

In Chinese lore the ant is 'the righteous insect' and represents orderliness, patriotism, virtue and subordination to authority, but the god Wang-ta Hsien is invoked against white ants and any insect that damages the rice crops.

Hinduism uses the ant as an example of the transience of existence. Hindus and Jainas feed ants on certain occasions associated with the dead. In Zoroastrianism the ant belongs to Ahriman as 'devouring beasts', the enemy of the agriculturist.

Homer says that ants show solicitude for their comrades, alive or dead, and that they exhibit ingenuity; they were worshipped in Thessaly and the Myrmidons were said to be descended from ants. Strabo recorded a myth that the Myrmidons were ants transformed into men after a plague had depopulated the whole island. In the Harranian mysteries, ants, dogs and ravens were the brothers of man.

Amerindian shamanism represents the ant as patience. It is a planner like the **Squirrel**, a builder like the **Beaver**, aggressive like the **Badger**, with the stamina of the **Elk**, the scrutinizing ability of the **Mouse** and the generous sacrificing nature of the **Turkey**. It developed its narrow waist through self-denial in order to provide food for the people who had to go underground during the world's cataclysms. Quetzalcoatl, the Central American God of the Elements and a Culture god, turned himself into an ant to steal the maize, which the ants had hidden in a mountain, to give to man. The Pima tribe of south Arizona is divided into two moieties, Red Ants and White Ants. There is also a tribe of Black Ants.

In Benin, in West Africa, ants act as messengers of the Serpent God; for the Ibo of Nigeria the white ant, or termite, is a ju-ju (or charm) which can be invoked to destroy the property of anyone whom one seeks to injure.

In Bear mythology bears eat ants to cure themselves of sickness.

Huge ants are guardians of treasures in Chinese, Persian, Indian and Greek legend. In Greek myth ants are an attribute of Ceres.

In some countries of Europe ants are lucky, in other places unlucky, for instance in Scotland and Bulgaria they are a bad omen, in Estonia good.

The *Ant Lion* is a fabulous creature with the forefront of a lion and the hinder part of an ant. Its father eats flesh but its mother eats grain. In the Bestiaries, as a thing of two natures the ant is said to be symbolic of 'every double-minded man, unstable in all his ways'.

Antalops. According to the *Book of Beasts* this is 'an animal of incomparable celerity, so much so that no hunter can get near it. It has long horns shaped like a saw and can cut down trees. It drinks at the Euphrates.' It goes on to say that on the river bank there is a fragrant shrub which it eats but gets its horns entangled within so that it cannot free itself; it then cries out in a loud voice and the hunter, hearing this, hastens to kill it. The Bestiary says the two horns are the Old and New Testaments, with which the faithful can cut down all growing sins and vices, but he must not allow himself to be drawn aside from the waters of salvation by the pleasures of the world and get entangled in the thickets of lust, pride and evil passions, or he falls a prey to the Devil. Depicting this scene was a favourite theme for mediaeval artists.

Heraldic Antelope

Antelope. In Sumerian and Semitic mythology the antelope is a
form of Ea and Marduk and Ea-Oannes is 'the antelope of Apsu',
'the antelope of creation', while the lunar antelope is sacred to
Astarte. In ancient Egypt it was sacred to Isis and could also
represent Osiris and Horus, as opposed to Set, to whom the
antelope, as a desert animal, was sacrificed. Throughout Asia Minor
it was a lunar animal associated with the Great Mother. In Hinduism
it is an emblem of Siva, and Soma and Chandra have chariots drawn
by antelopes.

Strabo describes the animal as between a stag or a ram but as
swifter than either; in Roman art the antelope is depicted as the prey
of lions, leopards and dogs; it is an animal of the hunt.

For the North Amerindians it is one of the totem animals of the
Plains Indians of the Comanche tribe. The Hopi have a Snake-
Antelope ceremony which takes place yearly in the Big Feast Moon.
Ritual visits are made by each society to the other. Two Snake
Maidens are greeted by two Antelope Youths, who hold an antelope

fetish and a snake. There is a mystic marriage in which the antelope is associated with the highest centre of consciousness at the crown of the head. The antelope is the Awakener, Summoner, and Life-bearer, and the marriage has a solar-lunar symbolism in the awakening of the life energies. Antelopes running simulate thunder and the rain-bearing clouds; they are also a fertility symbol.

Found frequently in Heraldry as a supporter, the heraldic antelope is a fictitious animal having the body of a stag, tail of a unicorn and head of an heraldic tiger with two serrated horns and a tusk on the tip of its nose; there are tufts on the back of its neck and on the thighs and tail. It symbolizes 'fierce and fall', strength and dangerousness.

Among African tribes the antelope is a significant animal, as it alone knows the dwelling place of the god who can take its shape. For the Bushmen the divinity can appear in the form of an antelope.

Ape. The ancient Egyptians venerated the ape, the baboon, as sacred to Thoth, God of Wisdom, and Hapi, God of the Nile. Thoth can be depicted either as the **Ibis** or the **Baboon**, which is often dog-headed; he invented numbers, time and writing, and is sometimes portrayed as an ape when he appears in the Judgement Hall of Osiris. Four apes sit by the Lake of Fire near the throne of Osiris, and the judgement and appeal is made to them by the soul of the deceased as it passes through to the Kingdom of Osiris. The soul must satisfy the apes and the 42 assessors before it can pass through.

The ape is depicted on ancient Assyrian monuments, and is mentioned in the Old Testament in I Kings 16: 22; it was traded from Tharshish for Solomon, though the 'ape' is probably a generic term applied to the whole monkey tribe.

In Hinduism the ape, or **Monkey**, represents benevolence and gentleness and is the emblem of the Monkey God Hanuman.

The four apes who sit by the Lake of Fire near the throne of Osiris.

Aesop uses the ape as a symbol of foolish maternal love, fondling her young so much that they are crushed to death. Pliny and Aelian also quote this excessive attention.

Early Christianity held the ape to represent the Devil, paganism, heresy, lust, vice, uncleanliness, malice, cunning and slavish imitation – hence to 'ape': in this context the ape is used in art and literature to satirize and parody humanity.

In mediaeval times, in symbolizing the Four Elements and Humours the ape was associated with Blood, the Sanguine and Air, with the Lamb, Lion and Pig the other animals, associated with melancholy, choler and phlegm respectively.

Heraldry depicts the ape usually 'collared and chained', with the chain round its loins.

See also **Monkey**

Apis. See **Bull**

Apocalyptic Animals. Animals appearing in the Apocalypse are:

The Tetramorphs: the Lion, Ox, Man, and Eagle surrounding the throne of Christ and later depicted as symbols of the Four Evangelists: Mark, the Lion, representing the dignity of Christ; Luke, the Winged Ox or the Calf, signifying sacrifice; Matthew, Man, representing the Priesthood of Christ; John, the Eagle, symbolizing the Ascension and divine nature of Christ (Revelations 4: 2–8).

The Lamb with seven horns and seven eyes depicts the Spirits of God (Rev. 5: 6–14). The Four Horsemen: the White Horse, the Conqueror; Red Horse, War; Black Horse, Famine; the Sickly Pale Horse, Death, together represent divine wrath and retribution (Rev. 6: 1–8).

Horses with lions' heads and serpent-headed tails (Rev. 9: 13–19).

A dragon with seven heads, to signify the seven deadly sins (Rev. 12: 1–6)

The beast with ten horns and seven heads, symbolizing the Roman emperors and rulers (Rev. 13: 1–10)

The beast with the horns of a Lamb, representing paganism (Rev.13: 11–20)

The white horse and rider, depicting Christ as warrior and eagerness (Rev. 6: 2). The Beast which rose out of the sea had seven heads; and the Beast which came out of the earth had two horns like a lamb.

Apop. See **Serpent**

Areop-enap. A Spider Creator-God of the South Pacific, who made the earth and the sky. See **Spider**.

Argonaut.   Or the Paper-nautilus, a sea-creature who uses its shell as a boat and its six arms as oars, with two special arms for sails.

Argus.   The 100-eyed monster, his eyes were used by Juno/Hera to decorate the peacock's tail after Hermes/Mercury had slain him to liberate Io. The eyes slept two at a time, symbolizing eternal or jealous watchfulness.

Armadillo. Among South American Indians the Armadillo represents women, and women eat its meat at the Festival of the Dead, while the **Ostrich** represents men. There is an Armadillo tribe, and its medicine-man can take the form of the animal to communicate with the spirit world. The armadillo also represents boundaries and the shield that protects humanity from all that is undesirable.

Asp or Aspis.   The name appears to have been used for more than one species of snake. The Bestiaries say that when the asp hears the music of the snake-charmer it presses one ear to the ground and puts its tail into the other, thus symbolizing the man who is deaf to the voice of the Lord, a symbolism also ascribed to the adder.

In Christianity it represents evil and venom, but in ancient Egypt it depicted solar power, royalty and dominion, while in Greece it was a protective and benevolent power.

See also **Serpent**

Aspares. Beautiful Hindu water-nymphs having the power of transformation into water-fowl; they have been associated with the Gandharvas and with warriors who fell in battle.

Ass.   The ass as depicted on ancient Egyptian and Assyrian monuments is not the humble donkey which Apuleius calls 'the most ill-starred of quadrupeds, pitiful and miserable', but the wild ass, the onager, a much larger animal and more ancient than the horse described in Semitic symbolism and rites. It was treated like a horse, drawing the heavy chariots of the Sumerians and used for the baggage-trains of their armies. The Egyptians were using these animals to draw war chariots and other wheeled vehicles in about 3000 BC; they were also used as the pack animals of transport for the poorer peoples and nomads. As a desert animal the ass was associated with Set, to whom it was sacrificed, and in later Egyptian times Set was personified by a donkey. The wild ass of the desert also symbolized desolation, wariness, speed, and solitude.

Pliny and Xenophon say that the ass was eaten by the Greeks but was a forbidden food for the Harranians. For the Greeks it represented the typhonic aspect, sloth and infatuation; it was sacred to Dionysos and Priapus as the procreative, and Typhon was depicted with the head of an ass; it was also sacred to Cronos/Saturn and Silenus is sometimes portrayed riding on an ass. At the Roman Vestalia, which was a holiday for millers, bakers and their animals, donkeys were garlanded and decorated with cakes.

The Chinese Taoist Immortal Chang Kwo-lao, a bringer of children, rides on a magical donkey which could be converted into paper and folded up and put away when not in use.

In Hindu mythology asses drew the chariot of Ravana when he abducted Sita; it is thus an inauspicious animal for Hindus except at Holi. In Buddhism the ass is a symbol of the ascetic, an example of simplicity, sleeping by the roadside on a bed of leaves.

The Three-legged Ass of Zoroastrianism is often equated with the **Unicorn**; it has three feet, six eyes, nine mouths, two ears and one horn of gold, which 'will vanquish and dissipate all the vile corruption due to the effect of noxious creatures'. Its body is white and is a symbol of purity and it is a champion of the oppressed. (*Bandahis* XIX).

In the East the ass is noted for its strength, courage and intelligence; the Western donkey being a degenerate animal. Plutarch says that the ass was revered by Jews because it found springs of water in the desert during the Exodus. The biblical wild ass is the Onager and is symbolic of wildness and desolation. It is first mentioned in the Old Testament in Genesis 12: 16. The domesticated ass was used for grinding corn, turning mill-stones and ploughing, but there was a prohibition against asses and oxen being yoked together for ploughing (Deuteronomy 22: 10). Ass's milk was used and the animal was ridden by people of rank and wealth, the white ass being particularly esteemed. The Romans believed that the Jews worshipped the ass and, later, early Christians were accused of worshipping it. Tertullian stated this and said that there were caricatures of 'the ass-hoofed God of the Christians' which also had ass's ears.

Epiphanius says that the Gnostics held that the Lord of Sabaoth had an ass's head. In mediaeval times there was a Feast of Asses at the Festival of Fools after Christmas, on January 14, in which sacred subjects were caricatured, and Baalam's Ass and the Flight into Egypt were burlesqued. The ass, or donkey, also symbolizes Christ's entry into Jerusalem. In the Bestiaries and later Christianity it represents the Devil as it 'brays about day and night seeking its prey'.

Muslims hold it as an accursed creature. It prays for misfortune for its owner and its bray is full of ill-omen.

In general symbolism the ass or donkey portrays stupidity, stubbornness, inferiority, lewdness, fertility; it is supposed to be deaf to music. An ass in a lion's skin depicts a blustering coward, or a fool pretending to be wise. The ass is one of the most frequent forms used in symbolic satire.

Attitude. The attitude or position in which an animal is portrayed conveys a definite symbolism, for example *rampant* depicts combat, energy, power, while *couchant* implies power at rest but vigilant. A deity standing on an animal is a frequent feature in Sumerian, Syrian and Hittite religions, and represents affinity with and power over the animal.

Auroch or Urus. Extinct in 1627, the auroch appeared in most of Europe, south-west and central Asia and north-east Africa. It was hunted in Egypt and Assyria. It was the largest and most powerful hoofed animal except for the **Elephant** and **Hippopotamus**. It is mentioned in the Old Testament in Numbers 23: 22 and Job 39: 10, and is suggested as having been the Re'em or Unicorn. Julius Caesar described it as smaller than an elephant and resembling a bull and as very swift and strong. Pliny also mentions its strength and speed.

Axolotl. The Aztec 'Servant of the Waters', it was an aspect and symbol of the god Zolotl who went through many other transformations in order to avoid death.

B

Baboon. Thoth, the Egyptian God of Wisdom who founded the arts and sciences and invented hieroglyphics, later identified with Hermes/Mercury by the Greeks, was depicted as a baboon, baboon-headed, or as a dog-headed baboon. He was also portrayed as an **Ibis**. As a baboon he greets the rising sun; as an ibis he sails over the sky.

See also **Ape**

Badger. An old myth said that the badger shows its age by the number of holes in its tail, one being added each year. It was also called *Bawsin*.

In China it is a lunar, *yin* animal full of mischief and playfulness and typifies the supernatural powers which it possesses. These qualities are carried over, in an even greater degree, to Japanese myth and legend in which the badger, together with the **Fox** and **Cat**, is involved in endless trickery and shape-shifting – a typical **Trickster**. He is a great illusionist, and one of his favourite tricks is to appear as a sage or holy man to induce people to revere him. Japanese jesters are sometimes called Badgers and as such figures of badgers are shown playing a tattoo on the stomach. Like the fox, the badger is also a 'rice spirit' and the wind-badger Tanuki is responsible for providing the growth of the rice crops.

Among the Hopi Northern Amerindians the Badger Clan is one of the four most important and the animal symbolizes the North. There are Grey, Brown and Black Badger clans.

For the Zuni the badger is stout of heart but not strong of will; it is the younger brother of the **Bear** and is guardian and master of the South, but is replaced by the wild cat in hunting rites. It also symbolizes aggressiveness, quick anger and attack and is a Keeper of the Medicine Roots.

In Europe it represents clumsiness and is also a weather prophet.

Baku. A Japanese fabulous creature, the Eater of Dreams. It has the face of a lion, body of a horse, tail of a cow and feet of a tiger. It is invoked to devour evil dreams and render them harmless, or to change them into good fortune when appealed to with the words 'Devour O Baku'.

Bandicoot. This small marsupial is the totem animal of an Australian Aboriginal clan; it emerged from the body of Karora the ancestor, as he slept underground, leaving a large hole filled with the juice of honeysuckle buds. The hole became a soak. The Bandicoot is said to steal vegetables from gardens and farms and represents extreme business.

Bantam. Symbolizes pluck, priggishness, standing up for one's self and taking on someone larger and stronger.

Barbary Lamb. A composite lamb-like creature, half-animal, half-vegetable, which hung from a tree, its tail end enclosed in foliage.

Bar Juchne. A fabulous bird of immense size whose extended wings eclipsed the sun. The Talmud says that one of her eggs once fell out of the nest and broke 300 cedars and inundated 60 villages. The bird is similar to the Arabian **Roc**, Persian **Simurgh** and the Indian **Garuda**.

Barnacle Goose. There are various myths accounting for the origins of Barnacle Geese, but all maintained that the birds laid no eggs and were hatched from barnacles. Geraldus Cambrensis said he 'had seen it with his own eyes'. One tradition said that they grew on trees which were always at the edge of the sea, thus they were also called Tree Geese, and were said to hatch from large fruit-like formations hanging from the branches, drop into the sea and swim away; if they dropped on land they died. Another account says that they were bred from the fungus of old ships' timbers and developed into shells, then barnacles, then geese. These myths are extremely ancient though they do not appear in Graeco-Roman lore but are confined mostly to Northern Europe. The birds, being like fish, may be eaten in Lent.

In the Bestiaries the barnacle geese grow on trees by the sea, hanging from the boughs until they grow their feathers, then they fall like ripe fruit and swim away. This symbolizes the doctrine of the Immaculate Conception, that is, being born without procreation.

Basilisk/Cockatrice. The Basilisk or Cockatrice is an old name often applied to the **Serpent** – originally distinct the basilisk and serpent later became indistinguishable, as is the case in the Old Testament (Jeremiah 8: 17). It is a symbol of evil and treachery. It is the King of the Small Serpents (the Dragon being King of the Larger Serpents). Pliny places it in Africa and says that its power of evil is such that it 'splits rocks' and that 'all other serpents flee from and are afraid of it'. It is a creature of extreme malignity, feared by

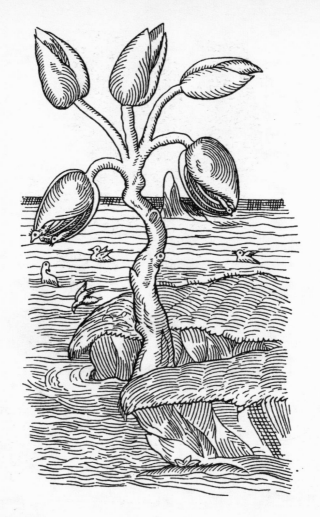

The Tree-geese

all. It can kill by the smell of its breath, by a glance from its eyes
or the touch of its tail, and its hiss burns people up; it also produces
hydrophobia and sends people mad. It frequents desert places, like
the scorpion, its eyes are yellow and toad-like and it is depicted as
having the head and claws of a cock and body of a serpent. It can
only be killed by a **Weasel** (it is suggested that this may refer to the
mongoose, the enemy of the snake) or by a **Cock**, or by seeing its
reflection on looking through crystal. Travellers in the regions where
it was found carried a cock for protection.

The Basilisk and Cockatrice were prominent in mediaeval lore and
symbolism, especially in devotional art and architecture. The
creature had an excrescence on its head resembling a crown. It was

A Cockatrice

hatched from an egg laid by a cock, in the seventh year of its life, when Sirius was in the ascendant. The egg causes to each cock intense discomfort in the bowels, is laid on dung or in some warm place and is hatched by a toad or serpent. Albertus Magnus says: 'I do not think this is true; yet it is reported as a fact by Hermes and accepted by many persons.'

Christianity used the Basilisk/Cockatrice as a symbol of the Devil who entered Paradise to seduce the first parents. It is a beautiful creature in form and colour, but beauty is often associated with evil. It also represents the Antichrist.

Bat. The bat has an ambivalent symbolism and mythology, being unlucky and unclean in some traditions and lucky and an acceptable food in others. Large bats were eaten in Assyria and Africa and were preserved in salt, but in the Old Testament bats – 'fowls that creep, going on all fours' (Leviticus 11: 19) – are unclean and an abomination (Leviticus 11 and Deuteronomy 14) and depict impurity and idolatory. The *Book of Baruch* says that they sat on the heads of Babylonian idols (6: 22). Bats' heads were used as charms in Egypt and hung in dovecotes to prevent the pigeons leaving it.

As a creature of night and dark places bats are symbolic of

desolation and desecration in many parts, but in China, though being a nocturnal and *yin* animal, its name is a homophone of happiness, *fu*, and thus becomes happiness and good luck. A pair of bats is the emblem of Shou-Hsing, God of Longevity, and indicates good wishes, while a group of five bats represents the five blessings of health, wealth, long life, happiness and peace; but in Buddhism the bat is a symbol of darkened understanding, while in Japan it is a state of unhappy restlessness and chaos.

The bat is important in Amerindian lore, and represents rebirth in the shamanistic ritual death at initiation as it emerges from the cave-womb of Mother Earth. It is also a rain-bringer. The Ruler of the Bats is a variegated bat-God among the Kiches of Guatemala, at enmity with the hero-gods Hun-Ahpu and Xbalanqua. Among southern tribes it is significant as having fangs like the Jaguar but also flying like a bird and nursing its young like a human.

A sacred bat figures in Australian Aboriginal myth in Queensland and it is the totem animal of a tribe, but it is a bringer of ill-luck for the Maoris of New Zealand.

In several parts of Africa bats are sacred as the abode of souls of the dead, while in other places they can represent perspicacity but also darkness and obscurity.

Ainu myth says that the bat did not come down from heaven with the other animals but was made by God in this world; it is a bird, being wise and brave, and makes war on the demons of disease.

In folklore bats are supposed to drive away locusts, so a bat hung up on a tree can ward them off. A bat buried at crossroads, with incense burnt over it, is a love spell.

Western lore associates the bat with vampires, witches, graveyards and death, and Christianity calls it 'the bird of the Devil' and the incarnation of the Prince of Darkness; Satan is depicted with bats' wings. It was supposed to be a hybrid of bird and rat and as such depicted duplicity and hypocrisy; it also represented melancholy as it haunts ruins and lonely places. It is associated with witchcraft and black magic, cunning and revenge. On the other hand, in the Bestiaries the *Vespertilio*, symbolizing evening, is a paltry animal but represents affection as groups of them hang close together.

Bear.   The bear is one of the oldest if not the oldest of the verifiable sacred animals; evidence of the Bear Cult exists from earliest times. Neanderthal man had sacred shrines and altars of the Master Bear and bear skulls and bones were ritually interned with human skulls. Ancient shamanistic cults covering a wide area from the North American Indians to Iceland, Finland, Siberia and Japan depicted the bear as a sacred animal; it was an Animal Master and instructed shamans. The Innuit (Eskimo) shaman is in touch with the Great Spirit, manifested in the Polar Bear. Bear gods are often hunter-gods,

working through the shaman, who often wears a bear skin. In the
Grisley Bear Dance, at the coming of spring, the she-bear
symbolizes maternal love and renewal of life as she emerges from
her winter hibernation with her already-born cubs. There were 'Bear
Madonnas' in rituals in which a woman wearing a bear mask holds
a cub. Male bears were sacrificed as a Vegetation Spirit for the spring
renewal of life.

Among Amerindians the Black Bear is a Guardian of the West,
'stout of heart and strong of will'; it is replaced by the Coyote in
hunting rituals. Bears are messengers of the Forest Spirit; they also
represent supernatural power, strength, fortitude and the
whirlwind. As associated with honey the bear also stands for the
sweetness of truth. The Bear Clan is the most important of the clans
of the Hopi Indians – Bear, Parrot, Eagle and Badger, which also
represent the four cardinal directions, the bear being the West. For
the North-west Coast Indians a Great Heavenly Bear keeps watch
and depicts the warrior spirit. It is the totem animal of the
Ouataouaks and is sacrificed and ritually eaten. The bear is expected
to accept being sacrificed as an honour and is invited to his own
feast, as with the Ainus of Japan. But the Cherokee portray the bear
as a buffoon who tries to behave like humans in going on two feet
but fails through clumsiness. The Cree tribe invoke the Bear Spirit
to obtain longevity and the Bear Sacrifice is an important Delaware
festival; there are bear tribes in California and among the Hurons,
the Iroquoians and the Ute of Colorado; the Shuswop of British
Columbia have a Bear Dance. The Innuit, when they kill for food,
propitiate the slain animals by returning the unusable parts to the
element from which they came, for example seals to the sea and
bears' heads left with the head pointing inland to the mountains,
to which they will return to become another bear. But the Great
White Bear of the Algonquins is a dweller in the evil underworld.

All Siberian shamanistic cultures, together with the Ainus, regard
the bear as their mythical ancestor and it is therefore considered
superior to man in many ways. It is closely associated with worship
of the dead and is generally looked upon as a person incarnate rather
than an animal. This also applies in the Amerindian, Finnish, Tartar
and Ugarian tribes, while the Samoyeds of the Ket River are also
descended from bears. For the Ainus it is the 'King of the Forest',
the most powerful and majestic of creatures, but for them bears are
of two kinds: the good who live in the middle mountain and the
evil who live at the bottom of the mountain and sometimes attack
people; the latter should not be worshipped. Wolves will help people
against the evil bears, and may be called upon for this purpose. A
bear cub is kept as a pet until the festival, then sacrificed as an
honour and invited to its own feast, but is apologized to and revered
in the rites; it is the Divine One Reigning in the Mountains.

The bear is particularly revered in Lapland. Lapps and Siberian tribes may not mention it by its real name, thus it is addressed as The Old Man, or the Grandfather, the Chief's Son, Crooked Tail and many other titles. This also applies among Amerindians where he is the Grandfather of all Animals; these conciliatory terms are used to propitiate the spirit of the hunted. In the *Kalevala* the bear is called the Honey-eater, the Fur-adorned and the Forest Apple. It is the Dog of God, having 10 times the strength of man and 12 times more wit. As with the Ainus, he is apologized to and revered when slain. In other parts of Japan the bear symbolizes benevolence and wisdom, while in China he is bravery and strength; Yu the Great dressed as a bear and incorporated the Bear Spirit. Mongols are descended from a woman who had two children by a bear.

Bears play a prominent part in Mediterranean mythology. Arcadians were descended from bears. The constellations Ursa Major and Minor were two she-bears in Crete who helped to look after the infant Zeus and hid him from Cronos. They were sacred to the lunar goddesses Artemis and Diana, and an attribute of Atalanta and Euphemia. In the cult of Artemis, Lady of the Beasts and protectress of wild animals, girls from five to ten years old were dressed in yellow robes and called 'bears' and imitated their actions in the rites of the festival of Brauronia; the girls had to spend a period serving Artemis in this guise before they could be married. Artemis is sometimes depicted with the head of a she-bear. The goddess Artio is also a she-bear. Artemis/Diana turned Callisto into a bear. There was also a Roman myth that it was Juno, jealous of Callisto, who turned her into a bear so that she would be shot, and yet another version said it was Zeus himself who made the transformation to protect her from Hera's/Juno's vengeance, and, again, that Zeus, protecting her from Hera and the hunters, turned her into Ursa Major and her son into Ursa Minor. In the Greek Rites of Isis festival a tame bear was dressed as a matron and carried in a litter in the procession. In Rome bears were used in the arena to fight, to kill criminals, for bear-baiting and performing and were occasionally kept as pets.

In Vedic times Ursa Major, the Great Bear, was called the Seven Bears.

The bear can be either solar or lunar in its symbolism; it is solar in hero myths but lunar when associated with the moon goddesses and in inundation mythology. Both aspects appear in Scandinavian and Teutonic traditions: the bear is sacred to Thor as God of Thunder and Lightning and to the lunar goddesses of the waters. The she-bear Atla symbolizes the feminine principle, while the he-bear Atli is the masculine. The she-bear is also an attribute of the Gaulist goddess Artio, who kept a tame bear.

In Celtic myth the bear is a lunar power, emblem of the goddess

Berne; it also represents Andarta – 'Powerful Bear', while the 'Son of the Bear' occurs frequently in Irish and Welsh names. The dual symbolism is also apparent in the Celtic association between the Bear and the **Boar**, with the Boar as Spiritual Authority and the Bear as Temporal Power.

The Old Testament depicts the bear as a symbol of great ferocity, the she-bear protecting her cubs. This is referred to in I Samuel 17: 34f; II Samuel 17: 8; Hosea 13: 8; Proverbs 17: 12; Isaiah 59: 11; and in the New Testament in Revelations 13: 1. Bears were used to punish the children who mocked Elisha. The fight between David and the bear was interpreted as the conflict between Christ and the Devil, since Christianity used the bear as a symbol of evil, cruelty, carnal greed and the Devil. It typifies Satan in Christian art and in the Bestiaries, which use the David symbolism to represent Christ throttling evil powers when 'he descended into Hell and delivered the captive spirits out of his jaws.'

The habits of bears give rise to much symbolism. Cubs, being born in winter during hibernation in a cave and emerging mobile with the mother in spring, became a symbol of resurrection, new life in spring and also of initiation and inspiration. It was believed that during this hibernation the bear nourished itself by drawing juice from its paws. It was also believed that the cubs were born as shapeless lumps of flesh and that the mother 'licked them into shape'; this was used to depict bringing order out of chaos. The belief in the amorphous birth of the cubs is used by Aristotle, Pliny, Aelian, Oppian and Isadore (Aristotle reported the same of the **fox**) and passed from them into European literature and into the Bestiaries, which used it as a symbol of transformation, of the heathen being converted to Christianity. Aristotle, Aelian and Pliny also say that the bear's breath is offensive to other animals, also that when bears fall ill they cure themselves by eating ants. The Syriac *Book of Medicine* says that the eye of a bear, placed in a hive, makes bees prosper.

In Heraldry the animal figures largely in connection with names derived from the bear and is used as heraldic jokes or puns, such as to bear and forbear. It is generally depicted as muzzled. The head alone is frequently depicted, and bears' paws are often found in crests and as charges on shields.

In Europe, in English Mummers' Plays the bear pursues little boys dressed as lambs, but is driven off by the Shepherd hero. In Spain, in the carnivals in the Pyrenees the bear is a notable figure; masked and with a blackened face he pursues the girls and is killed, but is then often revived by the Doctor. The bear is the national emblem of Russia.

Beaver. An important animal in North Amerindian lore. The Beaver, along with the **Otter**, **Hare** and **Spider**, was a member of the Council of Animals which helped humanity to Recover the Light. It is also one of the animals which helped to bring up the mud from the bottom of the waters to create the land in Algonquin myth; it is also a powerful Water Being among the Blackfeet and gave them their ritual Beaver Bundle. There are numerous Beaver Tribes and Beaver Clans and the animal is frequently cited as an ancestor by such tribes as the Cayuse and the clans of the Creek, Onondaga, Seneca Iroquois and Shuswop Indians. The beaver represents action, a lover of home and family and group achievement and it uses both earth and water energies.

In Europe it depicts industriousness – 'working like a beaver' – and in ancient times it was the subject of a strange belief that its testicles contained a precious substance which 'heals diverse diseases', thus it was hunted for them. The beaver knew why it was hunted, so when pursued it bit its testicles off. If again hunted it lay on its back to show the hunter that what he sought was no longer there. The myth is of very ancient date, and was recorded by the Egyptian priest Horapollo and by Apolonius, Pliny, Aelian and Juvenal. The Christian Bestiaries used this to moralize that man must separate himself from 'the works of the flesh which are adulteries, fornications, revellings and envies and throw them to the Devil who hunts the soul'. The beaver is depicted in European art in the act of self-mutilation; it also symbolizes vigilance and peacefulness.

Zoroastrianism gives the beaver prominence as a creature of the waters; it is the Luck of the Rivers and killing it brings drought and dire penalties to the killer.

Bee or Apes. Bees are probably the most universally symbolic of insects; objects of admiration, veneration and fear and subjects of cults, rituals and beliefs in birth, death and the soul; they are also connected with supernatural powers. On the practical level they provide valuable food and drink in honey and mead, and represent industry, order and, as they were believed to be parthenogenetic, purity, chastity and virginity. Spiritually bees, like birds, are winged messengers between this world and the realm of the gods. 'Telling the bees' of a death or important event is an ancient and widespread custom for conveying news to souls in the next world. Also, being winged, they are associated with the soul and thus with immortality; this symbolism is illustrated when bees were carved on tombs. Bees were the only creatures to come direct and unchanged from Paradise. The symbolism can, however, be ambivalent, for while bees have a spiritual import they also have erotic associations; they, with Cupids, are ravishers of flowers and hearts and personify a kiss which extracts honey but pierces the heart; a symbol which is found both in Greek and Oriental erotics. The sting of a bee has phallic connotations.

The earliest known use of the bee as a symbol occurred in Egypt, about 3500 BC, at the union of the two kingdoms of Upper and Lower Egypt when they had 'joined the Reed to the Bee'. The royal symbols of Lower Egypt meant 'he who belongs to the bee'. They are the tears of Ra, the Sun God. 'When Ra weeps again the water which flows from his eyes upon the ground turns into working bees.' The bee is the 'giver of life' and therefore birth, death and resurrection; it is also industry, chastity, harmonious living and royalty. In Egyptian hieroglyphics the hornet is sometimes used as an alternate translation.

Bees and honey are alluded to in the *Rig Veda*: Vishnu, Krishna and Indra are called *Madhava*, the 'nectar-born ones', and have the bee as an attribute. Vishnu can be depicted as a blue bee resting on a lotus – blue being the colour of the sky and ether – and Krishna as an avatar of Vishnu has a blue bee on his forehead. A bee surmounting a triangle represents Siva. Soma, the moon, is also called a bee. Erotic symbolism also occurs with Kama, God of Love, and bees as 'sweet pain' compose his bow string; he is followed by a train of bees.

The symbolism of industry and thrift also obtains in China, though the *feng* can be translated as a bee or a wasp. Swarms of bees are a lucky omen. The Chinese have a saying: 'Bees make honey and men eat it.' In some parts of the country beehives are turned round to face the opposite direction when their owner dies.

Both Pliny and Aristotle say that bees have something divine about them and that good souls could be reincarnated in bees; while Porphyry says that the souls of those who lived justly were called bees, 'for the bee is just and sober'. Again they represent industry, prosperity, purity and immortality. Demeter was 'the Pure Mother Bee'; the Great Mother was known as the Queen Bee and her priestesses were Melissae, the Bees. Pindar says that the Pythian priestess at Delphi was known as the Delphic Bee, and her emblematic bee appeared on Delphic coins. The officiates at Eleusis were Bees. The name Melissa is an ancient title referring to a priestess of the Great Mother or to a nymph (the full-grown larva of bees are called nymphs) and occurs frequently in Greek myth. In one myth the nymph Melissa was the first to discover honey as a food. The Muses, originally nymphs of springs and inspiration, later became associated with the various arts, and bees were called Birds of the Muses. The Muses, as bees, guided the Ionians from Greece to Asia Minor to form a new colony. Poets and eloquent people were said to have been touched on the lips in infancy by the Birds of the Muses. Pindar, Sappho and Homer are all referred to as having the gift of honeyed words or song. Sophocles, Plato, Virgil and Lucan were supposed to have been fed by bees or to have had their lips touched with honey in infancy. Priestesses of Apollo, God of Music, Poetry, Arts and Eloquence, were sometimes called Melissae.

There are various myths associating both Zeus and Dionysos with bees; both were said to have been fed by them. The Cretan Zeus was born in a cave of bees and was fed by them, and Zeus also had the title of *Melissaios*, Bee-man; he fathered a son, the hero Meliteus, by a nymph who hid the child from Hera in a wood, where Zeus had him fed by bees. Dionysos was fed on honey as a babe by the nymph Makris, daughter of Aristaeus, protector of flocks and bees; in yet another myth he was tended by Nysa, another daughter of Aristaeus. Ovid says it was Dionysos who first discovered the art of making hives for bees, that it was he who introduced honey and it was therefore right that honey-cakes should be offered to him. Pan and Pripaus were also said to be protectors and keepers of bees. Bees are depicted as flying round Eros/Cupid, who was stung by a bee. As emblems of the goddesses Demeter, Cybele, Diana, Rhea and the Ephesian Artemis, bees are lunar and virgin. The bee appears on statues of Artemis and some of her priests were called Essenes – King Bees – Pausanias says that the word 'Essene' means King Bee. With the Essenes 'King Bees' were priestly officials. Philo says that the Essenes kept bees.

The Romans held that sexual abstinence was required when handling hives, otherwise the bees would fly away. The bees were also to be informed before their hives were moved. Contrary to beliefs in other parts, swarms of bees denoted misfortune and foretold defeat in battle or death, but they could also announce the attainment of sovereignty as in the case of Dionysius of Syracuse. In iconography and sculpture, a headless bee and a headless frog avert the evil eye. According to Virgil the bee is 'the breath of life'; Porphyry equates it with justice and sobriety, Seneca with the monarchy.

There is a curious connection between bees and lions and bees and oxen which occurs in West Asia, Greece, in the Hebrew and Mithraic religions and in Etruscan art. Bees were thought to be born from the carcass of a lion or an ox in which the maggots finally turn into bees. In the same manner hornets were generated from horses, drones from mules and wasps from donkeys. There is a probability that in the Old Testament story of Samson, the lion and the bees had some association with the lion-and-bee connections evident in the earlier cults of the Great Mother. The bee-oxen relationship also occurs in Mithraism, where the vital principle springs from the bull and the bee represents the soul. Bees and oxen were regarded as sexless and androgynous.

In the Bestiaries the bees have a King which they love, serve and honour. Again, the bee is a symbol of industry and perfect social living, 'with equal sweetness for Kings and commoners alike'. The bee is weak in physical strength but 'strong in the vigour of wisdom and the love of virtue'. Christianity uses the orderly life of the hive as a symbol of the monastic communal life of industry and charity. Saints, famous for good works, were compared to bees, and eloquent Fathers of the Church had lips flowing with honey, while the Virgin Queen of the Bees is typical of the Virgin Queen of Heaven. Christ was called the 'aethereal bee'. Occasionally bees appeared in catacombs as symbols of the soul and immortality, but this was an adaptation of the ancient pagan usage. The bee also represents courage, prudence, economy, co-operation, sweetness and virginity. Regarded as never sleeping, it also depicts vigilance and zeal; flying in the air it portrays the soul entering the Kingdom of Heaven. The bee is the Christian and the hive the Church. There are numerous legends of God or Jesus creating bees and of imitations created by the Disciples or the Devil, the result being wasps. Bees resent screaming or quarrelling.

The symbolism of diligence is also present in the *Septuagint*: 'Go to the bee and learn how diligent she is, and what noble work she provides, whose labours kings and private men have for their use, she is desired and honoured by all.' Bees attack plunderers with great ferocity (Deuteronomy 1: 44, Psalms 118: 12).

One of the books of the Qu'ran (Sura XVI) is entitled 'the Bee', and bees represent the faithful, intelligence, wisdom, and harmlessness; they 'benefit fruit blossoms, practise useful things, work in the daytime, do not eat food gathered by others, dislike dirt and bad smells, and obey their ruler; they dislike the darkness of indiscretion, the clouds of doubt, the storm of revolt, the smoke of the prohibited, the water of superfluity, the fire of lust' (Ibn al-Athir).

In Celtic lore bees have a secret wisdom derived from the other world.

Bees and worms help the Aztec god Quetzalcoatl on his journey to the Land of the Dead, at which time he takes the form of a dog. Aztecs held that the soul becomes an insect, and as there are references to a Bee God, this may have been a bee-soul. An intoxicating drink was made from wild honey-bees by the Maya. (The European honey bee, *apis mellifica*, was not known before the Spanish Conquest.) Amerindians referred to the stinging bee as 'the white man's fly'.

The Australian native bee was stingless. In Australia and Africa bees are found on tribal totems and among the Kung Bushmen they are one of the vehicles of supernatural power.

In Heraldry bees are the most frequently used insect, usually on a shield but also on crests.

Bee-eater. According to Pliny and Aelian the bee-eater is noted for its filial piety. It is destructive to bees and is said to be able to fly backwards.

Beetle. A symbol of blindness. In the Authorized Version (AV) of the Old Testament it is listed as clean food (Leviticus 11: 22) and, although later translated as cricket or grasshopper, was more likely to have been the **Locust**. It is eaten in Africa and by Australian Aboriginals. Pliny says that beetles are killed by the scent of a rose, and Aelian tells us that 'you will destroy the beetle if you throw roses upon it.'

Behemoth. Referred to in the Old Testament (Enoch 66: 7–9), Behemoth is the male counterpart of the female Leviathan; together they dwell in the abyss and are at enmity. It is usually supposed to have been the **Hippopotamus**, and represents the power of the land as opposed to Leviathan's power of the sea (with Ziz the power of the air).

Bennu. The ancient Egyptian Sun Bird, probably the origin of the **Phoenix**; it was worshipped at Heliopolis. It rose from the flames of a tree at Heliopolis. It was a sacred bird, associated with Ra as Sun God; it also incarnated the soul of Osiris.

Bestiaries. A Bestiary, or Beast Epic is, as T. H. White says, 'a kind of naturalist's scrapbook which has grown with the additions of several hands', but it purported to be a serious work of natural history. Its origins can be traced back to ancient Egypt, Greece and Rome, to such sources as Horapollo, Herodotus,. Aristotle, Pliny, Aelian or to **Physiologus**, to mythology and travellers' tales. Later, Bestiaries were developed by the Fathers of the Church, who were responsible for the addition of the extreme moralizations drawn from the animals' characteristics. Christianity, at no time a religion of the world of nature (regarding her as subservient to man), used her as food for moral and spiritual teachings with the eventual result that more attention was paid to morals, symbols and allegories than to scientific accuracy, while the Bestiaries became a mixture of facts and fancies. They were systematized in the 11th–12th centuries and were fully illustrated, greatly influencing art and literature. They spread into most European languages, gathering more imagination and moralizing on the way, so that various creatures were apt to be represented under different and often contradictory guises, for example both the Crocodile and the Hoopoe can symbolize evil qualities on the one hand and virtues on the other.

They were further systematized into segments, with Bestiaries for Beasts, Volucaria for Birds and Lapidaria for Stones, but still all completely symbolic.

Bicorne. A fabulous panther-like animal which fed on hen-pecked husbands and became fat in consequence of over-eating and wore a cheerful grin. His counterpart, **Chichevache**, was thin and mournful.

Birds. In symbolism and myth, birds, with their powers of flight, universally represent the Spirit, the soul, ascent to the heavens and communication between heaven and earth, gods and men. Having wings, they can also symbolize angels and the higher states of being, and are a means of travel to the next world. In many traditions the soul takes flight in the form of a bird when it leaves the body. Euripides calls birds 'heralds of the Gods'; being air-borne, quick in flight, and alert they make excellent instruments of communication. They are also obvious vehicles and symbols for the spiritual flight and for visiting the other worlds of the shaman or medicine-man. (The word 'medicine' is here a poor translation, as it correctly means 'spiritual power'), and in mythology the Hero is often accompanied by a bird who informs and guides him (he understands the language of the birds). Birds universally act as messengers, informants or prophets, and frequently have the power of metamorphosis, or of being a form adapted by some divinity or supernatural being.

The bird which laid the Cosmic Egg from which the world emerged is an almost universal symbol; it is usually a bird of the waters, such as the Nile Goose, or one whose egg is laid on the waters, as with the Hindu Cosmic Egg which was laid on the primordial waters.

The Egyptian Soul-bird Ba

Birds are divided into two classes, the heavenly and demonic; beneficent or malign; those that help and work for humanity and those that are inimical; the clean and the unclean; though the symbolism is totally ambivalent; for example the **Raven**, an unclean scavenger associated with death and darkness, a bird of witches and evil in one tradition, can become the Hero-Trickster or a totem of the Amerindians, the messenger of the God Odin/Woden, or of the Sun God Apollo, or the Chinese solar raven in others. The same applies to the **Owl** as a bird of both wisdom and darkness. The Law of Moses (Deuteronomy 14: 11–20) divided birds into clean and unclean classes, the latter generally comprising birds of prey, carrion-eaters and fish-eaters.

There are also fabulous birds often symbolizing elemental powers, such as the **Thunderbird** and gigantic creatures like the **Roc**, **Simurgh** and **Garuda**, so huge as to blot out the sun and able to carry off elephants to their nests; they appear in many traditions and usually represent the power of the air, storms, thunder and lightning, the thunder being produced by the flapping of their wings and the lightning from their tongues or talons. Fabulous birds often depict celestial realms and powers and are at enmity with the chthonic serpent.

In tribal cultures birds are often totems and ancestors; in Australian Aboriginal lore all birds were originally aboriginals in the Dreamtime.

There is a natural association between birds and trees, and birds are often depicted in the Tree of Life, usually with the serpent at the roots. Birds are also portrayed with flowers, particularly in the East. In Western art this can be merely an attractive combination, but in Chinese and Japanese art the association has a deeper spiritual significance and identification.

Birds play an important part in Heraldry, the **Eagle** being the most prominent, but many being fabulous.

Bird of Paradise. The Bird of Paradise was reported by travellers in the East and was given its name for its great beauty, but the true species is not known. It was said to be about the size of a goose and had a sweet, pure note which turned to a moan if captured; it lived on dew. It had a brilliant plumage but no wings or feet, and suspended itself from lofty trees by wire-like feathers on its tail. It was called the Bird of Paradise because no one knew whence it came or whither it went; it was also known as the Bird of God. It was mentioned in association with the Nile but its tradition is widespread, and a Malay myth says that the bird drops its egg from the air and that when the egg reaches the earth it bursts and releases a fully-fledged bird.

Bishop Fish

Bishop Fish. A sea-monster of Europe which has the shaven head
of a monk and a large fish body. Also known as the Mitred Bishop,
the belief in the creature goes back to the 13th century; it was
reported as caught in the Baltic in 1433 and was taken to the King
of Poland who wished to keep it captive, but it appealed by gesture
to the bishops, to whom it was shown, to be allowed to return to
its native element, and this being granted, it made the sign of the
cross and disappeared into the sea. It was in fish form but wore a
mitre and carried a crosier; it also wore a dalmatica. Another was
caught in 1531 in the German Ocean, but would not eat and died
in three days. The Bishop Fish has its counterpart in the **Buddhist
Sea Priest**. Pliny maintained that the sea contains the counterpart
of every creature that exists on land and in the heavens.

Bison. See **Buffalo**

Bittern. Called 'a mere drum', derived from the belief that it 'drummed' by shaking its beak in the marsh. In the Old Testament it symbolizes desolation in Zephaniah (AV) 2: 14, Isaiah 34: 11 (the **Pelican** in the Revised Version) – a desolation 'both the cormorant and the bittern shall possess'.

Blackbird. Frequently mentioned in the Greek Anthology, together with the **Thrush**; it was sacred to the gods for its sweet song, but it is also noted as a destructive bird. It is killed if it eats the pomegranate.

Blood.   The blood of the victim plays a highly important symbolic role in religious rites. Representing the life-force, the soul, it is the chief and most sacred offering in a sacrifice. It is also a means of transference of power; to absorb the blood is to absorb the power of either the deity, the sacrifice or an enemy. The blood of sacrificial animals could also symbolize the red, solar energy. The shedding of blood in sacrifice propitiated the divinities of the dead and satisfied the ghosts; the blood of the sacrifice restores lost vital force.

Boar.   Has an ambivalent symbolism; the Golden Boar is one of the great solar animals while the White Boar, dweller in the swamps and representing the watery element, is lunar. In some traditions it depicts all that is evil and unclean, in others it can be divine, appearing on altars and images of gods, also on coins and standards; but it always symbolizes strength, fearlessness, savagery and wildness.

Going back to Vedic times, the Storm God Ruda was 'the Boar of the Sky' and in Hinduism Varahi, the third incarnation of Vishnu, or Parjapati, was as a boar which saved the Earth from the waters of chaos and was the first tiller of the soil. As a fertility symbol it is also an emblem of Vajnavrahi, Goddess of the Dawn, who as the sow is the source of life.

In one version of the Sumero-Semitic myth, Tamnuz, like Adonis, was slain by a boar while out hunting; in both cases the boar represents the 'wild boar of winter' with the coming of spring. The same symbolism applies to the killing of the Boar of Calydon. In Graeco-Roman myth boars were sacred to Ares/Mars as war, destruction and strife; the boar was the form taken by Ares when he fled from Typhon. The boar which slew Adonis was sacrificed to Aphrodite, and the animal is an attribute of Demeter and Atalanta. It is the animal of the hunt *par excellence*, and is depicted in the boar-hunts of Adonis, Meleager and Hippolytus. Rows of boars' teeth adorned the helmets of warriors and, according to Homer, Odysseus wore one. At the early Olympic Games a boar was sacrificed and competitors swore on pieces of the sacrificed animal that they would not be guilty of foul play in the games. An animal so sacrificed could not be eaten. If an oath-taker played false he too would be torn to bits. For the Syrian Adonis the wild boar becomes taboo and is then ritually killed and eaten at the feast of commemoration. This is referred to in the Old Testament (Isaiah 66: 17).

The boar which killed Adonis is paralleled in the Celtic myth of Finn arranging for Diarmaid to be killed when boar-hunting. Few animals are more important for the Celts than the boar; it was a sacred, supernatural, magical creature, symbolizing the warrior, warfare, the hunt, protection, hospitality and fertility. The boar's head signifies health and preservation from danger, it contains the power of the life-force and vitality. The boar and the **Bear** together represent Spiritual and Temporal Power. The boar is often depicted in association with the tree, wheels and ravens; it appears on the helmets of warriors and on trumpets. It is the animal of Celtic ritual feasts and food for the gods, esteemed the fitting food for gods and heroes. Bones were found placed ritually in graves, the head, again, being of special importance. Figures of boars appeared on British and Gaulish altars. In Irish myth there are divine, magical and prophetic boars, and supernatural and otherworld pigs which bring death and disaster. In Celtic saga there are also the magical Pigs of Manannan and other legends (see **Swine**), according to which eating the flesh restored health and happiness. The boar was ritually hunted and slain and there are many accounts of a Great Boar hunted by a hero. Twrch Trywth was a king turned into a boar who was chased by Arthur and his warriors across Ireland, Wales and Cornwall, where it disappeared into the sea. A Gaulish god is depicted with a boar and sculptures of boars are found in Celtic forts and in France and Portugal. Druids called themselves boars, probably as solitary dwellers in the forest.

The boar is prominent in Scandinavian and Teutonic lore. It is a storm animal and funerary but also represents fertility and the harvest; it was sacrificed to Frey at Yule – he rides the Golden Bristled Boar, swifter than a horse. The boar is sacred to both Frey and Freyja and to Odin/Woden. Boars' masks and helmets put warriors under the protection of Frey and Freyja and the golden bristles of the boar Gulliburstin made the sun's rays with their glare. There was a Teutonic custom of solemn affirmation by the golden-bristled boar, it being a revealer of secrets and a detector of falsehood. The magic boar Saehrimnir was eaten each day by the warriors in Valhalla, and, like the Pigs of Manannan, it revived and was hunted and eaten again. The boar's head was the feast at Yuletide banquets. A similar rite appears in both Vedic mythology and the Adonis story.

Contrary to the reverence with which the boar is held in Celtic and Scandinavian traditions, in Egypt it was the epitome of evil, an

attribute of Set in his typhonic aspect when he swallows the eye of
the God of the Day. For the Hebrews it was the most unclean of
animals and the enemy of Israel, a destroyer of the vines, and
Christianity confirms the evil symbolism with the boar as brutality,
ferocious anger, cruel princes and rulers and the sins of the flesh;
it is also the Antichrist and divine wrath; for Jews, Christians and
Moslems it is a symbol of destruction.

The symbolism becomes favourable again in Zoroastrianism
where the 'shining boar' is associated with the Sun in the
Zendavesta. The boar and the **Stag** were created by Ormuzd for the
killing of serpents which, with the **Dragon**, represented Ahriman
(*Bandahis* II.47).

In China the boar depicted the wealth of the forests, and a white
boar was lunar; this also applied to the 'white boar' used as a term
for the moon in Japan, where it also symbolized all the warrior
qualities, courage and conquest.

The wild boar is frequently portrayed as an heraldic animal; it is
one of the heraldic Beasts of the Chase – 'the untamed creature of
the woods', often called by the French name *sanglier*. It also appears
as the domestic animal and the boar's head occurs as a crest.

Bones. Bones of animals were used from earliest times as tools,
weapons, harpoons, needles and scrapers and were hollowed out to
use as containers. They were also found ritually interred and in
caves, suggesting either veneration or a funerary feast, many of the
deposits having been arranged with great care and showing
symbolic designs. Among bones found were those of bear, ox,
bison, horse, ibex, woolly rhinocerous, mammoth, hyena and dog.
The skull was of particular significance as symbolizing the vital life-
force of the head and it was a frequent fetish and used as a drinking
vessel in rites. Bones represent the indestructible life principle, the
essential and resurrection, but on the other hand they can signify
mortality and transiency.

Booby. The booby was so called by early mariners because they
thought it stupid when it defended its nest instead of running away;
the bird then became a symbol of stupidity.

Borak or Buraq. Al Borak was the milk-white steed that carried
the Prophet Muhammad to visit the heavens at night; it is sometimes
depicted with wings. In Indian iconography it is portrayed with
peacock's feathers, ass's ears and a horse's body.

Brahminy Duck. See **Sheldrake**

Bucoros. The Rhinoceros-bird, it is drawn or sculpted on house
gables in Borneo as a luck-bringer, its beak pointing towards foes.
The head is carried on magic staffs which figure in mimetic dance.

Buddha. The Buddha passed through animal incarnations in earlier lives as a tortoise, monkey, elephant and great hare.

Buddhist Sea Priest. See **Sea-Buddhist Priest**

Buffalo or Bison. In North Amerindian lore the buffalo or bison portrays supernatural power, strength and fortitude; it also represents the whirlwind. It is the most important totem animal among the Plains Indians, for whom it is sacred and their chief support. The Cree, Pawnee and Sioux have the Cosmic Buffalo as Grandfather and Father of the Universe, he controls the gate of coming into the world and going out for all animals. Black Elk says: 'The Buffalo represents the people and the universe and is he not generous in that he gives us our food?' He also represents prayer and abundance, and a white buffalo is particularly sacred as a sign of prayers granted and prophecy fulfilled. Elaborate ceremonies, dances and tests of endurance accompany Buffalo Festivals and Dances. In the Buffalo Tribe of the Mandan Okapi every man must possess a buffalo hide and horns for use in the mask-dance of sympathetic magic for hunting. The dance imitates the stamping and bellowing of the buffalo until their gradual exhaustion and death. There is an association between the Bison and Corn Spirit and the Buffalo Dance and Green Corn; the two are connected in the Creek and Pawnee rites.

Among Zulus the soul can pass into a buffalo and the animal is the alter-ego of the Bantu tribe. Certain African pastoral tribes who hold the buffalo in reverence sacrifice and eat the male animal once a year at festivals, and it is sacrificed (but not eaten) at funerals, although the female is never sacrificed.

There was also a buffalo sacrifice on ritual occasions among the Malaysians of the Straits of Malacca. The animal had to be without blemish.

Vana, Vedic God of the Dead, rides on a buffalo, and in Buddhist iconography the Buddha is sometimes depicted as buffalo- or bull-headed.

The Taoist Lao Tzu rides on a buffalo or **Ox**, and was riding a green (sometimes yellow) buffalo when he disappeared in the West. The buffalo and ox are interchangeable in the 'Ten Ox-herding Pictures' in which the buffalo symbolizes unregenerate human nature and starts as wholly black and wild and during the process of taming is depicted as gradually becoming white and tame until in the tenth picture he disappears completely.

In Europe the buffalo was known in the North in Roman times, and is mentioned by Martial as appearing in the amphitheatre in Rome.

Bull. As the bear is the primary symbolic and sacrificial animal of the hunter, so the bull is that of pastoral and agricultural communities, and it was reverenced and worshipped from earliest times. It was obviously venerated for its usefulness, strength and virility and in many early civilizations was regarded as a divine incarnation, but its symbolism is ambivalent, for while the bull usually embodies the masculine procreative power, the solar generative force, strength, warriors, royalty and the Sky Gods, it also represents the earth and the humid, seminal power of rain, and so becomes associated with the lunar Great Mother. Riding a bull, or bulls drawing a war chariot, depicts the masculine and solar, but when ridden by a goddess, such as Astarte or the Sidonian Europa who was identified with her, the symbolism becomes lunar. Both gods and goddesses can be represented as crowned with a bull's head, while its horns are both solar power and the crescent moon.

The bull cult appears extensively in Sumero-Semitic religions as a sacred, fertilizing power. The Celestial Bull ploughed the great furrow of the sky; the Sky Gods ride on bulls and are Bulls of Light; Enil or Enki is 'the savage bull of the sky', but the lunar god Sin also takes the form of a bull. The Hittite Sun God's chariot is drawn by bulls, but bulls are also harnessed to the chariot of the Weather God and his Queen. This Weather God aspect was later developed in the Roman Jupiter Dolichenus. Dionysos Zagreus was called 'the bull' by his female devotees and Plutarch says that he was also called the 'son of a bull'. An ancient tradition said that he was sacrificed and torn to pieces in the form of a bull, and Euripides maintained that the meniads devoured the bull they dismembered.

The roar of the bull or the stamping of its hoofs is a symbol of thunder which brings the fertilizing rain. Dumuzi, the Sumerian God of Crops and Herds, is the 'wild bull' whose voice is the thunder; he is the consort of Inanna, Queen of Heaven. As a sacred animal the bull was often placed standing alone on an altar and it sometimes wore the conical hat of divinity. The Canaanite cult of the Storm and Vegetalian God Baal represented the god as a bull, as did the Syrian and Phoenician worshippers of Baal or Bel. The Canaanite Monster of the Wilderness, part bull, part man, resembled the Cretan Minotaur, offspring of Pasiphae by the bull sent by Poseidon from the sea for King Minos. The Semitic Moloch was also bull-headed. Human-headed bulls guarded the palaces of the Assyrian kings.

In Zoroastrianism the bull was the first animal created, it was slain by Ahriman but from its soul rose the germ of all creation. It was the soul of the world, but its generative power was lunar as it was associated with the moon and the fertility of the rain clouds.

The Anatolians caught wild bulls for sacrifice to the gods; it was the focal point of the hunt, and the Alexandrians held a *corrida* in an arena in which the bull was captured and sacrificed – rites now

The Minotaur

decadent in bull-fights. Captured wild bulls also appeared in the Roman arenas, and fights were staged between bulls and men and bulls and other animals; they were also trained for circuses. Gilbert Murray says: 'the tremendous *mana* of a wild bull occupies almost half of the stage of pre-Olympic ritual with its strength, fury and sexual potency.'

Of all the many and varied animals venerated in Egypt the bull was one of the most revered. The early kings of Egypt called themselves bulls and later the Pharaoh was called 'the bull of his mother' and the bull was often used to depict him in art. The sacred bull Apis was, according to Herodotus, 'a black bull with a triangular white blaze on his forehead and on his back was the shadow of the figure of a falcon; in his tail were double hairs and on his tongue a beetle.' (These features can be seen in the Egyptian figures in the British Museum.) The seat of the cult was Memphis, while at Heliopolis the Bull-God Mnves or Menwer was worshipped, as was the Bull-God Bacchis at Hermonthis. Strabo tells us that there were many places in which a sacred bull or cow was kept and venerated. According to Plutarch Apis was the result of a virgin birth since he was conceived 'by a ray of generative light from the moon falling on the cow, his mother'. He was an avatar of Osiris and 'the second life and servant of Ptah'. In *The Book of Making the Spirit of Osiris* the moon is addressed as 'that bull that groweth young in the heaven each day . . . when thou art seen in the sky on this day many conceptions take place.' The solar bull was sacred to the Sun God Ra who, as the Bull of Heaven, daily impregnated the Sky Goddess Nut. The black of the bull Apis signified the dark of the moon from which the new moon was born; the lunar bull brought the revivifying night dews.

The bull sacrifice was the central ceremony in Mithraism, and Mithra is portrayed either as carrying, mastering or slaying the bull which symbolizes both victory over man's animal nature and life through death as well as the life and fertility of the blood. At initiation rites, initiates were baptized in the blood of the bull. Mithraism passed into Roman cults, and the bull was an attribute of Jupiter as Sky God, who is sometimes depicted as having bulls under his feet. The lunar bull was sacred to Venus as fertility, and Europa, as the dawn, was carried across the sky by the solar bull.

In Hinduism the bull symbolizes strength, speed, fertility and the reproductive powers of nature; it is an attribute of Agni 'the Mighty Bull' and a form taken by Indra in his fertile aspect. Siva rides the bull Nandin as Guardian of the West and of all quadrupeds. The bull is also the vital breath of Aditi, the all-embracing, and, in the Vedas, Rudra, both destructive and beneficent, is called a bull – he united with the Cow-goddess to father the Marints. The power given by the sacred drink Soma is frequently equated with that of the bull, and in the Vedas Soma is deified as the Moon-God.

Yama, God of the Dead in Buddhism, is sometimes bull-, or buffalo-headed, and the bull is his attribute, representing the ego, the moral self (see also **Buffalo**).

Celtic and pre-Celtic cults gave great importance to the bull, which, in its solar aspect, was associated with horses, stags and swans. Warriors needed to possess the qualities and characteristics of the bull, and bull-slaying and sacrifice appeared frequently in Celtic rites; the animal was also ritually killed for divination. There were the Three Bull Protectors of the Island of Britain mentioned in one of the *Welsh Triads* and there was a three-horned sacred bull. For the Druids the sacrificial white bull was the sun, with the **Cow** the earth. In Scandinavia the bull was an attribute of Thor, as Sky and Thunder God, and was sacred to Freyja as Goddess of Fertility.

Yahweh is the 'Bull of Israel' and thus represents the might of Yahweh. In Christianity the bull depicts brute force and is the emblem of the martyr St Eustace.

In Heraldry the Bull Calf, Cow or Buffalo cannot be depicted *proper* except in the case of piebald bulls. The bull is often used as a crest and is also portrayed collared and chained.

See also **Buffalo** and **Cow**

Bustard. According to Aelian the bustard is hostile to the dog but is grossly deceived by the fox.

Butterfly. In changing from the mundane **Caterpillar** and going through the stages of dissolution before emerging as the celestial winged creature the butterfly symbolizes rebirth, resurrection and the powers of regeneration. As emerging from the chrysalis it represents the soul leaving the body at death. A white butterfly could be the soul of a child who died unbaptized, but in Christian art the butterfly depicts the risen soul; the stages of its development are life, death and resurrection. Sometimes it is shown on the hand of the Christ child.

Chinese symbolism uses the butterfly as immortality, leisure and joy, while depicted with the chrysanthemum in art it portrays beauty in old age; with the plum it is longevity. Japan follows much of the Chinese symbolism but the butterfly can also represent a false lover, a vain woman or a Geisha, though a pair of butterflies are conjugal happiness. A white butterfly can embody a soul of the dead.

Psyche, the soul, could be represented by a butterfly in Greek art and was a symbol of immortality. The Graeco-Roman Horae, spirits of the seasons, were sometimes portrayed with butterfly wings. Butterflies can also symbolize a life of pleasure, irresponsibility, 'a butterfly existence', or spiritedness. A butterfly in the house is a good omen and heralds the coming of spring, but a swarm is unlucky.

In Pima myth the butterfly is a form of the Creator. It is also a totem of a tribe, and Butterfly Dances are performed by the Amerindian tribes of the southwest, such as the Hopi. In many parts butterflies and moths are the souls of the dead.

An Australian Aboriginal myth says that when death first occurred in the world it was assumed that the dead had been taken into the spirit world to come back in another form. The caterpillars volunteered to go up to the sky in winter to find out what had happened. On the first warm day the dragonflies reported that the caterpillars were coming back in new bodies – these were multicoloured butterflies.

Buzzard. The totem of the Papago tribe of North American Indians of the Arizona-Mexico region and also sacred to a Californian tribe; it was killed annually at a festival, without shedding blood, and the feathers were used for a garment for the medicine-man; the body was ritually buried, in sacred ground, to the lamentations of women. Buzzard also appears in the creation myth of the various animals and birds, being sent to bring up earth from below the primordial waters, or after the Flood, but Buzzard stopped to eat and so was condemned to feed on corpses.

As a carrion-feeder it is one of the unclean birds.

C

Caduceus. The double **Serpents** of the Caduceus of Hermes/ Mercury symbolize the opposites in dualism; the complementary nature of two seemingly opposites, they are the serpents of healing and poison, fire and water, binding and loosing, sleep and awakening, good and evil. They are hermetic and homoeopathic – 'nature can overcome nature'. They are also suggested as two snakes pairing, depicting not only the generative forces of nature but also the ultimate union of opposites, the androgyne. The caduceus is carried by messengers as a symbol of peace and protection; it is pre- eminently their attribute.

Calf. A symbol of an acceptable sacrifice or gift. In Egypt it was the vehicle to which Apis (see **Bull**) was transferred. Vedic symbolism uses the calf as the mind of Aditi, with the bull as his vital breath; the All-Embracing. In Christian iconography the calf without blemish can represent Christ. Some African kings or chiefs are called 'Great Calf' or 'Great Black Calf'.

Calygreyhound. An heraldic animal with the body of an antelope, claws of an eagle on forelegs, or hoofs of an ox on hindlegs. It symbolizes a swift mover.

Camel. The personification of Africa. The camel symbolizes obedience and subservience; it can be a guardian of the waters and springs in Arabia, but there was a demarcation between the camel- owning plains tribes and the shepherd tribes of the mountains. The camel is the most valuable animal in the Middle East; it is not only a sacrificial animal but also provides food and milk, the hide is used for leather and its hair is woven into a coarse cloth, it is also believed to be apotropaic and a cure for rheumatism; the camel's droppings are used for fuel. The dromedary is domesticated and used for transport, ploughing, riding and racing. In Arabian myth it is a noble creature, ennobled by God himself, while for Islam it is an animal of Paradise; the Prophet swore by a camel and rode on one. The mosque at Kaba was built on the spot where Muhammad's favourite camel Al Kaswa knelt at the flight from Mecca.

The camel was domesticated in Egypt about 3000 BC and was common in that country and in Mesopotamia; it was sent as a tribute to Assyria. In the Old Testament it is first mentioned in Genesis 12: 16, though this was thought to be a later addition to the text. It is referred to in Genesis 32: 15 as a milk animal and Isaiah mentions troops of camels. Job owned 3000 and camels carried the gifts of the Queen of Sheba for Solomon (I Kings 10: 2). As a sacrificial animal it was unclean for the Jews.

Pliny describes the different types of camel known to the Graeco-Roman world, where it was occasionally used in agriculture for ploughing but essentially as a pack animal and for riding both in war and peace. It is depicted in Roman-Christian art and appears in scenes with Orpheus; it also occurs on amulets of the Graeco-Jewish period; it was used on Roman coins as the personification of Arabia.

Christianity, associating the camel with the Magi and John the Baptist, who was clothed in camel's hair, used it as representing royalty, dignity, stamina, temperance and obedience.

Cameleopard. The Giraffe was said to be the misbegotten offspring of camel and leopard. There was also the Camelopardel, which had two long horns curving backwards. The animal was said to be the size and height of a camel with the skin of a leopard; this is generally assumed to be an early description of a giraffe. It appears in Sumerian and Egyptian iconography and in Heraldry. The name is a Roman word-combination.

Capacti. A Mexican monster whose body was used to create the earth.

Capricorn. A goat-fish which was intended to be a goat, but when pursued by Typhon leapt into the sea while still only half a goat, so the other half became a fish. It is a form of the Babylonian Ea-Oannes and the Indian Varuna as the life-principle of the waters. It is also the sign of the Zodiac when the sun is reborn at the winter solstice; it is the cardinal-earth. As half-fish, half-goat it also depicts the dual nature of land and sea, of height and depth. It is sacred to Cybele as a symbol of safe travel.

Caribou. The totem animal of the Amerindians of the far north, the Innuits (Eskimo) and Kutchin tribes whose living depends largely on the caribou. It features also largely in Chipewayan animal spirit beliefs.

Carp. In China and Japan the carp has an important symbolism. In the former it represents literary eminence, perseverance in difficulties, courage. The carp, swimming upstream against the current to spawn, is said to 'leap to Dragon Gate' and become a dragon, hence a scholar who is successful in the literary examinations is 'a carp that has leapt the Dragon Gate'. It is also depicted as two joined together with only one pair of eyes; this is the 'fish sharing eyes' which signifies conjugal fidelity, domestic felicity and abundant progeny. Twin carps represent the union of lovers. In Japan it also symbolizes courage, endurance, dignity, good fortune and resignation to fate; it is an emblem of the Samurai as having these qualities. At the Boys' Festival paper carp kites are flown as typifying courage and tenacity.

Cat.   The changing dilation and contraction of the cat's eyes make it a natural symbol of both solar and lunar powers: solar as the varying strength of the sun and lunar as the waxing and waning of the moon. As a nocturnal animal it also represents the splendour of the night, but its movements typify stealth. The black cat is totally associated with the lunar aspect, with death, evil and the power of witches. The good luck of the black cat is a modern development. There is a supernatural element connected with the cat; it is said to be psychic and, like the rat, to have foreknowledge of impending disaster. Sailors will not use the word at sea, and care must be taken over what is said in front of a cat. It has been persecuted and avoided as a witch's familiar; cats and dogs as familiars are also rain-makers, hence 'raining cats and dogs', but in other connections the two animals are in opposition as hereditary enemies; here the dog is solar and the cat lunar.

The cat appears in Greek art in the 5th and 4th centuries BC, but is little mentioned; it is depicted in Pompeii as a pet in Roman art, and the Goddess of Liberty has a cat at her feet symbolizing the rejection of all restraint. Artemis took the form of a cat when fleeing from Typhon. Pliny and Seneca mention cats, and they feature in Gallo-Roman sculpture as an attribute of the Moon Goddess Diana. The cult was spread by Roman colonists.

The Egyptian veneration of the cat was widely established from 1570 BC. It was sacred to Set, the power of darkness, and to the goddess Bast or Bastet; at Bubastis she has a cat's head and human body; she also appears as Ubastet or Pasht (this has been suggested as the origin of the word 'puss'). Bast represented the benign aspect of the sun as the cat basks in the solar rays. Originally a lion-goddess she was Goddess of Joy and guarded against disease. Herodotus said that cats were so cared for in Egypt that the people would save cats from a fire in the house rather than the house itself or any other possessions. Cats were mummified; this implied the protection and favour of the Mother Goddess Isis, and the cat also portrays pregnant women since the moon makes the seed grow in the womb.

The cat does not play a large part in Celtic tradition but it was associated with chthonic powers and was thus funerary, also a prophetic animal. In Roman Gaul and in Irish lore there was a 'Little Cat' as a guardian of treasure; it turned into a flaming object and burned the thief to ashes. There was an island inhabited by men with cat-heads. In Celtic saga there were Monster Cats to be fought by the Hero, the cat taking the place of the **Dragon**. The Welsh Great Cat was born of the enchanted sow Henwen, originally a human; it could eat nine score warriors. Monster cats and sea-cats appear in Irish tradition of probably Celtic origin. In Irish myth the eldest son of a hog had a cat's head and was known as 'Puss of the Corner'.

In Scandinavia, cats are an attribute of Freyja, the northern Venus, who symbolizes love and passion and who controls the night; her chariot is drawn by cats.

The Amerindian Wild Cat is a Hunter-god, younger brother of the Coyote, it portrays stealth; as the Tiger Cat or Cat-a-Mountain it is fierceness, ingratitude. The Wild Cat replaces the Badger (who is not strong of will) in Zuni hunting rituals. The Peruvian cat Ccoa is a storm spirit with a large head and with hail raining from its eyes and ears. The Guirivulu is a cat monster of South America, its tail ends in a claw; it can change into a snake and live in the waters. The Wild Cat is also a totem animal of an Australian Aboriginal tribe.

In the East, the Hindu Goddess of Birth, Shasti, rides a cat as a symbol of the prolific. With the Chinese the cat, as a nocturnal animal, is *yin* and associated with the powers of evil and of transformation, it is a shape-shifter. Seeing a strange cat foretells change and a black cat denotes misfortune or illness. The cat maintains its symbolism of transformation in Japan but it also becomes peaceful repose. In Japanese myth and legend the cat, with the fox and badger, is associated with endless trickery, shape-shifting, bewitching phantoms and vampires. The cat is, with the venomous snake, under a curse, as they were the only two creatures who did not weep at the death of the Buddha, but the cat is popular with Japanese sailors as it can keep off evil spirits of the deep and has control over the dead. For the Ainu of Japan cats are capable of bewitching people, possessing them, or causing misfortune. Their nature is demonic as they originally rose from the ashes of a demon defeated and burned by the Mole deity, but another myth says that cats were created to deal with rats who bit off the Devil's tongue. As coming from demons they must be treated with care.

Zoroastrianism divides the animal kingdom into those who serve Ormuzd, the good, and those of Ahriman, the evil. Dogs belong to Ormuzd but cats to Ahriman and there are Divis who are cat-headed with horns and hoofs who depict the 'false gods' of Persian myth. This symbolism is reversed in Islam, in which dogs are unclean but the cat, having received a blessing from the Prophet, may be kept by Muslims.

The domestic cat is not mentioned in the Bible but has a single reference in the Apocrypha in Baruch 6: 22 which probably refers to the Wild Cat, associated with the bat as unclean and as being among the animals appearing on Babylonian images – cats, bats and swallows.

Christianity connects the cat with Satan, the Hell-Cat, darkness, lust and laziness.

In British Heraldry the Wild Cat, the Cat-a-Mountain or Cat-a-Mont appears frequently but most often in Scottish armory; it is always represented full-face, like the leopard.

It is suggested that the nursery rhyme 'Hey diddle diddle, the cat and the fiddle . . .' had Egyptian origins – the Cow being Nut, the Heavenly Cow, the lunar Great Mother, and the cat-headed Bast, with the Dog representing the jackal or dog-headed Anubis; the fiddle is the sistrum of Isis and the dish and spoon ritual vessels. The sacred Cow–Dog–Cat theme appears in Roman, Gallic, British and Celtic traditions.

Caterpillar.   Mentioned in the Old Testament in connection with the **locust** as powers of destruction, devastation and voracity (Psalms 78: 46; Joel 1: 4). In Australian Aboriginal myth the caterpillars volunteered to go to the skies to see what had happened when death first occurred; they came back as **Butterflies**.

Cattle.   Among domesticated animals the cultivation of cattle is the most widespread. 'Chattels' are symbolic of wealth and property and a medium for barter. In the Bible the term 'cattle' is used to distinguish the domestic from the wild animal – 'the beasts of the field'; it is always employed in connection with adult animals. Among the pastoral tribes there can be almost a kinship between earth and people, and in the case of ritual slaughter the killer is unclean even when the sacrifice is for a communal feast. In Madagascar there are myths of descent from cattle, and the animals are used for food, labour and sacrifice. On the other hand some civilizations, notably the East Asiatic, refrain from using cows' milk, regarding it as pathological, and use cattle for work only. Cattle play an important part in Hindu festivals, in which they are ritually sprinkled, decorated with garlands and have their horns painted and are then driven out to graze where they please.

Cayman or Caiman.   In Central and South American tribes the cayman is a Shaman's tool, Shamans being possessed by ferocious animals such as the cayman or jaguar in which form they can travel through time and space. The cayman is sometimes depicted with human hands and bird claws. The cayman is an attribute of America personified.

Ccoa.   A storm spirit cat of Peru depicted with a large head with hail raining from its eyes and ears.

See also **Cat**

Centaur. The combination of the human and horse; the body represents the lower animal nature incorporated with the higher nature of judgement and virtue; the savage and the benign in association. The head, hands and trunk of the man comprise the thinking, manipulating and emotional powers of the human with the strength and speed of the horse. Centaurs are sometimes regarded as divine beings: Pindar calls Chiron 'Son of Crones' and 'The Beast Divine', but the first centaurs, offspring of Ixion by Juno in the form of a cloud, were hardly divine, as the cloud bore 'a monstrous son', 'unblest of the Graces' whom she named Cantauros. He mated with the mares of the dales of Pelion and 'thence there sprang a wondrous warrior-like tribe like unto both their parents – like to their dams in their nether parts and the upper frame their sire's'. Chiron, 'the justest of the centaurs' personified wisdom and had knowledge of medicine and archery; he was tutor to Achilles, greatest of the warriors, and to Asclepios, greatest of physicians, and to other heroes. The Centaurs inhabited the mountains of Thessaly; they were fierce but wise, benevolent but sensuous. As sensuous they are associated with the Sirens in the orgies and processions of Dionysos/Bacchus, symbolizing animal instincts and passions. Centaurs acted for underworld deities and so appear on tombs and funeral monuments. Chiron was immortalized by Zeus among the stars as Sagittarius.

Centaurs have an affinity with the Vedic cloud-horses, the Gandharvas. There were also hippo-centaurs, ass-centaurs, fish-centaurs, all of mixed human-animal form; they also appeared as both male and female.

Christianity used centaurs to symbolize the Devil, shooting 'the fiery darts of the wicked' at believers, and as man torn between good and evil, animal and spiritual nature, sensuality, passions, brute force, the heretic. They appear in Christian architecture as shooting at lions, dragons, stags and other wild animals, depicting the conflict of fierce passions or the fight against the lower nature.

Centipede. The Centipede spirit Wu-kung Ching is one of the Seven Devils of Mount Mei. Originally an officer of the advance guard, he changed himself into a poisonous centipede to slay the Count Yu Chan, but was eventually killed himself. The centipede is feared by the Chinese **Dragon**.

Cephus. A combination of satyr-head and dog-bear body; originated in Ethiopia and worshipped by the Egyptians at Memphis.

Cerastes. A two-horned small desert snake of Egypt, not found in

Europe, it was the Greek name for the African snake with a horny protuberance above each eye. Herodotus says it is harmless to man and Aristotle points out that the horns are merely protuberances but large enough to suggest horns. Pliny says the snake buries itself in the sand and moves its horns to attract birds to strike. It was used as a detector of poisons in food and drink, as it perspires in the presence of poison; it also wards off the evil eye. It has been suggested that it was the 'asp' of Cleopatra's suicide.

Cerberus. See **Dog**

Chameleon. In the Four Elements the chameleon is the personification of Air. Pliny says it lives on air and that it changes to every colour except red or white, while Aristotle says it varies only from black to green. Its changing colour is used as a symbol of inconstancy; also the fluctuations of fortune. Its two eyes, seeing independently, represent seeing into both the past and the future.

In African myth Chameleon was given a message of resurrection and immortality for man from God, but he told it to **Lizard** in garbled form and dawdled on the way, so Lizard got to man first with a message of death instead of immortality. It is regarded with fear in West Africa as having magic properties. Among the Bushmen it is a rain-bringer. Christianity depicts it as Satan, taking on different guises to deceive humanity.

Charadrius or Caladrius. A type of plover, mentioned by Aristotle and in the *Septuagint* and *Pentateuch*. The bird was said to be white with no dark spot on it, though one version says it has a yellow beak and legs and a long neck. Brought to the bed of a sick person it predicts recovery or death; it looks steadfastly in the face of one who will recover and draws the malady out, flying up to the sun and causing the disease to be consumed in the solar heat. If it turns its back the patient will die. The *Physiologus* says: 'So Jesus Christ, without spot or blemish, came down from heaven and turned his face away from the Jews but looked in favour on the Gentiles and healed them of their spiritual infirmities.' The bird is portrayed in churches and illustrated in missals and psalters. The marrow, thigh bone and lungs of the bird cure blindness and symbolize the eyes of the spiritually blind being opened to truth, as in the case of St Paul. The Charadrius was also associated with courts and kings as curing the jaundice caused by over-indulgence.

Cheetah.   A natural symbol of swiftness and speed. Cheetahs were trained for hunting in Assyria and Egypt but were replaced by the dog when hunting gazelles and antelopes. In Egypt in the 3rd century BC a procession in honour of Dionysos had lions, cheetahs and leopards. The cheetah is a totem animal in Africa, and tribes have totemic rites and dances of hunting, miming the movement of the animal and its cries and characteristics.

Chichevache. The counterpart of the **Bicorne**, the Chichevache is a fabulous creature that lives by eating virtuous or ill-treated women and consequently is short of food and is emaciated.

Chimera or Chimaera. A fabulous animal usually portrayed with the head, mane and legs of a lion, the body of a goat and tail of a dragon, but also as having three heads – according to Hesiod those of lion, goat and dragon – or as a lion-dragon with a goat's head in the middle of its back. It lived in the mountains of Asia Minor and was slain by Bellerophon, from the air, mounted on Pegasus. It breathed fire. It appeared in ancient Greek poetry as a creature of great strength and swiftness, and symbolized storm, wind and dangers on land and sea. As an imaginary thing it represented the non-existent, hence 'chimerical'.

Cicada. A demon of light and darkness and the cyclic periods of the two, but also a symbol of poetry and the coming of summer. Hesiod says that when it pours out its song, shrill and continuous, summer has come. It is sacred to Apollo and an emblem of Tithonus, who obtained immortality but not eternal youth and so grew older and weaker until he turned into a cicada. It is also a symbol of bad poets and their ceaseless chatter. Aristotle says that, like the **Grasshopper**, it has no mouth but instead a tongue-like formation which enables it to feed on dew only. In China cicadas are kept as pets in grass cages; they represent resurrection, immortality, eternal youth and restraint on greed and vice. Jade images of cicadas were placed in the mouth of the dead to ensure immortality. In Greek myth it also signified immortality as being bloodless and living on dew. It is unlucky to kill one. This prohibition also obtains in Polynesia, where no noise may be made to interrupt its singing. The Green Cicada is an Australian Aboriginal totem; among moietes a Cicada must marry into a Crow tribe.

Cinnamon Bird. Herodotus says that this is a large bird which came from some unidentified land to Arabia, carrying cinnamon with which to line its nest. The nests, built high, are brought down by various methods by spice hunters.

Clam. The Giant Clam is the totem and ancestor of a Melanesian clan and was one of the agents used by Old Spider Woman in creating the earth.

Cock. As the herald of the dawn the Cock is pre-eminently a solar bird, with the exception of Celtic, Scandinavian and some ancient Greek symbolism in which it has chthonic associations as a bird of the underworld. Elsewhere it incorporates the masculine principle, courage, vigilance – an 'awakener' – war and aggression. It is one of the chief sacrificial creatures and was frequently depicted as a guardian in early times and as such was sacrificed and buried under foundations of buildings to ward off evil. It is also a weather prophet and, having second sight like dogs, cats and rats, it can warn against danger. Cock crow at midnight presages a death; cock crowing also marked one of the night watches. Cocks fighting represents the battle of life. Cock fights took place annually at Athens in the month of Poseidon as a symbol of battle and pugnacity. The cock's head is an ancient Sun God symbol.

The colour of a cock is highly symbolic; the white cock was sacred to the moon and to goddesses such as Athene and Demeter, but on the other hand it was connected with Apollo as the rising sun. In Egypt white or yellow cocks were sacrificed to Anubis, Osiris and Nephthys. The black cock has always been strongly associated with witches, the Devil and Black Magic. In Scandinavian lore the golden cock Vithafmir at the top of the Yggdrasil guards against evil powers, but the underworld red cock Fralar lives in Valhalla and will wake the heroes for the last great battle.

In ancient Greece the cock was solar as sacred to Apollo, but it had otherworld connections which gave it a chthonic significance. Socrates said he would sacrifice a cock to Asclepios at his death. The cock, with various other fertility symbols such as the pomegranate, eggs, shark and mullet, was a forbidden food at feasts of women at the Haloa winter-festival. Cocks drew the chariot of Hermes/ Mercury as an emblem of the God of Merchants, and accompany him in Graeco-Roman art. Greek symbolism also used the cock as depicting a bombastic talker. In Greece a white cock was sacrificed and buried in ceremonies aimed at averting threatening winds and squalls, though the normal storm sacrifice was a black animal.

Poultry-keeping had been established in Greece before the Persian war – Aristophanes calls the cock the Persian Bird – and it was common in Rome, the Romans later taking it to all their colonies. Cocks were sacrificed to the Lares and were kept at the temple of Hercules, with hens kept at the temple of Hebe. Cocks were also symbols of the Sun God Mithras.

Sacred in early Britain, the cock had the chthonic aspect of the Gallo-Roman Mercury, was an attribute of the gods of the underworld and of the Celtic Mother Goddess; the cock was sacrificed on Bride's Day.

Early Hebrew marriage rites had a cock and hen carried in front of the bridal pair to signify fertility.

In China, the cock as a homophone of 'fortunate' was employed in funerary rituals to ward off evil spirits; it represents the sunset, though the red cock is the original form of the sun and protects against fire; here it is the *yang* principle, courage, valour, fidelity, also war and aggression. With a crown on its head it portrays the literary spirit; with spurs the warlike character. In some initiation rites a white cock was sacrificed to represent the death of the old life and the purity of the new. A cock and hen in a garden depict the pleasures of rural life.

For the Japanese the cock is a Shinto symbol, standing on the drum which calls the people to prayer in the temples. In Buddhism the cock represents carnal passion and pride and is depicted at the centre of the Round of Existence with the pig and the snake.

Christianity equates the cock with the solar power as putting to flight the powers of darkness; it depicts vigilance also and those two aspects are shown in the cock as a weather-vane on churches, with the bird turning in all directions to watch for the forces of evil; it also acts as a guardian in the hours of darkness when the bells are silent. The cock greets the dawn of Christ in the East. Bede says that it depicts 'the souls of the just awaiting the dawn'. In the New Testament it is associated with Christ's passion and represents resurrection; as connected with St Peter it symbolizes human weakness and repentance. In the Bestiaries it is called *Gallus* and is mentioned as the only bird to be castrated. Cockcrow is 'pleasant and useful', it 'consoles the traveller and forewarns the anxious; it calls the priest to his devotions; gives hope to the sick, reduces fever and restores faith.' Peter washed away his previous sins by testifying after cockcrow.

In Heraldry the cock features more often as a crest than on shields, with beak and spurs depicted as 'armed'. It can be represented without comb and wattles. It symbolizes both soldierly courage and religious aspiration.

The blood of a cock is an essential ingredient in ju-ju rites, particularly at initiation; it was taken over into voodoo.

Cockatoo. The totem of an Australian Aboriginal tribe, Cockatoos' feathers were carried by tribal messengers as emblems of their mission.

Cockatrice. See **Basilisk**

Codfish. In the lore of the Nootka North American Indians the Sky Codfish is a mythological being who causes eclipses by swallowing the sun.

Colour. The actual colour of an animal or bird, or the tincture in which it is depicted in iconography, holds its own important symbolism; this obtains especially where sacrificial animals are concerned. Different colours fit different needs, for instance, when rain is needed the animal should be black, like the black clouds, while purificatory rites are naturally associated with that which is white, or, as in South America, a grey llama was sacrificed to the

God of the Sea, white to the sun; a red-coated sheep is also sacrificed to the sun.

The cow of Minos was each day white, red and black, as dawn, noon and night.

White was the colour most frequently preferred to signify purity, not only that of the sacrificial animal, but also of the new life for the people after the sacrifice. White also represents perfection, holiness, redemption, the sacred, propitiation and surrender. It is the solar colour, associated with the Sky Gods and with the dawn, although it can also be lunar, as in the case of the White Tiger in China, which is a *yin* animal, symbolizing the West, the dying year and mourning. In Japan, on the other hand, white animals are solar and bring good fortune. Albino animals were widely venerated, for example, in Patagonia a white rhea was sacrosanct; the whole species would die out if one were killed. White often represented the sacred and good as opposed to black as the profane and evil, as in the case of the white cock, one of the most preferred sacrificial animals, as against the black cock of witches and black magic. White horses were particularly sacred, and the white elephant has special significance in the East.

Colour was important in Celtic representations of the underworld, and the White Bull was the chief sacrifice of the Druids at the cutting of the mistletoe. White doves are an almost universal symbol of peace and are particularly associated with the Mother Goddesses and Queens of Heaven and were sacrificed to them; they were emblems of femininity and maternity. In Greece a white cock was sacrificed and buried to avert storms and threatening winds, though the normal storm animal was black, again like the storm clouds. Virgil said: 'To storms a black sheep; white to the favouring West.'

For African tribes, sacrificial animals and birds must be of one colour. The milk of a white cow is a potent offering in spells and invocations, but the blood and gall of a black ox are used in rain-making magic.

Black is naturally associated with the night, the underworld and death; it is also the colour of pitiless Time, which is the dark aspect of the Great Mother in her dual role of birth and death, and of Cronos/Saturn as Time. Black oxen draw the chariot of death and were sacrificed to underworld deities such as Pluto. The Egyptian Apis Bull was black except for a white blaze, symbolizing the dark of the moon from which the new moon is born. The Chinese Black Tortoise is *yin* and depicts the North and winter. Among birds, black, dark-coloured or night-birds are generally allied to powers of darkness and considered unlucky, the brighter colours being lucky. Black dogs are widely known as haunting wild places, and they often presage death; they, with black cats and cocks, are particularly known as witches' creatures or familiars.

Red, the colour of blood, represents all War Gods, the Sun and Fire, the masculine principle, but it can also symbolize the desert, evil and calamity. In Celtic myth death was the Red Horseman, but the Red Dragon of Wales depicts sovereignty. In China the Red Phoenix is the sun, joy and happiness.

Blue, as the colour of the sky, can portray both Sky Gods and Queens of Heaven. In China the Azure Dragon signifies the East and spring.

In divination from the entrails of animals, colour, size and shape were of great importance in reading the omens.

The tincture in which an animal is portrayed in Heraldry holds a special symbolism; *or* is gold; *gules*, red; *azure*, blue; *vert*, green; there are also variations which can be highly symbolic or merely a case of distinction.

Composite Animals.   Composite creatures take on the symbolism and powers of every feature represented, the qualities, virility, strength or weakness of each part depicted. They also signify the land, sea and air powers portrayed by bodies, wings and fins, for example the swiftness of the horse-body, the wisdom of the human head and the powers of ascension of wings.

Half-human, half-animal figures also represent the instinctual, intuitional animal powers combined with the human intellect, also the combination of the dual nature in humanity, the higher and the lower and the conflict between the two.

In deities the particular quality of the god or goddess is represented by the animal feature, for example the fish-tail of the Babylonian Ea, God of the Waters, or the solar falcon head of the Egyptian Sun God Ra. Most Egyptian deities appear in zoomorphic form.

Egyptian Composite Creature, with the head of a crocodile, mane of a lion, fore-feet and body of a cheetah and hindquarters of a hippopotamus

Celtic cult animals have horns, symbols of supernatural power or divinity, and are depicted as birds, horses, and serpents. Among northern nomadic people several heads may be portrayed as a single body.

Animal-headed divinities have been suggested as originally totem animals. Diodorus says that they originated as rallying signs on battle standards. Composite figures appear universally.

Condor. The embodiment of the Inca Gods of the Air. Peruvian clans used the feathers as ritual ornaments. There is a Condor clan of the Amerindian Eagle Tribe.

Coney. The Coney of the Bible is the Rock Hyrax, the **Rabbit** being then unknown, and is an unclean animal for the Jews but is included in Solomon's wise creatures; although a 'feeble folk' (Proverbs 30: 26) they are extremely wary. The Hebrew name *Shaphan* signifies 'the hidden'. The Arabs of Sinai called the coney the 'brother of man' and it was forbidden to eat it.

Conflicting Animals. Certain animals are traditionally in conflict; they usually symbolize powers which are naturally at variance, such as light and darkness, life and death, good and evil, the solar and lunar, masculine and feminine. Of these antagonistic creatures probably the most notable are the Solar Eagle in enmity with the chthonic Serpent, and the Solar Lion confronting the Lunar Unicorn. There are also the opposites of the fierce and the gentle, the Lion and the Lamb, or Wolf and Lamb.

Early and mediaeval zoologists assumed that there were natural enemies. Lucretius says that the universe operates on a system of sympathies and antipathies. This may be likened to the Chinese *yin-yang* cosmic order, though here the opposites are held in tension rather than in conflict. Magic may be said to operate on much the same scale, finding the power of control of one thing over another.

Zoroastrianism has the belief in a dualistic conflict between good and evil, Ormuzd and Ahriman, which operates through the whole universe so that in the animal kingdom certain animals are by nature assigned to one or the other – the Bull, Horse, Dog are pure, the Lion and Cat impure. The Boar and Stag were created by Ormuzd to kill the Serpent of Ahriman. The conflict symbolizes the fundamental tensions between opposites in life and the interplay of the negative-positive forces and sexes apparent both in society and individuals.

When normally conflicting animals are depicted together, such as the Lion and the Lamb, the symbolism is that of the Golden Age, Paradise, peace and friendship. Many myths of conflicting monsters, or man against monsters, may be seen as the conflict between light and darkness, summer and winter.

Bear-headed Fish (*from an Indian mural depicting the constellations*)

Constellations. In mythology various constellations are represented by animals, such as the Great Bear and Little Bear, the Dog Star and the various signs of the Zodiac. Not only were animals elevated to the skies to become stars or constellations, thus retaining their powers over the earth and affecting the fate of man and beast in astrology, but there was an ancient and widespread belief in star-ancestors and animal ancestry which occurred in such widely differing cultures as the Greek, Egyptian, Amerindian, Australian Aboriginal and African. An early missionary among the Greenlanders wrote: 'Their notions about the stars are that some of them have been men and others different sorts of animals and fishes. But every reader of Ovid knows that this was the very mythical theory of the Greeks and Romans.'

The Great Bear, Ursa Major, is depicted as the Heavenly Bear, and she and Ursa Minor represented two she-bears in Crete who looked after the infant Zeus and helped to hide him from Cronos. In another version of the Graeco-Roman myth, Zeus changed Callisto into Ursa Major to protect her from the jealousy of Hera/Juno; her son became Ursa Minor. Poseidon placed Delphinos among the stars as the Dolphin.

The Sumerian Mushussu, a three-headed dragon, was identified with the constellation Hydra. The winged horse, Pegasus, was taken into Olympus and later transformed into a constellation. The Dog Star, Sirius is the constellation of Canis Major. The Egyptian Bast represents the star Sothis. Sagittarius, half-man, half-horse, the Centaur Chiron, a sign of the Zodiac, was immortalized by Zeus and placed in the heavens.

Animals as heavenly bodies are particularly prolific among tribal and totemistic societies. In Amerindian myth the culture-hero often disappears after the completion of his mission and leaves the earth to become a star. The Innuits (Eskimos) have the Great Bear as a

Reindeer; the Pleiades are baying hounds round a Bear. Capella is a Reindeer buck behind a sledge with a man driving two more Reindeer. The seventh star of the Great Bear is a fox gnawing antlers. The Gemini are two Elks running from two hunters driving Reindeer teams; Corona is the paw of a Polar Bear. Delphinius is a Seal; Cassiopeia is four Reindeer bucks in the middle of a river.

Among South American Indians the Southern Cross is the toes of a Great Ostrich and the Centaur its leg. Orion is a Turtle. In Central Brazil the Southern Cross is a Ray Fish; the two stars of the Centaur above it are an Ostrich upon which Scorpio, a Jaguar, is leaping. The Milky Way is the Ostrich Way with the Southern Cross as its head and the two stars of the Centaur its collar. But among the Hopi of Arizona the Milky Way was the result of negligence on the part of Coyote who let the stars escape from a sealed pot. In some tribes Orion is Birds-meet-each other; in others it is the Black Vulture with the Southern Cross as the Ostrich; the large stars of the Centaur a Roebuck and the Pleiades a flock of Parakeets. Scorpio is the Great Serpent.

The Southern Cross appears in Australian Aboriginal myth as an Eagle's foot or an Emu. Mars is an Eagle; Corvus is a Kangaroo; Altair an Eagle-in-action; the star at the head of the Cross is a fleeing Opossum and the Milky Way has a Crocodile in it. Aldebaran represents the Rose-crested Cockatoo; Sirius is an Eagle.

In Polynesia the Milky Way is the Long-blue-cloud-eating Shark. The Pleiades is the Hen-with-six-chickens for the Dyaks; in the Torres Straits the Great Bear becomes the Shark.

The Pleiades as the Hen-with-Chickens also occurs among the Ibos in Africa. Other tribes have the Great Bear as a Camel and Cassiopeia as an Ass. The Pleiades are also Ants; Orion a Fish or a Dog or a Palm Rat or a female Hartebeeste; the sword is also three male Tortoises with his belt as three female Tortoises. The Bushmen have Aldebaran as a male Hartebeeste.

In Chinese mythology, the twenty-eight constellations were represented as sub-human or animals such as the Dragon, Crocodile, Badger, Fox, Dog, Wolf, Leopard, Hare, Porcupine, Rat, Bat, Griffon, Gibbon, Cock, Crow, Horse, Ox, Dew-worm, Deer, Monkey, Snake, Stag, Goat, Tapir, Swallow, Tiger and Pig. They could also be represented as human or composite.

Coot. A symbol of stupidity and of baldness. The Bestiaries say that the coot is an example of compassion, for when the **Eagle** rejects its weaklings they fall to the ground and the coot then brings them up with her own brood. It is called the *Falica*, and here typifies intelligence and foresight. As it stays in one place and does not stray – 'so do the faithful live, all knit together in one flock.'

Cormorant.   An unclean bird for the Jews; a symbol of desolation in the Bible.

Corn-crake or Land-rail.   Mentioned in early Greek literature as accompanying the **Quail** and used interchangeably with the Quail in Old Testament translations of Exodus 16: 13, Numbers 11: 31–2, Psalms 105: 40.

Cougar.   See **Panther**

Council of Animals.   In Merovingian days it was the custom for all animals to assemble round their King at Whitsuntide, Nobel the Lion. It was a type of *Champ de Mars* and it not only decided on all the undertakings for the following year but also was a special tribunal at which accusations were made, complaints heard and justice meted out to all. It was at this tribunal that Reynard the Fox was tried (see also **Fox**).

The Amerindians had a Council of Animals which, with the aid of the Otter, Spider and Hare, helped mankind to Recover the Light.

Cow.   As representing both the horned Moon Goddesses and the nourishing Earth Mother, the cow is both celestial and chthonic, it symbolizes all their nourishing, procreative and maternal qualities but is also associated with their birth-death-and-rebirth aspect.

In ancient Egypt the cow was pre-eminently the Great Mother Hathor, who was depicted as a cow, or with the head and horns of a cow, the horns representing the crescent moon. There was also Nut, the Celestial Cow, the Lady of Heaven whose four legs are the four quarters of the earth. The double-headed cow signified the Upper and Lower Egypt. Hathor, Nut and Isis could all be portrayed as cows or with horns. Hathor was not only a Sky Goddess and Goddess of Love, but was also associated with the dead and cemeteries, and in this guise provided nourishment for the soul. The Celestial Heifer, the cosmic goddess Mehurt, gave birth to the sun. She, too, was usually pictured as a cow or cow-headed. The Heavenly Cow was also associated with the Bull of Heaven, giving birth to a calf each day – the sun. This has affinities with the myths of the Sidonian Cow-goddess, identified with Europa as the bride of the Bull-Zeus. The Syrian Astarte and Ishtar were also depicted as cows and with the lunar horns.

Although the **Bull** was one of the foremost sacrificial animals, the cow was seldom sacrificed. Herodotus says that though the Lybians ate oxen the cow was sacred and they would not touch its flesh, and that the Phoenicians sacrificed and ate bulls but not the sacred cow.

Nowhere is the cow more venerated than in India. It is a sacred animal which the *Rig Veda* says is 'not to be killed'. From Indo-Iranian times it has been treated with respect and care as a source of life-giving milk, the holy milk which nourished kings and priests.

Nandini, the wish-fulfilling cow, gives milk and an elixir. Aditi, the All-Embracing Mother of the gods, and Prithivi, Vedic Earth Goddess, are also associated with the plenty, fertility and nourishing qualities of the cow. For the Hindus the cow is full of power and can transmit this if driven over the threshold of a new house, or after prolonged absence. Its urine is apotropaic and is used in purification rites and sprinkled after a death or a birth in the house. An offer of milk must not be refused as it is associated with Lakshmi, Goddess of Fortune; it is used at weddings both as a drink and for finger-dipping. The Cows of the Dawn represent the rays of the sun. In the Himalayan region the Holy Cow leads the dead along the difficult and dangerous road to the Gates of Judgement. In the *Rig Veda* clouds can be symbolized by cows as the nourishing and fertilizing rain.

The Greek Hera and Io took the form of the cow, and cows were sacrificed to Hera/Juno and Hercules. Hera took the form of a white cow when she fled from Typhon.

The cow appears frequently in Celtic mythology as a provider of nourishment for entire communities, like the magic cows of Manannan, one speckled, one dun, with twisted horns, who were always in milk. The chthonic cow is depicted as red with white ears, and there are otherworld cows which emerge from under the waters of a lake and numerous cows connected with otherworld beings, with magic and supernatural powers. The *Welsh Triads* refer to sacred otherworld cows and to the Three Prominent Cows of the Island of Britain.

In Scandinavia the Primordial Cow, the Nourisher, sprang from the ice and licked it to produce the first man. The enchanted Cow of Norse myth could wreak more devastation in battle than an army of warriors; it belonged to King Eystein and was slain by the magic of Ivar, eldest son of Ragnar.

The cow is naturally a *yin* animal in China and represents the earth principle, with the horse as the *yang* and the heavens.

The Amerindian White Buffalo Cow brought the Sacred Piper to the people for their rites.

In Zulu myth mankind was 'belched up by a cow'.

Coyote. Coyote, Raven and Hare, or Rabbit, are together the main **Trickster** Heroes of the North Amerindians. Coyote appears mainly in the western mountain regions and the Plains. He is the archetypal Trickster Culture Hero; a Fire Theft hero but also a flood-bringer and the spirit of night. As a 'Medicine Dog' he has magical powers; as the Trickster he is the acme of humour, always getting into absurd situations, never learning from mistakes; he has a love of poetry and of the ridiculous, is a humorist and clown but also a demiurge and creator, and while he is associated with the introduction of death, pain and evil into the world, he is also a hero-saviour and can lead one out of danger. He is the totem animal, or the Brother, or Old Man Coyote or Little Wolf among numerous tribes.

The Chinook Coyote, however, differs from that of the Californian tribes in that he is not a Trickster and not mischievous or of an evil nature; he is an important Hero-Creator who sprang from a fog after the Flood and plaited feathers which became people of various tribes. In the Californian region he has a relationship with the Creators such as Eagle, Wolf, and Fox, but while they are responsible for the good and wise things, Coyote brings about the bad and introduces death.

In Hopi lore he is the Trickster who was responsible for the formation of the Milky Way by his negligence in taking the lid off a sealed pot and letting the stars escape.

Coyote appears with the Jaguar in ritual processions in Mexican iconography.

Crab. The oblique movement of the crab symbolizes dishonesty, people such as money-changers, unreliability and crookedness. It also represents the oblique retrograde movement of the Sun after the summer solstice in the sign of Cancer.

Buddhism uses the crab as typifying the sleep of death and the period of existence between incarnation and regeneration into the next life.

In Sumeria crabs, lobsters and scorpions were associated with the goddess Nina, Lady of the Waters.

For the Incas the crab was the terrible aspect of the Great Mother, the devourer of the world of time and the waning moon. In Amerindian myth it is a controller of the lower waters but it never reaches the bottom, its power being annulled by the magic of the White Diver Bird.

The Bestiaries say that the crab tricks the **Oyster** by inserting a pebble in its shell when it opens, and is thus a symbol of trickery, deceit and cruelty, cheating another's innocence.

The crab is the totem of a Melanesian clan by whom it may not be eaten; it appears as a huge Crab-goddess or demon; it causes elephantiasis.

Cramp Fish. See **Torpedo**

Crane. In most mythology the crane is a messenger of the gods and represents the ability to enter into higher states; it is also credited with great intelligence, discipline and vigilance.

Cranes were reported to post sentries while they slept, the sentry holding a stone in one claw and standing on the other foot so that if he fell asleep the stone would drop and wake him. Aelian affirms this but Aristotle does not mention it, while Pliny adds that the

The Crane and Serpent (*from a Bestiary*)

crane also fills his beak with sand for the same purpose. Cranes were
also believed to carry a stone in their beaks when migrating so that
they did not cry out and attract the attention of predators. When
flying they form a triangle, the old in front, the young protected in
the middle. Their discipline taught men the rules of government.
They are also weather prophets, alighting before bad weather, and
sailors returned to port if they saw cranes flying in a contrary
direction. Hesiod says that they signal the times of sowing and
shearing and that 'the voice of the Crane crying year after year from
the clouds above' is the signal for ploughing to begin.

In Graeco-Roman myth there is an enmity between cranes and
pygmies which is similar to the Indian account of the hostility
between the **Garuda** Bird and the dwarfs, the *Kirata*. In Greece the
crane was sacred to Apollo as spring and light. The Crane Dance
in Greece symbolized the start of the year.

The Old Testament portrays the crane as a chatterer (Isaiah 38:
14) 'as a crane so did I chatter', and in Jeremiah 8: 7 it represents
orderliness and appointed time.

The crane is of great importance in Chinese symbolism; it is 'The
Patriarch of the Feathered Tribe', a messenger of the gods and an
intermediary between heaven and earth. It carries souls to the
Western Paradise and signifies immortality, longevity, the protective
maternal instinct, good fortune, vigilance, happiness and high
official position. White cranes are sacred and live in the Isles of the
Blest. In art the crane is usually depicted with the sun and the pine
tree, both *yang* symbols. In both Chinese and Japanese myth it
attains a fabulous age – 1000 years or more. Japanese symbolism
follows the Chinese in most respects, but in Japan it is called
'Honourable Lord Crane'.

Celtic mythology has both solar and underworld symbolism for the crane. It is associated with the solar deities, especially in their healing aspect; it is also depicted with weapons and battle objects. It is a supernatural creature and appears riding on the backs of human-headed horses and in connection with magic cauldrons. On an ancient altar in France three cranes are depicted standing on the back of a bull. But the crane is also a form of Pwyll, King of the Underworld, and as such a herald of death.

A completely contrary symbolism obtains in Gallic lore where the crane is a bad omen, depicting meanness, parsimony and evil women. It is an attribute of the Gaulish Mercury and Mars, and as such is connected with war and death.

Christianity uses the crane to represent vigilance, loyalty, good order in monastic life. In the *Physiologus* the care and vigilance of the crane is opposed to the **Fox** as the Devil, and the fable of the crane extracting a bone from the throat of the fox is likened to saving a soul from the jaws of hell. The Bestiaries say the crane symbolizes care and courtesy, supporting the weaker when they tire on a long flight and setting sentries during the night watches.

In Ainu myth the cranes came down from heaven and were the bringers of clothing for the people; garments were found in the nest of the original pair – their nest is supposed to be lined with wool.

The Amerindians associate the white of the crane's feather with divine wisdom and life.

The crane is an attribute of the female figure of Vigilance. The crane's foot symbolizes the branching out of the lines of the family tree, hence the *pied de grue* – pedigree.

In Heraldry the bird is usually represented as holding the stone of vigilance in its claw, but heraldry makes little distinction between the crane, **Stork** and **Heron**, except that the heron always has a tuft on its head.

Crawfish or Crayfish. As a fertility symbol the crayfish was a forbidden food in Greece at the women's festival of the Haloa. Among the Ainu it is a minor God of the Rivers, the 'deity who walks backwards'. In Amerindian myth the crawfish dived and brought up mud from the waters for the Great Spirit to create the earth after the Flood.

Cricket. The Japanese Tree-cricket or *sami* is popular in mythology: its singing symbolizes the chanting of a Buddhist priest. In China it depicts summer and courage. In China and Japan crickets are kept as pets in little grass cages. In the West the cricket is a symbol of the domestic hearth.
See also **Grasshopper**

Crocodile. From the earliest times the crocodile was both feared

Egyptian Crocodile God Sebek with a mummy on his back; to the left stands Isis, while Osiris, in the character of Menu, 'the god of the uplifted arm' and Harpokrates sit in the disk of the moon (*from a bas-relief at Philae*)

and revered, but attitudes adopted towards it varied greatly. It was venerated in some parts and hated and killed in others, sometimes treated as a god, at others seen as embodying all that is evil. There were strange beliefs associated with the crocodile. Aristotle and Herodotus state that it was not able to move its lower jaw and that it had no tongue, and this was generally accepted, though Aelian says later that it had 'a kind of shabby representation of a tongue' while Pliny says it 'lacks the use of a tongue', as does also the **lizard**, so both typify silence.

As pre-eminently a creature of the Nile, the crocodile features largely in Egyptian mythology, but again is ambivalent as a symbol of both the sunrise (and thus associated with the Pharaohs) and Set/Typhon, the power of evil and the demonic foe of Horus. This dual symbolism also occurs in connection with Sebek the crocodile-headed God, who on the one hand was a son of Neith and an ancient solar deity (identified with Ra as Sebek-Ra), but on the other hand was associated with Set as evil and brutality. Crocodiles were sacred to him and were kept in a lake by his temple. Crocodiles were also worshipped at Ombi; as sacred they were decorated with jewels, gold bracelets and ear-rings, and were fed by the priests on bread, flesh and wine. Remnants of the cult at Thebes remained in Egypt until modern times. The crocodile-god required placation by sacrifices and offerings; shrines were dedicated to him, and the *Book of the Dead* gives a spell which enabled the deceased to take on the form of 'the divine crocodile which dwelleth in terror and seizeth its prey.' There were also four crocodiles, living at the four corners of the earth, which threatened the newly dead in order to seize upon the magical words and powers they needed for entrance to the next world.

The crocodile also symbolizes vicious passions, deceit, treachery and hypocrisy: having swallowed the moon he weeps, hence 'crocodile tears'. Sometimes depicted with an open mouth, it signifies going against the current and therefore liberation from the limitations of the world. As a creature of both the land and water it portrays the dual nature of man.

In Africa it is sacred among the Bantus and is used by magicians. Among West African tribes if a crocodile or leopard is seen when out hunting it must never be named and it is forbidden to eat the flesh by those for whom it is a ju-ju. The liver and entrails of the crocodile are extremely powerful in magic and can, when manipulated by a witch doctor, cause death to anyone.

The Australian Aboriginals say that the crocodile was originally a man who jumped into the water and changed into a crocodile. In Oceania, notably in Sumatra, the crocodile is worshipped as a god, a dangerous one to be propitiated; it is therefore addressed in flattering terms when crossing rivers or on any encounter.

The *Physiologus* uses the crocodile as hypocrisy; it says that the 'crocodile tears' are shed by the creature after it has devoured a man. In the Bestiaries it is the Cocodryllus and breeds in the Nile, it is amphibious with horrible teeth and claws and symbolizes the Devil, Death and Hell. Being swallowed by a crocodile or any other reptile depicts the descent into Hell. As crocodile dung was used as a cosmetic to reduce wrinkles, the Bestiaries say it represents pride, corruption, hypocrisy, avarice and luxury.

In Mayan festivals the crocodile in effigy was a feature of clowning; snapping its jaws and going among the people and threatening them, it played much the same part as the Hobby Horse in English festivals.

In some countries the crocodile can be the abode of the souls of ancestors; it can also be equated with the Dragon.

Crossbill. Christian lore said that the Crossbill was stained by the blood of the crucifixion in trying to extract the nails from Jesus' hands and feet, just as the **Robin** tried to pull out the thorns of the crown. Its beak was crossed in its effort to extract the nails.

Cross-breeding. According to the Bestiaries cross-breeding is 'bastardizing nature' and is a greater sin than fornication in that it injures natural affinity, destroying sex and creating a eunuch.

Crow. Aelian says that the crow's monogamy and conjugal affection make it a symbol of constancy, and hence it was invoked at weddings. This also appears in other cultures such as in Egypt where a pair of crows denoted conjugal happiness; for the Aryans the crow was a marriage gift as it provided food and fertilizing dung and urine – symbol of life itself. In Hinduism it is an attribute of Varuna.

Although sacred to Apollo, who took the form of a crow when fleeing from Typhon, the crow was unlucky in ancient Greece, and though also sacred to Athene she never permitted crows to alight on the Acropolis; it was an omen of death if a crow perched on a roof. The bird was little mentioned in Greek augury, but a single crow was a bad omen, as was a crow appearing on the left side.

Chinese symbolism depicts the crow in different colours: when black it is evil, malice and bad luck, but if portrayed in red or gold it is solar, the sun and filial piety. It has, however, been queried as to whether it should be the **Cock** and not the crow that was meant to be associated with the sun, since stylized creatures found in ancient works of art can easily be confused. The three-legged crow, or cock, lives in the sun, its three legs representing the three phases of the day. A black crow and white heron together depict the *yin-yang* principle. For the Japanese the crow signifies ill luck on the one hand, but on the other it can be a messenger of the deities, and in Shintoism is associated with temples. The crow is sometimes portrayed in front of the sun.

The white crow appears in Celtic lore as Branwen, sister of Bran. Crows can be a form adopted by fairies, usually with ill intent, and are therefore dreaded. The **Owl** is the mortal enemy of the crow since it steals the crow's young in the nest at night.

The Bestiaries say that the crow is a soothsayer and that crows are devoted parents and hence a symbol of love and duty to one's offspring. They teach that Nature divides her riches equally but that humanity shows discrimination in the wrongfulness of primogeniture. Crows were said to lead **Storks** on migration. Like the Turtle **Dove**, the crow is used as a symbol of fidelity as it is said to remain alone if it loses its mate – this also makes it signify solitude. Christianity also uses the crow on the dark side as the Devil plucking out eyes.

Among Amerindians the crow is a keeper of the sacred law and has knowledge of the mysteries of creation, protecting the ancient records. It sees the past, present and future at the same time. It is also a shape-shifter and an omen of change. The black feather of a crow symbolizes death and will bring death to an enemy, but as a scavenger it is a cleanser and beneficent. Crow brought the first grain and beans to the Algonquins and is a messenger to the Spirit world. It is the central figure in the Ghost Dance. The Crow Tribe of Montana was named after the Absaroke bird, no longer found in that region.

The crow is a totem animal with the Australian Aboriginals. Among moieties a Crow must marry a Green Cicada. The bird is also associated with sorcerers.

Almost universally associated with prophecy, eating the heart of a crow bestows prophetic powers; it is also a weather prophet and its cawing predicts rain.

Cuckoo. Symbolizes spring in southern Europe and summer in the northern regions. Traditionally the cuckoo turned into a **Hawk** for the winter and dwelt with the fairies. On hearing the first cuckoo money should be turned in the pocket. The cuckoo sucks other birds' eggs to keep its voice clear. The arrival of the cuckoo is the occasion for the sowing of crops; if it comes early it presages frosts and a bad harvest, but if late it is a good omen. The bird itself is ambivalent, sometimes regarded as evil and demonical, at other times venerated, as in the case of the Phoenicians, for whom it was the kingly bird, mounted on royal sceptres. In Greece it was a symbol of wedlock and was one of the transformations undertaken by Zeus in order to win Hera; it therefore figures on Hera's sceptre.

Pliny says that the cuckoo is a magic remedy for fleas and that a cuckoo in a hare skin cures insomnia.

In Hindu myth the cuckoo symbolizes the sun hidden by clouds and hence fertilizing rain; it is supernaturally wise, knowing past, present and future. A cuckoo and bee accompany Kama, God of Love.

Among the Ainu it descends from heaven each spring and tells the people it is time to start work in the gardens.

The cuckoo is sometimes associated with fertility charms and with marriage rites; its egg is also used as a charm. Its habit of laying its eggs in other birds' nests gives rise to a symbolism of unfaithfulness in marriage – the cuckold. In Japan it depicts unrequited love. It also symbolizes mockery and a fool.

D

Dance. Dances are frequently performed in imitation of animals at tribal festivals, particularly those of the Amerindians and Australian Aboriginals. The animals are usually totems or objects of the hunt, or both. There are such well-known dances as the Snake, Bear, Buffalo, Dog, Deer, Kangaroo, and Cassowary and other birds. The dances are associated with fertility rites for both people and animals, or, in hunting tribes, both the hunt and the quarry are mimed and the dancing continues until the symbolic exhaustion of the hunted is attained.

Deathwatch Beetle. Its ticking in a house foretells death. In Japan it is called the Poverty Insect; for the Japanese it does not presage death but the coming of the God of Poverty.

Deer. Universally a symbol of swiftness, agility, gentleness and timidity. Although deer were depicted in early Egyptian temples they died out in that country before the Christian era; they were sacred to Isis. Deer are mentioned frequently in the Old Testament; they were clean meat for the Hebrews. The biblical Hart or Hind is thought to have been the Fallow Deer. In Isaiah 35: 6 it depicts agility – 'leap as the hart'; it portrays the loving wife in Proverbs 5: 19, and in Psalms 42: 1 it represents the soul panting and thirsting after God. The sureness of the hind's feet appears in II Samuel 22: 34; Psalms 18: 33 and Habakkuk 3: 19. It typifies the beloved in Canticles 2: 9 and 17; and 8: 14. The symbolism continued with the spread of Christianity.

The Greeks held the deer sacred to the Moon Goddesses Artemis, Aphrodite, Athene and Diana, but it was also sacred to Apollo at Delphi and to Icarus. A hind suckled Telephus. It was believed that if wounded by an arrow the deer would find the herb dictanum or dittany which effected a cure by ejecting the arrow from the body. Aristotle says this also of the wild goat, and Pliny of the deer.

A deer is the mount of Vayu, Vedic God of the Wind, who is usually portrayed riding on one. The deer has particular significance in Buddhism as associated with the Buddha's first sermon in the deer park at Sarnath which set the Wheel of the Law in action; deer are depicted on either side of the Wheel; they also represent meditation, gentleness and meekness. The deer is also, however, one of the 'three senseless creatures' of Chinese Buddhism as typifying love-sickness, with the **Tiger** as anger and the **Monkey** as greed. In China the deer also represents high rank, official success, and wealth.

In Celtic tradition deer are frequently the means of taking souls to the otherworld. There are Celtic, Irish and Gaelic goddesses associated with them, such as Flidass, Goddess of Venery, who has a chariot drawn by deer. They are supernatural animals of the fairy world and are fairy cattle and messengers. Stag hunts often end in some supernatural situation. Deer skin and antlers were used as ritual ornaments and vestments.

As a totem animal the deer plays an important part in Amerindian culture. There are deer tribes and clans, and the deer is head of the four-footed animals of the Indians of the southeast Woodlands. The Deer Dance of the southwestern tribes secures food and fertility for both people and animals; the deer, being a rain-bringer, also brings thunder and lightning and has powers of either causing or curing illness. Among the South American Indians it can be a demonical animal, incarnating the soul of a sorcerer or sorceress, usually the latter. Dead ancestors can also be incarnated in deer. The Aztec God of Hunting, Mixcoatl, is accompanied by a two-headed deer. The White Deer of the Algonquins dwells in the evil underworld. In Mexico a deer slain in the peyote hunt is mourned and the bones, representing the peyote roots, are buried as part of ceremonies of apology and propitiation so that they may be born again. These rites of propitiation to the spirit of the slain are similar to those of the Ainu Bear Sacrifice. In Ainu myth the deer was created to provide food for the people. Originally they were not deer but God's hunting dogs to hunt hare; they were then white. The bones and hair of deer consumed in a heavenly feast were distributed over the mountains and changed into living deer.

See also **Stag**

Descent from Animals. The theme of descent from animal ancestors is widespread in mythology and fairy tale, particularly among tribal cultures, and there are numerous myths of marriage between humans, animals and birds, such as that of a woman who met a bear by which she had two children who were the ancestors of the Mongols. Descent from animals accounts for the similarities between humans and animals, as an Amerindian said: 'we know what animals do . . . because long ago men married them and acquired the knowledge from their animal wives'. Various clans of the hunting tribes say they are descended from half-animal, half-human ancestry and can be born either as humans or animals, but in either case they are of the same blood.

Alaskan tribes have an Animal Ceremony with masked dances representing the various clan ancestors. There are Amerindian tribal descents from the Bear, Wolf, Beaver, Coyote, Eagle, Owl, Frog, Raven, Dog, Jaguar, Cayman, Seal and others.

The seal occurs in Celtic and Gaelic lore and fairy tale as an ancestor; the wolf founded an Irish tribe and the 'Son of a Bear' occurs frequently in Irish and Welsh names.

In the East some Indian families claim descent from the Nagas, and the Tiger can also be an ancestor. Various sea-creatures are progenitors in Oceania, such as the Clam, Octopus, Shark, Lizard and Eel, while the Miao and Yao tribes of China rose from a Dog who won a Princess by helping her father against his enemies. The Bear is pre-eminently the animal of the Ainu, but there were also other ancestors.

Madagascar has Cattle and Sheep ancestors, and a Malagasy myth traces the descent of one tribe to a Moth. Sheep can also incarnate souls of ancestors.

Emu and other creatures occur in Australian Aboriginal tradition, as does the Serpent Old Woman ancestor, while in Africa the Leopard and Hyena appear in this role.

Even belief in descent from insects occurs, as the Myrmidons were originally Ants.

Devil Fish. An heraldic creature, half-devil, half-fish.

Dingo. An Australian Aboriginal totem animal. At ritual ceremonies members of the tribe perform sacred dances during which they howl like the dingo and walk on all fours. Among moieties a Dingo must marry a Water-hen.

Divi. See **Cat**

Divination. Animals and birds were closely involved with the ancient and universal practice of divination, which assumes that deities, or powers other than human, can and will communicate with humanity and express their desires. Divination also sought to reveal hidden secrets, to foretell future events or discover the probable success or failure of undertakings. It was largely the province of the priests, shamans and magicians but also affected everyday life in the occurrence of personal omens. The Oracle at Apollo's shrine at Delphi was probably the most famous, but in Babylon and Assyria divination was an important factor in religion. The Roman College of Augurs treated divination as a science. Justin says that the Celts were 'skilled beyond other people in the science of augury.' The Etruscans kept 'haruspices' – models of livers which could be consulted at any time. Divination from the liver had its own name, 'hepatoscopy'.

Innumerable methods were employed but the use of sacrificial animals was one of the most usual. This was called 'exispicy' and was the means of augury from the entrails of the sacrifice, particularly the liver and kidneys. The shape, colour and size of the entrails all had special significance. Porphyry says that diviners ate the hearts of animals and birds because in this way they partook of the souls and powers of these animals and so received the influence of the gods through them. Bones were also involved, particularly the shoulder-blade of a sheep, or if not available or affordable the breast-bone of a fowl might be used as a poor man's substitute. The shell of the tortoise was widely used in the East, but generally the East employed non-animal systems, such as astrology, the casting of lots or the prophecies of oracles or shamans.

Augury involved the flight of birds, or of a bird; the posture when settled or any movement while settled; if they are scattered it means ill-luck and enmity, if together it signifies good luck and peace. The croak of a raven repeated three times when flying over a house is an omen of death; a crow settling on a roof and cawing is the same. The laugh of a woodpecker denotes intrigue, if the sound is to the right it is a sign that the intrigue, if against one, will fail, or that one could succeed in intrigue oneself; the laugh to the left has the opposite significance. A hawk pursuing its prey to the right bodes success, to the left failure – an ancient Babylonian belief. Numbers are also significant: one or two croaks of a crow or raven are favourable, three means death. Magpies are well-known for number symbolism. A crowing hen is 'neither good for God nor men'.

The Roman College of Augurs distinguished between bird prophets as either *Oscenes*, or 'talkers', and *Alites*, or 'flyers'; among the talkers were ravens, crows, owls and magpies; the flyers were eagles, vultures and migratory birds, although the latter could come into both categories as some talked as they flew, such as geese and swans. Patterns of migration were also of great significance.

The way a cat faces when washing itself shows which way the wind may be expected to blow. The howling of a dog at night portends death and was associated with Hecate.

Dodo. Extinct in the 17th century, the bird is used to symbolize extinction, the dead and gone, 'as dead as the Dodo'.

Dog. There is evidence that the dog was domesticated in 7500 BC; it appeared in pre-dynastic Egypt and pottery dogs were seen 1000 years earlier. It is not only the oldest animal companion of humanity but also has the widest range of uses in friendship, guarding, hunting and herding, but in symbolism and myth it is ambivalent, revered and a close companion in some societies and despised and execrated in others; it can also be either a solar or lunar animal. Solar dogs chase away the **Boar** of Winter, are fire-bringers and masters of fire, destroying the enemies of light; lunar dogs are associated with Artemis, Goddess of the Moon and of the Hunt, and are also intermediaries between moon deities. Apuleius says that 'the dog . . . his face alternately black and golden, denotes the messenger going hence and thence between the Higher and Infernal powers.' It is a guardian of the underworld, attends on the dead and leads them to the next world. Plutarch says that dogs symbolize 'the conservative, watchful, philosophical principle in life'. They embody the qualities of fidelity, watchfulness and nobility (dogs and falcons were emblems of the nobility); they are also credited with psychic powers and the dog is often a culture hero or mythical ancestor. It continues its companionship in life by accompanying the dead to the underworld and interceding for them there. Pliny says that the dog and the **Horse** are the most faithful to man.

The significance of the dog varies in Sumero-Semitic symbolism. It was revered in Babylon, but in Semitic iconography it accompanies the **Scorpion**, serpent and baleful reptiles; it is evil and demonic. In Phoenician art it is associated with the sun and is an emblem of Gala, the Great Physician, and a class of priests were called 'dogs'. The Arcadian Belit-ili either has a dog sitting by her or her throne is supported by dogs. The dog is also an attribute of Astarte or Ashtoreth. Tacitus mentions Heracles of the Assyrians as being accompanied by a dog, as was also the Tyrian Hercules or Melcarth. In Hittite ritual a figure of a little dog was made of tallow and placed on the threshold with the invocation: 'You are a little dog of the table of the Royal Pair. Just as by day you do not allow other men into the courtyard, so do not let the Evil Thing in during the night.' Al-Nadim says that dogs were sacred to the Harranians of Syria in their mysteries, they were regarded as brothers of the mystae and were forbidden as food.

The Semitic antipathy towards the dog was carried over into Judaism where, except for in Tobit, where Tobias has a dog companion, the dog was held in contempt as unclean and a scavenger and was ritually taboo (Matthew 7: 6), associated with whoremongers (Deuteronomy 23: 18) and sorcerers, fornicators and idolaters (Revelation 22: 15).

Dogs were venerated in Egypt and were shown as guarding, hunting and herding. They were sacred to Anubis, who was depicted as dog- or jackal-headed, and to Hermes as the messenger god; they were also an attribute of the Great Mother Amenti. A dog guided the hawk-headed solar god to keep the sun on its right path. A human soul could enter a dog.

In Graeco-Roman myth the dog is again ambivalent, the term 'cynic' – that is, 'dog-like' – is derogatory and implies impudence and flattery. Homer says the dog is shameless, but on the other hand it is associated with Aesculapius or Asclepios the skilled physician and healer, and the dog also heals by rebirth into a new life. Its fidelity survives death. It also accompanies Hermes/Mercury as messenger god, presiding wind and the Good Shepherd. Sirius, the Dog Star, accompanies the hunter Orion. Hecate has the dogs of war, and dogs were sacrificed to her at crossroads. The dogs of Hades symbolize dawn and dusk when hostile and demonic powers prevail, and the monster dog Cerberus guards the entrance to the underworld; he also attends the underworld deities Pluto, Hecate, and Serapis. He is depicted with three heads with serpents' manes; he prevented the living from entering Hades, but Orpheus, Aeneas and Odysseus got past him to visit the dead. He barked when exposed to light and his saliva gave rise to the poisonous aconite. He was overcome by Hercules but eventually returned to the underworld. War dogs are depicted at the altar of Zeus in Pergamon accompanying Hecate, Artemis and Asteria. Epona rides on a horse with a dog on her lap. In Rome dogs were used as house guards and kept as pets, they were also trained to perform in circuses and to draw carts. Portrayed frequently in funerary art the dog was a symbol of fidelity and of the love that outlives death. Dogs and goats were sacrificed at the Roman Lupercalia.

Nowhere is the dog more venerated and cared for than in Zoroastrianism; it is an integral part of Parsee life. The *Avesta* and other sacred books say the dog symbolizes sagacity, vigilance and fidelity and is the pillar of the pastoral culture. It must be treated with the utmost kindness and reverence. 'Four-eyed dogs', that is, those with a fleck above each eye, were especially esteemed and kept as temple dogs to join in the rites. The death of the body and the transit of the soul required the presence of a dog. The sag-dig, either a white or 'four-eyed' dog, is introduced to the death-bed and accompanies the funeral procession. The death of a woman in childbirth requires two dogs for the two souls. In creation the dog ranks next to the human. Every household should not only give food to any hungry dog but the dog should be fed with 'clean food', specially prepared, before the family itself is fed. At religious ceremonies a complete 'meal of the dog' is prepared with consecrated food and the dog was served before the worshippers joined in the communal meal. A prayer is said as the dog eats. As the dog can see spirits it can act as an intermediary between people in this world and the next and can also ward off evil spirits and protect from the powers of darkness. Dogs guard the Cinvat Bridge which must be crossed into the next world and where the good and evil are separated; they protect the righteous but do not stop the evil spirits from tripping up the bad, who then fall into the pit.

The Vedic God of the Dead, Yama, is attended by two ferocious dogs, each having four eyes; they act as his messengers and range round looking for those about to die. Indra, chief of the Vedic gods,

Chinese Celestial Dog-Demon

has the hunting dog as his attribute and companion. The hero of
the Mahabharata refuses to enter Indra's heaven unless his faithful
dog can go in with him.

T'ien Kou, the Chinese red Celestial Dog, has a dual symbolism.

He can be *yang* and help Erh-lang drive off evil spirits, in which case he represents fidelity and unswerving devotion, but as guardian of the night hours the dog becomes *yin* and depicts destruction and catastrophe; he is connected with comets, meteors and eclipses, caused when he goes mad and bites the moon. In his destructive aspect the Celestial dog carries off new-born children if they are not protected, but he can be driven off by the Taoist Immortal Chang Hsien or by being shot with a bow and arrow of mulberry or peach wood, or dog hair can be used as an amulet. The Dog Spirit, the Dog Star, Kou Ching, controls the fate of the family astrologically. For the Japanese the dog is a protector and guardian. In Polynesia it is an inventor and fire-bringer. The Buddhist Lion Dog is a guardian and defender of the Law.

The dog is important in Celtic myth and appears frequently with hunter-gods, such as Sucellos, the 'Good Striker', and with the Horse-goddess Epona. Dogs are associated with the healing waters and Nodens, God of Healing, could manifest as a dog. Dogs are also psychic animals and connected with divination and they are frequently metamorphosed people in Celtic lore. There are endless accounts of ghost, supernatural or enchanted dogs who could be either helpful or malevolent.

The Scandinavian, Teutonic Odin/Woden has two dogs and two ravens as counsellors and messengers. Garm, a monster dog, is guardian of the underworld. He called the underworld to battle but was slain by Tyn, who was also killed. Larger dogs and winged demons await the wicked at the gates of Hell. Dogs have been found buried in graves.

In Christianity the dog represents fidelity, watchfulness and conjugal fidelity; it is also depicted with the Good Shepherd as a guardian of the flock and in this aspect can also symbolize a bishop or priest. Black-and-white dogs signify the Dominican Order. The dog is an emblem of St Bernard, as rescuing alpine travellers, and of St Roch, who was fed by his dog. In the Bestiaries dogs typify sagacity, fidelity and priests as watch-dogs since they drive away the trespassing Devil and protect the treasury of God. The fable of the dog trying to grasp the reflection of an object mirrored in a pond and losing the real object is used to symbolize 'the silly people who leave the Law for some unknown thing'.

Islam holds dogs in contempt as unclean and a term of opprobrium for unbelievers; they may only be kept as guard dogs, but salukis and greyhounds were used for hunting by Moslems.

The dog represents loyalty, service and compassion among Amerindians and is a guardian and protector; it also tolerates human failings. It is the totem animal of the Dog Ribs. It is a culture hero, an intercessor and messenger, a rain-bringer and the inventor of fire, it can also appear as a mythical ancestor. A white dog was sacrificed by the Iroquois at the New Year festival to take the prayers of the people to the next world. The Haichol Indians of Central America speak of themselves as descendants of the dog survivors of the Great Flood. The Aztec God Quetzalcoatl enters the Land of the Dead in the form of a dog, helped by worms and bees. In one tradition the Dog God Xolotl is his twin brother. Figures of dogs were buried with the dead both as companions and food, a custom found particularly prevalent in coastal Peru. A spotted dog was sacrificed at the Mayan Fire Festival. There is an Amerindian Dog Dance.

Ainu mythology has watch-dogs stationed on the road to the otherworld at various points so that they can direct souls on their way and see that they go to the rightly deserved place. The dog is also considered psychic and can detect the presence of any ghost.

Dogs, either **Dingos** or non-native, are an essential accompanist to any Australian Aboriginal tribe. The dog or dingo is also a totem animal. In New Zealand the Maoris believe that the dog has a soul which goes to the next world.

Among African tribes the dog is often a culture hero and the inventor and bringer of fire. The Yoruba have a God of the Forest, Aroui, who has a dog head, and in Bantu myth the Dog and **Jackal** were originally brothers until the dog ingratiated himself with man.

The dog is the personification of fidelity. In art it signifies marital fidelity when included in portraits. Dogs appear frequently in Heraldry, especially in England as the Talbot, the hound of early days; Greyhounds, Bloodhounds and Foxhounds are also portrayed, but the dog is not depicted *rampant*. When shown nose-to-ground it is termed a 'hound on scent'.

The Black Dog, a huge, shaggy ghost-dog with fiery eyes, is a frequent theme in hauntings and is usually a portent of death; it can be harmless if not touched, but to touch it is to die. Similar to the Black Dog is the Scottish Highland Ce Sith, a fairy dog as large as a bullock with dark green hair.

The Devil's Dandy Dogs are a pack of fire-breathing, fiery-eyed hounds led by the Devil over the moors of West England on stormy nights. They will tear anyone to pieces who gets in their way, but prayer is apotropaic. These are paralleled in the North of England by the Whisht Hounds who hunt high on a wild night and presage death; they are said to be the souls of unbaptized children. Shuck is a huge ghost dog of East Anglia, wholly black and fiery-eyed, an apparition of ill-omen.

See also **Wild Hunt**

Dolphin. The 'King of Fishes' is pre-eminently the symbol of sea-power and, as 'the arrow of the sea', it is swiftness. Pliny says it is 'the swiftest of all other living creatures whatsoever and not of the sea-fish only . . . it is quicker than any fowls, swifter than the arrow from the bow.' The dolphin is a saviour, a guide to souls in the underworld and to the Isles of the Blessed, it is also a saviour of the shipwrecked and regarded as kinder and more sensitive than humanity.

The Sun God Apollo, who was also the God of Music, is closely associated with the dolphin, which was sculptured on the walls of his temple at Delphi; he could assume its form. In this aspect he is known as Apollo Delphinos, founder of the Delphic Oracle. Delphi was regarded as an omphalos, the World Centre, with the Greek words *delphis* (dolphin) and *delphys* (womb) bringing in the symbolism of the masculine, solar Sun God and the feminine, watery power of the womb as the centre of life. Also in line with their connection to Apollo dolphins were said to be music-lovers. Aelian refers to 'the music-loving dolphin', and in the aspect of music lovers and saviours dolphins rescued Arion from the sea; in Greek art Arion is depicted riding on a dolphin. Telemachus was also saved by a dolphin, after which Ulysses bore a dolphin on his shield. In one tradition the Isthmean Games were founded in honour of Melicantes, whose dead body was carried ashore by a dolphin. Poseidon/Neptune naturally has the King of Fishes as his emblem, and he placed Delphinos among the stars as the Dolphin. It also represents Aphrodite/Venus, the 'woman of the sea', and here there is an amatory significance associated with Eros. The Mediterranean nymphs, the Nereides, ride on dolphins, and Thetis is portrayed riding naked on a dolphin. There is also an association with Dionysos. The dolphin depicted Minoan sea-power.

Sumero-Semitic symbolism uses the dolphin as an alternative to the **Fish** in representations of Ea-Oannes; it is also employed in connection with Astarte as associated with the waters and with Ishtar.

Roman art often depicts cupids riding on dolphins and they appear in funerary art as guides on the journey of the soul to the Isles of the Blessed. Egypt has the dolphin as an attribute of Isis. Dolphins appear frequently in Celtic art and on Gaulish coins, they are often ridden by a male figure. Like the **Salmon** they were associated with well-worship.

Early Christianity was symbolized by the fish, with Christ as the saviour of souls bearing them across the waters of death; the dolphin can take the place of the fish in this context, also of the whale that swallowed Jonah; in this it takes on the significance of the death and resurrection of Christ. Christians adapted the myth of the rescue of Arion from the sea to represent Christian converts saved by the waters of baptism. A dolphin with a ship or anchor typifies the Church guided by Christ; the ship is sometimes replaced by the ark of salvation and rebirth. A dolphin pierced by a trident, or on an anchor, symbolizes Christ on the Cross. The Bestiaries say that there is nothing faster in the sea and that the dolphins can out-speed ships, also that the dolphin should properly be called *Simones*. In mediaeval art it depicts social affection.

Amerindian tradition also has the dolphin as a messenger between this world and the next. It is the essence of the Great Spirit, the breath of life, the life-force, rhythm.

Amazonian tribes believe that the river dolphin can change into a mortal at night and join in the festivities and dancing; in this form it can seduce maidens.

Among the Ainu of Japan the dolphin is the God of the Sea, the Bear being the Mountain God.

The dolphin is the totem animal of an Australian Aboriginal tribe on Mornington Island.

In Heraldry the dolphin is usually depicted *embowed*; it first appeared in English heraldry in the middle of the 13th century. In France the use of the dolphin was restricted to the Dauphin, though it also appeared on the arms of the family of La Tour du Pin. Among the Elements the dolphin is the personification of Water.

The Dolphin and Anchor is a well-known symbol of speed and slowness, the two together forming the medium between extremes, or 'hasten slowly'. Two dolphins facing in opposite directions represent the duality of nature. In early times the dolphin could be called the 'sea-goose', with the porpoise being the 'sea-pig', though the two were frequently interchangeable.

Dolphins also forecast the weather: when seen on the surface they are harbingers of bad weather. The Venerable Bede said: 'When dolphins leap more often from the waves, the wind will rise from the quarter towards which they leap.'

The dolphin is *par excellence* the helpful animal; it is the 'peak of creation', symbolic of virtue, otherworldly wisdom, joyousness and playfulness. It was said to have had human form until it took to the sea. In early times it was a capital offence to kill one, and it remained a certain means of incurring misfortune.

Donkey. See **Ass**

Dove, Pigeon. The dove is one of the most venerated creatures, symbolizing the spirit, the soul, bringing the spirit down to the earth and the transit between one state and another; it also represents peace, innocence, gentleness, timidity and chastity, though in some traditions (and especially as the pigeon) it can represent lasciviousness. Doves were universally sacred to the Great Mother and Queens of Heaven and were depicted with them as symbols of maternity and femininity. They were also sacrificial birds and associated with funerary cults. As the pigeon the bird can represent cowardice – 'pigeon-hearted' or 'pigeon-livered'.

The veneration of the dove was established early in Mesopotamia, where a terra cotta figure of a dove has been found dating from 4500 BC; in Egypt it was recorded at about 2500 BC. White doves were sacred in Syria and Babylon and were used as messengers. The black dove or pigeon symbolized widowhood in Egypt. Pigeons were sent to the four directions at the coronation of Rameses III and at Egyptian festivals. The Phoenician sanctuary at Eryx honoured the dove as the companion of Astarte, and the Syrian Atargatis bore a sceptre with a golden dove on it.

The dove is symbolically associated with the Tree; in Egypt with the Tree of Life, sitting in its branches and appearing with the fruit of the tree. But it is with the Olive that it has a particular affinity as a symbol of peace and the Golden Age. The dove with the olive branch in its beak depicts peace *par excellence*; it also represents renewal of life. The exception to the rule occurs in Japan, where an ancient legend marks the dove as a messenger of war and sacred to Hachiman, God of War, although a dove bearing a sword announces the end of a war. In another context the bird symbolizes longevity and deference; this latter significance was taken from China where it represents not only longevity but also faithfulness, filial piety and orderliness. It is an emblem of the Earth Mother and of spring, fecundity and lasciviousness.

Doves fed the infant Zeus on ambrosia and were his messengers when Rhea hid him from Cronos. The dove with the olive branch is an emblem of Athene as renewal of life; it is sacred to Adonis, to Bacchus as the First Begotten of Love and to Venus as voluptuousness, and doves and swans can draw her chariot. According to Aelian white turtle doves were sacred not only to Aphrodite and Demeter but also to the Fates and Furies. The Oracle at Dodona, the oldest of the oracles of Zeus which was founded at the time of Deucalion, was said to be a dove which lived in the oracular oak and spoke with a human voice; the priestesses there were called 'Doves'. Strabo says, however, that the oracular response was not by the voice but in the flight of the doves. Another tradition says that the oracles were delivered through the sound of the rustling of the leaves of the tree caused by the doves. The Romans kept doves as pets and used them as messengers. Nero sent the results of the Games to his friends by carrier-pigeon. In Minoan art the dove is associated with the Great Mother and appears with snakes; together they symbolize the air and earth.

Domesticated by the Hebrews, the turtle dove and pigeon were the only birds that could be sacrificed according to the Law of Moses (Leviticus 5: 7). They were the poor man's sacrifice and a 'burnt offering' for the purification of the leper. They are also the most frequently mentioned birds in the Bible and were held particularly sacred. In the Old Testament the dove symbolizes freedom, escape and rest (Psalms 55: 6), also simplicity, harmlessness, innocence, meekness and constancy. The dove embodies the soul of the dead. In the New Testament it depicts the Holy Spirit (Matthew 3: 16). It can also signify mourning, a moaner (Isaiah 38: 14). It appears on Torah shrines. The Dove as associated with the Deluge myths appears in Babylonian, Greek, Hebrew and Caldean traditions. The dove was called the 'Turtle' until the 17th century.

Christianity not only took over the Old Testament symbolism but added to it, especially as a symbol for the Holy Spirit at the Annunciation, a theme which appears frequently in Christian art, either with the dove hovering over the Virgin Mary's head or with its beak inclined to her ear – which was used later to signify the Immaculate Conception. It also typifies the Holy Spirit at the baptism of Christ. Seven doves denote the seven gifts of the Spirit, and a flock of doves represent the faithful. The dove appears with the olive branch as peace, deliverance and forgiveness, just as Noah's dove brought back the symbol of peace between God and man. The Bestiaries say that this signifies not only triumph over death and the pure soul as opposed to the black raven of sin, but that the faithful can find no resting place outside the Church, just as the dove found no resting place outside the Ark. The Bestiaries employ the dove extensively in their symbolic moralizing. They also call the bird a Turtle, Turtur or Columba – 'a simple fowl, free from gall' and asking for love. It depicts preachers who share its good qualities: 'It flies about in flocks in the same way flocks of preachers belonging to the Faith follow the steps of good works and virtues.' There are the Three Doves: Noah, symbolizing Rest; David – Peace; Christ – Salvation. 'As the dove separates the wheat from the chaff, so does the preacher separate the true grain of Christian doctrine from the husks of Judaism. The two wings are the active and contemplative lives; the ring round the neck is the encircling sweetness of the Divine Word; the gold and silver plumage the precious treasures of purity and innocence; the whiteness and variable tints are chastity in conflict with fickle passion; its red feet depict the blood of the martyrs; its two eyes survey the past and discern the future, looking into the soul and up to God; their yellow colour indicates maturity of thought since yellow is the colour of ripeness.'

The *Physiologus* says that the Turtle dove, as a dweller in solitude, typifies shyness and loneliness. If she loses her mate the female refuses to take another and so represents chastity and continence, but 'women are seldom able to come up to the standard of doves.' This constancy is made an allegory of the followers of Christ, who withdraw from the world and devote themselves to meditation. In poetry the turtle dove is often used as a symbol of fidelity. In art and architecture two doves are often depicted together to represent conjugal love and affection, while one alone represents mourning. The dove is closely associated with Grail legends.

In Arabic lore the dove released by Noah from the Ark dipped its feet in the water and scalded its legs so that feathers would not grow on them. Noah blessed the dove and made it dear to men's hearts. Islam reverences the bird, which flies in flocks about mosques.

Yama, Vedic God of the Dead, sometimes used a pigeon or **Owl** as a messenger instead of his two **Dogs**.

For the Ainu the Green Pigeon is a case of metamspychosis as it is the soul of a Japanese man who was lost and died in the mountains and therefore must not be eaten. It likes only salt water.

The pigeon is a totem of a Melanesian clan associated with the **Sea-eagle**. People may kill and eat the eagle but not the pigeon, as it was once a living man. Russian peasants would not eat the pigeon since the Holy Spirit dwelt in the form of a dove.

In Heraldry the dove is always represented with a tuft on its head; this is suggested as a mark to distinguish the domestic dove from the wood-pigeon. The dove is frequently depicted with an olive branch in its beak, usually found *close*, but if with outstretched wings *volant*; it is then termed 'dove rising'.

Dragon. The dragon or 'winged serpent' (occasionally called a worm as with the Lambton Worm) is probably the most complex, widespread and ambivalent of mythical monsters, appearing in the mythology and symbolism of all nations. Originally it was a wholly beneficent creature, its serpent-like body representing matter and the life-giving waters, while its wings identified it with the spirit and the breath of life. It was an attribute of the Sky Gods and their earthly counterparts and representatives – the emperors and kings. It occurred as a divine or imperial emblem in Babylon, Egypt, China, Japan, Greece and Rome, and also for the early kings of England and Wales. Later it became ambivalent, symbolizing either the supreme celestial creative power or evil and destruction, wasting the land by fire or by trampling it to death; this dual symbolism was that of the beneficent sky and the fertilizing rains on the one hand and the malefic forces of lightning and flood on the other. This division is apparent in the Eastern and Western attitudes to the dragon; in the Orient it maintains its beneficent aspect, representing celestial power; in the West it is evil, chthonic and baleful.

When dragons appear as monsters they are autochthonous 'masters of the ground' and must be fought for mastery of the land or to win the guarded treasure. In this role they play a considerable part in the sagas of heroes and conquerors, in the legends of saints, in knight-errantry and chivalry. The well-known legend of St George and the Dragon has its counterpart in many ancient traditions: the conflict between Horus and Typhon, Bel and the Dragon, Marduk

and Tiamat, Perseus and Medusa, Bellerophon and the Chimera,
Apollo and the Python, Hercules and the Hydra, Thor and the
Dragon; added to these there are endless 'local' slayers of dragons.

Killing the dragon depicts the conflict between light and darkness;
overcoming the dark nature and attaining self-mastery, or, if the
dragon is a guardian, it symbolizes the winning of the treasure of
inner or esoteric knowledge, or in rescuing the princess it releases
pure forces kept in bondage by the powers of evil.

The dragon is frequently a fire-breathing monster. Euripides
describes it as breathing forth fire and slaughter; in the Old
Testament Moses has fiery serpents and Isaiah a fiery flying serpent.

Dragons represent the power of darkness in Sumero-Semitic myth,
they are the Adversary. In Babylonian lore Marduk, the Sun, slays
Tiamat, the force of evil and chaos. The Egyptian dragon was an
emblem of Osiris as God of the Dead, but it was also an imperial
attribute. The dragon of darkness, Apophis, was overcome each
morning by the Sun God, Ra. In Graeco-Roman myth it was an
attribute of Heracles/Hercules as a slayer of monsters. Ceres flew to
heaven in a chariot drawn by two dragons and later lent it to
Triptolemus to distribute corn all over the world; Medusa fled from
Jason in a chariot drawn by winged dragons and Apollo may be
taken as a dragon-slayer when he killed the Python, the dragon and
Serpent being largely interchangeable in mythology.

In Semitic lore dragons were associated with death and
destruction. The Hebrew symbolism of the malefic powers of
darkness depicted by the dragon was carried over into Christianity
when it was equated with 'that old serpent', the power of evil,
symbolizing the Devil, the Tempter in conflict with God and the
powers of righteousness. In the Old Testament the 'place of dragons'
was associated with the 'shadow of death' and the waters of the
deep. In the Middle Ages the dragon was synonymous with sin,
paganism and heresy, the Devil and all evil that is overcome by St
Michael. In the Apocalypse the dragon is again the 'old serpent',
the deceiver. St George is only one of the saints involved with
dragons. SS Cado, Clement, Keyne, Margaret, Martha, Samson,
Sylvester, Guthlac and the Apostle Philip were all associated with
the dragon in one way or another. In the Bestiaries the dragon or
Draco is 'the biggest of all serpents, in fact of all living things on
earth'. It has a crest and its strength is in its tail. It symbolizes the
Devil, who also has a crest, or crown, because he is the King of Pride.

In contrast, the Celtic and Teutonic dragon represents sovereignty,
power or a chief, such as Pendragon, the Celtic word meaning
'chief'. The Red Dragon of Cadwallader or Cadwaller is the emblem
of Wales – 'upon a mount vert, a dragon passant, wings expanded
and endorsed gules – the Red Dragon Dreadful'. It was blazed on
King Arthur's helmet in battle, later it was associated with Geoffrey

Dragon *(from the royal throne of Bhutan)*

of Monmouth and Owen Glendower. The Saxons had the white dragon as a royal standard. In early Britain it depicted supreme power.

The Heraldic dragon varies greatly, especially in the shape of its ears, but the wings are always those of a bat; the tongue and tail can be barbed; it breathes out fire and is a symbol of power, wisdom and one who has overcome an adversary or fortress. The Tudor Red Dragon indicates Welsh origins, and a Welshman always holds the position of Rouge Dragon in the College of Heralds. Dragon-Tygre and Dragon-Wolf are composite creatures and support the arms of the City of London.

In Hinduism the dragon is manifest power and the uttered word, it is an attribute of both Aruna and Soma. Vitra is the Dragon of the Waters which had to be slain by Indra to release the waters.

It is in China that the dragon reaches the height of its symbolic and mythological significance. It represents the highest spiritual power and is the emblem of the delegate of that power on earth – the Emperor. It is the masculine *yang* power, with the phoenix as the *yin*, the Empress. The dragon typifies the supernatural, infinity, the rhythms of Nature manifest in the divine power of change and transformation. It is the Celestial Stag, the sun, the heavens and their fertilizing rain, but it is also present in the waters of the deep; it is also the chief of the Four Spiritually Endowed or Auspicious Animals and is one of the Twelve Symbolic Creatures of the Zodiac. Dragons influence and control every aspect of life. As supreme power they live in palaces and in earlier times offerings were made to them; there are also dragon palaces under the sea. They symbolize all that is sacred and can be deities of the five regions: North, South, East, West and Centre. They are also shape-shifters and can make themselves invisible or manifest at will. Dragons can be of different natures; the Azure or Celestial Dragon *T'ien Lung* lives in the sky and guards the mansions of the gods, preventing them from falling; it represents infinite supernatural power and is the vital spirit; Fu-tsang guards hidden treasure. The *lung*, or Imperial Dragon, has five claws and its head points southwards and its tail to the North; it symbolizes the fertilizing rain and the East, the sun. The ordinary dragon has four claws, it is the *mang* and depicts temporal power. The three-clawed dragon was an early form in China and later became the Japanese dragon. *Li* is hornless; it lives in the sea and controls the deeps and symbolizes the scholar, while *Chiao* lives in the mountains or on land and depicts the statesman. According to Wang Fa the dragon has 'nine resemblances': 'His horns resemble those of a stag, his head is that of a camel, his eyes those of a demon, his neck that of a snake, his belly that of a clam, his scales those of a carp, his claws those of an eagle, his soles those of a tiger, his ears those of a cow.' In Chinese art two dragons are often depicted facing each other, these portray the *yin-yang* and eternity; chasing each other's tails they signify the two-way creative force and action of the dualistic powers. The dragon is often represented with the 'dragon ball' or 'flaming pearl' which has been suggested as representing the moon as rain-bringer, rolling thunder, the dragon swallowing the pearl as the waning moon, or the cloud-dragon swallowing the sun, but in Taoism and Buddhism it is the 'pearl of perfection', the 'pearl which grants all desires' and symbolizes widsom, enlightenment and the spiritual essence of the universe. The dragon and **Phoenix** portrayed together are the union of all opposites, Heaven and Earth, Emperor and Empress, macrocosm and microcosm, the rhythms of involution and evolution, the Androgyne. Depicted with the **Tiger** the dragon becomes lust and the tiger anger.

Both China and Japan have a tradition of the dragon being able to change into a bird. A monastery in Kyoto depicts a composite creature, half-dragon, half-bird, like the Chinese winged dragon. The Japanese dragon, derived from the Chinese, lives in deep lakes and springs. The three-clawed dragon, the Tatsu, represents the Mikado, imperial and spiritual power.

Dragons are also depicted in Cambodia in the sculptures of Ankor Wat and in the Brahmanical caves at Ellora.

The dragon fears iron and centipedes, but it has only one enemy, the **Elephant**; when they fight both die, as the dragon overcomes the elephant but as the elephant falls it crushes the dragon.

The Dragon and **Crocodile** were often treated as one in early times.

Dragonfly.   The dragonfly can share the symbolism of immortality and regeneration with the **Butterfly**. It appears frequently in Japanese art and poetry and is the national emblem of Japan, 'The Island of the Dragonfly' (*Akitsu-Shima*). It also portrays irresponsibility and unreliability. In China it is summer, weakness and instability. For Amerindians it represents swiftness, activity and the whirlwind, but its shifting colours symbolize illusion, the essence of change; it is in touch with the elemental worlds.

Duck.   Pliny and Aelian call ducks 'prophets of the wind' and the bird was regarded as a weather prophet. Aelian also says that it was brought as a tribute to Indian kings. It was frequently used as a subject of the Greek comic poets; it was sacred to Poseidon. In Egypt it was associated with Isis. For the Hebrews it was a clean food and also represented immortality.

As flocking on the surface it was taken to symbolize superficiality, a chatterer and typifying deceit. This theme of deceit is evident in the French *canard* – a false report. Sequana, Goddess of the Seine, has a barge drawn by a duck.

In China and Japan the duck symbolizes conjugal happiness, fidelity, felicity and beauty. The duck and drake together depict the union of lovers, co-operation, fidelity. In Chinese art two ducks are sometimes depicted with one pair of wings between them, this is called 'birds sharing wings', an object of good omen signifying complete conjugal unity and fidelity. The duck is *yin* to the **Cock's** *yang*.

Among Amerindians the duck is a mediator between Sky and Water, and it was one of the various creatures in Amerindian mythology which was credited with diving below the Waters of the Flood to bring up the first mud to make the earth. The Hopi associate the duck with the maize cycle as representing the necessary fertilizing water.

Duckbilled Platypus. Represents a pair who, against the tribal marriage arrangements and taboos, eloped but later repented. She was turned into a duck and he into a great water-rat and together they were banished to a distant river. She laid two eggs which contained strange creatures with fur bodies, webbed feet and duck bills.

Dugong. The sea-cow was clean food for the Hebrews; its skin was used for leather; it has been suggested as the covering for the Tabernacle (Exodus 25: 15) and for sandals (Ezekiel 16: 10).

The Bestiaries say that dugongs are known as swine to the vulgar, as they eat like pigs.

E

Eagle. It has been said by Professor D'Arcy Thompson that 'the complicated mythology of the Eagle baffles analysis.' Both its mythology and symbolism are world-wide. *Par excellence* the solar bird, it is the symbol of all Sky Gods, of the sun, majesty, authority, spiritual power, ascension, victory, courage, pride, strength and the spiritual instinct in humanity to soar heavenwards.

As solar and spiritual power the eagle represents light in conflict with the chthonic dark forces. The eagle against the **Lion** or **Bull**, in which the eagle always wins, depicts the triumph of the spirit and mind over the physical. The eagle is universally the enemy of the **Serpent** and iconography often portrays the eagle with the serpent in its talons, representing the victory of the celestial powers over the chthonic, good over evil, and light over darkness – but together they can typify cosmic unity, totality, the union of spirit and matter, intellect and instinct, spiritual and temporal power.

When surmounting a pillar the eagle is an emblem of the Sky Gods as the sun dissipating the powers of darkness. The double-headed eagles are attributes of twin gods and can depict dual power or omniscience. The symbol is of Oriental origin; it appeared among the Hittites, who introduced it into Byzantium, and it was depicted with Hittite goddesses and was also an attribute of Nergal, the beneficent noonday sun and differing from the Lion as the scorching, destructive summer noonday sun. The eagle represents omniscience and is often portrayed with either the serpent of darkness or the lunar **Hare** in its talons, symbolizing solar power.

As a symbol of sovereignty and victory the eagle is a natural emblem of War Gods such as the Assyrian, Babylonian and Canaanite Sun God Ninurta or Ningvisu; it is also a symbol of the Assyrian Asshur, a Storm God bringing lightning and the fertilizing rain. The Sun God Marduk is often depicted as an eagle.

According to the Egyptian High Priest Horapollo, the eagle was a symbol of the King and the royal bird of the Thebans, also a symbol of the Nile. It also represented the Sons of Horus.

In Greek mythology the eagle is the only bird that dwells in the heavens. It signified bravery and was sculpted on the tombs of brave men. On Plato's tomb it represented the aspiring soul. It is the bird of Zeus/Jupiter, though originally it was an emblem of Pan, who yielded it to Zeus. As an attribute of Zeus, and as his lightning-bearer, the eagle sometimes has his thunderbolt in its talons. Virgil calls it God's weapon-bearer. When depicted with Ganymede the bird becomes funerary; Ganymede watering an eagle represents the overcoming of death; the Rape of Ganymede by Zeus in the form of an eagle is an allegory of the rape of the soul from the body at death and its subsequent journey heavenwards.

Roman emperors adopted the eagle as representing imperial power, and introduced the *aquilia*, the eagle-standard of the Roman army. As a symbol of apotheosis an eagle was released at the funeral of an emperor to signify the soul departing skywards. As in Greece, the eagle was a solar storm-bird and lightning-bearer, holding Jupiter's thunderbolt; it symbolized victory, dignity, favour and quick perception. In Mithraism both the eagle and **Hawk** are attributes of the solar Mithras, and appear on Mithraic monuments.

There are various myths connected with the eagle, probably the best known being that of the renewing of its youth. When growing old, or some say every ten years, it flies straight up to the sun and is scorched, then plunges down into the sea, emerging completely rejuvenated. The myth is probably of Hebrew origin as it does not appear in Greek and Roman classics but is referred to in the Old Testament and is extensively used in Christian symbolism and literature. The Bestiaries quote it as a symbol of man renewing himself at the spiritual fountain; it also represents resurrection and new life in baptism, the soul renewed by grace. This myth is also taken as symbolic of the sun going down to the waters of the sea at night and rising rejuvenated next morning, having gone from West to East under the earth during the night.

Aristotle and Pliny both refer to the belief that the eagle's beak grows distorted and so causes starvation. Horapollo says: 'Desiring to represent an old man starved to death, they paint the eagle with its beak distorted.' Augustine says it dashes its beak against a rock to break off the excrescence and so feeds again. This is repeated in the *Physiologus*. Aelian says that the eagle is exempt from thirst but can perish from hunger, and that, if sick, it feeds on tortoises as a cure. Pliny and the *Physiologus* both say that the eagle and **Vulture** do not lay eggs but give birth to live young.

Eagles were said to gaze unblinkingly at the sun, it has also been said that when the young are fledged they are taken up to the sun and forced to look straight into it; if any weaklings fail the test and fall to the ground they are abandoned as unworthy, but the **Coot** will take pity on them and bring them up with her own brood.

In Hebrew tradition the eagle symbolizes the East and renewal.

In the Old Testament the eagle and vulture appear as interchangeable and both typify strength, size, swiftness and high flying
(Exodus 19: 4; Jeremiah 49: 22; Obadiah 1: 4), and in Psalms 103: 5
there is allusion to the renewal myth. The bird is unclean for the
Jews. Herod had a golden eagle put in his temple, and the eagle
appears on Torah shrines and on the Arch of Titus.

Christianity adopted many of the eagle myths for teaching the
faithful. Plunging into the sea and renewal of life signified, as
mentioned above, new life through baptism, and also resurrection.
Gazing unblinkingly at the sun is Christ gazing upon the glory of
God. Abandoning the young that fail the test represents the Last
Judgement. Grasping the serpent in its talons is victory over sin, but
when tearing at its prey it depicts the Devil. The eagle symbolizes
the Spirit, ascension, aspiration, spiritual endeavour. It is one of the
four creatures of the Apocalypse and in the Tetramorph it represents
St John the Evangelist. Its use as a lectern represents the inspiration
of the Gospels.

The eagle appears in Irish and Welsh traditions, but less often in
the Celtic. In Norse mythology it is seen in the boughs of the
Yggdrasil as light in conflict with the serpent of darkness. It is an
attribute of Odin/Woden who, in the form of an eagle, carried off
the mead. The North Wind is the eagle, huge and invisible,
associated with storms and darkness, described in the *Kalevala*. In
Finland the Supreme God can manifest as an eagle. The giant Thjazi
took the form of an eagle to abduct the goddess Idhunn.

In the East the Aryan solar, storm-cloud bird, the **Garuda**, on
which Vishnu rides, is often represented as an eagle; it is also an
emblem of Indra. In Buddhism the eagle is a vehicle of the Buddha
and an attribute of Amoghasiddhi. In the *Zendavesta* the eagle
guards the two gates of the world. The Arabic *Nasi*, the eagle, was
a Supreme God.

As solar the eagle is *yang* in China and represents carnage,
fearlessness, the warrior, authority, tenacity and keen vision; with
the **Raven** it was associated with war gods.

For the Ainu of Japan the Golden Eagle is the Great Spirit, the
Bird of Paradise who lives in the heavens; he is a divinity and his
wings are spotted gold. He never touches the earth but likes gazing
at it because it is so beautiful. He is a guardian and friend of the
Ainu, sent specially to help them, and is venerated and prayed to
because he once saved the people from starvation.

Among Amerindians the eagle is of outstanding importance; the
greatest of the birds; the eagle-feather head-dress represents the
Thunderbird, the Great Spirit, a messenger between earth and sky.
It is the Master of the Height and of the upper air; its feathers carry
the thoughts and prayers of the people to Father Sun. There are
three branches of the Eagle Tribe – the Condor, Eagle and Gray

Eagle. In some cases the White Eagle can represent man and the Brown Eagle woman. In the Amazonian region there is a harpy-eagle, greatly venerated as the most powerful bird of the region. It is depicted with the **Jaguar** (animal power) and the **Anaconda** (reptile power). The South-east Woodlands Indians have the eagle as the Bird of Peace with the Falcon as war, and it heads the bird category among animals. There is an Eagle Dance of the Creek Tribe. The Hopi say that the eagle holds this world and the next in its talons; while for the Zuni the White-cap or Bald Eagle is 'passing stout of heart and strong of will' and is Master and Guardian of the Upper Regions. In Mayan Culture there were military orders of Eagles, Jaguars and Coyotes. In Aztec tradition the eagle depicted celestial power, the bright sky, the rising sun which devours the serpent of darkness. Aztec art portrays the warrior clans by the eagle, with the jaguar, devouring hearts. The eagle and jaguar together flanking a figure appear in Toltec art to represent day and night. Eagle feathers are sacred objects used by shamans in healing and in Shamanism the bird embodies the power of the Great Spirit, the freedom of the skies and the state of illumination, under-standing and completion attained in initiation.

The **Sea-eagle** carries the souls of the Australian Aboriginals back to Dreamtime at death. The eagle and the **Hawk** are equated with the divine.

Alchemy uses the symbol of the soaring eagle as the liberated spirit, while the double eagle is the male-female mercury and the crowned eagle with the **Lion** represent quicksilver and sulphur, the volatile and the fixed, wind and earth.

Most important of the birds in Heraldry, the eagle is usually depicted 'displayed'. When it has a beak of another colour it is 'armed', or if the legs are different it is 'membered'.

Earwig. Represents the scandal-monger.

Echidna. An ancient Greek composite creature, half-woman, half-serpent, born of Gaea and Tartarus, who with Typhon gave birth to the **Hydra**, Cerberus (see **Dog**), the **Chimera** and the Nemean **Lion**. She was killed by the monster **Argus**. She also produced the Gryphon Vulture which tore out the liver of Prometheus but was killed by an arrow of Hercules.

The Australian echidna appears in aboriginal symbolism as lunar, playing the same part as the **Hare** or rabbit in other cults, and represents initiation, death and resurrection.

Eel. Sacred eels were known to the ancient Greeks, and in Phoenicia were kept at the Sanctuary of the War God and were decorated with gold ornaments, as were the sacred fish at Hieropolis. Eels were also held sacred in parts of Polynesia and had associations with Flood myths. It also plays an erotic role. It is an animal ancestor in Tahiti. In Madagascar it is a forbidden food. In China the eel depicts carnal love. It has a generally phallic significance and also symbolizes slipperyness.

The eel – or *Anquillae*, according to the Bestiaries – can be drowned in wine, after which drinking the wine gives 'a loathing for liquor'.

Egg. The Cosmic Egg, laid by a divine bird as the origin of the world and the world as egg-shaped are ancient and widespread myths, occurring in Egypt, Phoenicia, India, China, Japan, Greece, Central America, Polynesia and Finland. The Golden Egg is the sun and the serpent encircling an egg is the *Ouroboros*, representing totality, primordial unity. The Cosmic Egg is often laid on the primaeval waters and is symbolically split to form the earth and the dome of the sky. The Vishnu Purana says: 'In the egg were the continents and seas and mountains, the planets and divisions of the universe, the gods, demons and mankind.' The Cosmic Egg is the hidden origin and mystery of all being; matter in its inert state, the perfect unity of opposites.

Eland. The sacred Master Animal of the Bushman's mythology; the first created and favourite animal, associated with the moon. Eland masks and horns are worn at ritual ceremonies and dances; the animal is a mediator between man and God, and there is a close identification between the hunter and the hunted with ritual atonement and appeasement. The eland is a symbol of strength and vitality, it is a healer and rain-bringer.

Elements. The elements are sometimes represented by animals. In the West they are: Earth – Serpent or Scorpion; Air – Chameleon (nourished by the wind); Fire – Salamander; Water – Dolphin or Fish. In Chinese symbolism the Four Spiritually Endowed Creatures combine the elements. The Blue or Green Dragon is the Air; the Phoenix combines Fire and Air; the Black Tortoise – Earth and Water; the White Tiger – Fire and Water. There is also a Dragon of the Waters, of the Earth and the Mountains. In Graeco-Roman symbolism the elements are usually female or divine figures, but Dolphins represent the Waters; Fire a Phoenix and Air a Peacock.

Elephant. A natural symbol of strength, the elephant also depicts long memory, patience, wisdom and conjugal fidelity. A myth concerning the elephant was that, like the **Elk**, it originally had no joints in its legs and had to sleep standing. This was affirmed by Strabo and Aelian but denied by Aristotle and Pliny. Later the *Physiologus* repeated the belief and it was therefore accepted in mediaeval times. Pliny also says that the elephant is a religious animal, worshipping the sun and stars, invoking the heavens and

The Indian Elephant, Ganesha

bathing in rivers at the new moon to purify itself. Aristotle called it the most intelligent of all animals, gentle, tame and teachable.

Although not directly mentioned in the Bible, in Maccabeus the elephant is referred to as brought against the Jews by Antiochus Epiphanes. It was a war animal, used as shock troops, forming a spearhead for horses and infantry. Ivory is mentioned as symbolizing wealth, luxury and soft living. The elephant was also used as a war animal in the Seleucid dynasty, which took the animal as its emblem; it was also employed as a draft animal and ridden by mahouts, drawing chariots and working.

In Graeco-Roman art Dionysos/Bacchus is portrayed as riding in a chariot drawn by elephants; elephants were also used in circuses. They symbolized victory over death, longevity and immortality. At Pompeii, Venus is depicted with elephants. As they were believed to worship Helios, the sun, they also typified life and light and in this context they carried torches in Roman processions and drew emperors' chariots; elephants also appeared on Roman coins as symbols of imperial power and munificence. Africa is often represented in Roman art as having an elephant's head or head-dress, and both Africa and India are personified by the elephant; Africa can also be depicted holding an elephant's tusk in her hands. Asia is also personified wearing the elephant head-dress of the Ptolemies. The chariot of Fame is drawn by elephants.

Hinduism has the elephant as the vehicle of the god Ganesha, who is depicted as elephant-headed. He rides on, or is attended by, a rat, and both the rat and elephant are symbolic of wisdom. As God of

Wisdom Ganesha is often mentioned in prefaces to books or in textbooks. Indra, guardian of the East, rides the white elephant Airavata, and the King of Heaven visits the earth on a great white elephant. Siva is sometimes depicted wearing an elephant's skin. The elephant represents royalty, intelligence, the strength of sacred wisdom, prudence, might and longevity.

The elephant is sacred to the Buddha. A white elephant appeared to his mother, Queen Maya, to announce the birth of a royal world-ruler, and the Buddha could be spoken of as the Great Elephant in one of his incarnations. The White Elephant is also the Jewel of the Law, the *vahan* of the Bodhisattva; it is compassion, love, kindness, self-restraint and patient endurance. In China the Buddha P'u Hsien rides a white elephant, and the animal signifies sovereignty, sagacity, prudence, strength and energy. In the East white elephants are revered and given special treatment and are said to bring distinctive fortune.

The elephant is the enemy of the serpent, trampling it underfoot, and this is adapted in Christianity as a symbol of Christ's triumph over sin. In the *Physiologus* and in the Bestiaries two elephants represent Adam and Eve having knowledge of sin, but 'the new elephant, Our Saviour, raised mankind to its first estate, debasing himself that we might be exalted.' The elephant is also used as representing baptismal regeneration, since it 'gave birth in water'. It rarely appears in Christian architecture but is portrayed on chasubles as a symbol of priestly chastity.

There is a belief in tribal Africa that the souls of men can enter animals by witchcraft, and elephants can be possessed in this way in order to damage the plantations of enemies.

The elephant is not unusual in Heraldry, though the head is used more frequently than the entire body. In the Elephant and Castle form, the 'Castle' is the howdah, which is seldom omitted.

Elk. Amerindian and Siberian symbol of stamina and strength, the warrior energy, supernatural power, the whirlwind. Totem of the Omahas.

The elk was said to suffer from vertigo, which it cures by putting its left hind foot in its left ear, after which it can run away, hence the hoof of the elk when ground and taken as a medicine is a certain cure for vertigo, epilepsy, *mal de mer* and falling sickness.

Julius Caesar said, in the Gallic Wars, that the elk sheds its antlers and that its legs are without joints so that it sleeps standing up, leaning against a tree. To capture the creature the hunter must undermine the tree, then the elk, leaning against it, falls down and cannot rise again.

Tartars take the names of such animals as the elk and **Reindeer** but do not necessarily make them a cult object.

Ember Goose. The Northern Diver is symbolic of Ember Days in Norway as it appears at that time. It is also the *Adventsvogel*, heralding Advent in Germany.

Emu. An Australian Aboriginal totem bird and ancestor. The Chirunga or Tjuringh, the sacred objects of the tribe, are marked with the footprints of the mythological ancestor, Emu himself, when he and the sun originally rose from the sacred soak. Sacred pictures are drawn of the emu and its eggs and rites performed round them. Among moieties an Emu must marry a Rat.

Enfield. A composite heraldic beast with characteristics of the fox-greyhound, lion-wolf and eagle talons.

Erinyes or Eumenides. The three avenging Greek goddesses, the Furies. They were called the 'kindly ones' to placate them: it was unlucky to name them. They were composite creatures with snake-hair, dog-heads and bat-wings, and were born from the blood of Uranus. They cannot die while there is still sin on earth.

Ermine. Being white, the ermine symbolizes purity. In mythology it died if it became soiled, hence it also represented chastity. When appearing in portraiture it symbolizes the virtue of the subject.

F

Falcon.   The falcon, **Eagle** and **Hawk** share many of the same solar attributes and powers of ascension, inspiration, freedom and victory. In Egyptian mythology the falcon or the hawk replaces the eagle as the King of Birds and the solar principle, and represents Horus the all-seeing, who is depicted either as a falcon or falcon-, or hawk-headed. The wings outspread are the heavens and the eyes of Horus are the sun and moon; this image was carried on early standards. As solar the falcon is also identified with Ra, and it is an emblem of the Theban God of War Mont or Menthu, who is falcon- or bull-headed.

Falcon and eagle are joined also in Celtic lore as one of the primordial manifestations. They are both, as pure principles, opposed to the **Hare** (symbolizing lasciviousness), and the bird with the hare in its talons represents the victory of the spiritual over the carnal. In Scandinavian lore Odin could travel to earth as a falcon, which is also an attribute of Frigg and an aspect of Loki as fire.

In China the falcon is ambivalent, as both the beneficent power of the sun and also the destructive forces of war. For the Ainu of Japan it helps humanity by frightening hares off crops and gardens; its claw is a specific against snake bite.

Among Amerindians the falcon is the younger brother of the eagle, though for the Indians of the South-east Woodlands it heads the category of birds and is the supreme Bird of War, with the eagle as Peace.

Heraldry makes no distinction between the falcon and hawk. The falcon is frequently 'belled' and 'jessed'; when blindfolded it is termed 'hooded'; represented with its prey it is 'trussing' its prey. The falcon head appears frequently in crests.

Fawn.   A fawn's skin was the sacred vesture of the lower degree of the Greek Mystae, for, when born from the thigh of Zeus, Dionysos was placed by Hermes/Mercury on a fawn skin, and wore a magic fawn skin which arrows could not pierce (this is in other cases replaced by the skin of a tiger or leopard). Fawns were sacrificed to

Dionysos/Bacchus by the Meniads, and fawn skins were worn by the
Bacchant and Orphic devotees. The fawn was their emblem and was
also associated with Diana/Artemis as Goddess of the Hunt.

The fawn or **Deer** is a favourite form adopted by nymphs and
fairies to allow them to escape. It was the shape taken by the fairy-
mother of the Gaelic bard Ossian (Little Fawn), and she bore him
while in this guise; for this reason he could never eat venison.

Feather, Flight. Feathers can contain the spirit of the bird, its
powers and properties, the part representing the whole; wearing
feathers or a feathered head-dress, or feathers attached to a figure,
puts the wearer in touch with the *mana* and qualities of the bird and
transmits its knowledge. For example, the white feather of the crane
carries its symbolism of divine wisdom of communion with the
gods, while the black feather of the crow can carry death to an
enemy, and the blue feather of the jay revives and is an awakener
of life.

Feathers symbolize the soul, the power of flight to other realms, the
heavens, lightness, height, truth which must rise, instinctual knowledge
('a little bird told me'), magic power and the element of wind.

Flight represents the unrestricted powers of the soul or mind. It
runs through all myth and religion and is one of the fundamental
longings of humanity. It also signifies aspiration towards the divine,
transcendence, the release of spirit from the confines of matter, the
flight of the soul at death and the passing from one state to another.

Plumes crown many ancient Egyptian deities as a symbol of
sovereignty and solar power; they also typify truth, flight,
weightlessness, height and dryness. The feather of truth is an
emblem of the goddess Maat; it is weighed against the soul at death
in the judgement hall of Osiris. Deities depicted with feathers are
Amen Ra, Anheru, Osiris, Horus, Shu, Hathor, Amsu, Mentu,
Nefertium and Maat.

Feathered robes have the magic power of transporting the wearer
through the air. The Scandinavian Freyja had one such robe, and
shamans often use feathered robes to obtain the power of flight and
to visit the spirit world or to go on long journeys to gain knowledge
of distant places. In Shamanistic and Amerindian traditions feathers
are not only symbolic but are regarded as actual transmitters or
carriers of spiritual power. The eagle feather is the most significant
of all, representing the **Thunderbird**, the Great Spirit, the universal
spirit and also the solar power. This last is portrayed in its full
significance in the Plains Indians Feathered Sun, with stylized
feathers pointing both inwards and outwards from centre to
circumference; combining the symbols of the eagle and the sun it
represents the universe, the Sacred Centre, the radiation of power.
Toltec feathered sticks depicted prayer and contemplation.

In Chinese Alchemy the Feathered *hsien* or Immortal signifies freedom from earthly limitations, that is the spiritualized body. Some Polynesian deities have feathers as attributes as they are sacred emblems and talismans. This is particularly true of red feathers, either in bunches or individually.

Feathers are often the insignia of a chieftain in tribal societies.

In Heraldry single feathers are frequently seen as charges on a shield, notably the three ostrich feathers of Edward the Black Prince; these heraldic symbols are also associated with the Fleur-de-Lis as an emblem of the Prince of Wales. Cock feathers appear on charges, but for the most part feathers are, naturally, usually found on crests. The usual number of feathers on a plume are three, five or seven.

Ferret. Signifies persistent pursuit. Ferrets and **Weasels** were kept in households in earlier times to perform the functions of the modern-day domestic cat, that is, keeping down rats and mice.

Fetish. Like magic, fetishism is based on the desire to manipulate forces and powers beyond immediate human understanding and control. Its main purpose is to ward off evil or bring good luck, and fetishes have been used by all types of people and cultures from ancient times to the present. All talismans, amulets and charms have the character of fetishes. Almost any material can be used, animal, vegetable or mineral, stones, wood, metals, bones (particularly skulls), antlers, feathers, claws, teeth, shells – all are taken as imbued with a spirit which serves the possessor or can act as a guardian. Fetishes are used by individuals, tribes, societies (especially secret ones), in initiation, in hunting, by medicine-men, in rites of propitiation and in, and against, witchcraft. The later development of the fetish became the idol. Offerings are made to tribal fetishes and those representing the animals of the hunt are carried by the hunters as sympathetic magic. Fetishes can be carried about or hung over windows or doors through which forces of evil or disease might be likely to enter, or they can be stuck on poles. Local gods can be represented by some fetish object.

Firedrake. A Norse monster which *Beowolf* calls: 'the ravager of the darksome night', it is a fire-breathing type of **Dragon** guarding a hoard of gold. It was slain by Beowolf and his companion Wiglaf.

Firefly. In Buddhism the firefly portrays shallow knowledge which is incapable of lightening the darkness of ignorance. In Japanese mythology spirits can take the form of a firefly, and the firefly can take the form of a fire-flower, or fireflies can be stars which have left the sky to wander on earth. During the summer there is a Firefly Battle at Uji which is an occasion for Firefly Viewing.

Fish. The fish is one of the most widely-employed symbols, hallowed in religion and myth. The fish is ambivalent, representing both the male and female principles; it is pre-eminently a symbol of fecundity, phallic, but also associated with the feminine primordial watery element from which all life rose; it is also associated with all lunar deities. Fish was the sacred food at the rites of these divinities, especially of the lunar goddesses of love and fecundity such as Atargatis, Ishtar, Nina, Isis and Aphrodite/Venus. Their sacred day was Friday, on which day fish was eaten in their honour, and fish was the eucharistic meal of the priests of Atargatis. Sacred fish were kept in ponds at the temples and could not be touched on pain of having the body covered with ulcers and tumours, but at mystic celebrations priests and initiates ate the sacred food to absorb its divinity. The priests of the Sumerian Ea-Oannes, Lord of the Deep, wore a fish-skin robe with a fish head, which later became the form of the mitre of Christian bishops. Ea the goat-fish is both phallic/masculine and connected with the feminine waters and Ishtar.

The positions or accompaniments of fishes have their own significance. Swimming in the waters they depict the devotees or disciples living in the waters of life. Fishes swimming downwards denote the spirit descending into matter, while swimming upwards is the evolution of spirit-matter returning to the First Principle. Fishes with birds are chthonic and funerary, and represent resurrection and ascension. Fish- or Sea-gods ride on fishes or dolphins and portray the freedom of movement in the waters. The fish appears with the axe in Assyrian and Cretan iconography, and it is suggested that this typifies the union of the lunar and solar powers of water with the Sky Gods. Two fishes represent temporal and spiritual power; if they are swimming in opposite directions they are the duality of nature. Three fishes can be depicted as intertwined or as being united in one head – both depictions signify the unity of the Trinity but the one-headed-three is the more universal, being found in Egyptian, Indian, Mesopotamian, Burmese, Persian, Celtic and French iconography.

In Buddhism the fish has the special significance of representing taking refuge in the Buddha, the Law and the Sangha. Buddha is also a Fisher of Men. On the footprint of the Buddha the fish portrays emancipation from desires and attachments.

In Hinduism Vishnu first incarnated as a fish to save mankind from the Flood; he founded a new race and a new cycle. Varuna, God of the Skies and Waters, is represented by a golden fish; he redeemed Manu from the Flood. The fish is also a symbol of fertility and wealth and an attribute of divinities of love.

Egyptian kings were not allowed to eat fish, though it was eaten by the populace. The barbel was regarded as unclean and

Three fishes, symbolizing the trinity of divine power

symbolized hatred; it was an attribute of Typhon, the irrational, unrestrained element in nature. The fish was also the phallus of Osiris but was associated with the feminine aspect of fertility as an emblem of Isis and Hathor. Two fishes depicted the prosperity of the Nile and the creation principle.

Lucian says that the Syrians worshipped fish and held them sacred and would not eat them. Dagon, God of the Sea for the Philistines, could be depicted as a fish or part-fish. For the Hebrews certain fish were clean food, others forbidden: 'Whatsoever hath fins and scales shall ye eat: and whatsoever hath not fins and scales shall ye not eat; it is unclean to you' (Deuteronomy 14: 9–10). In the Torah fishes represent the faithful of Israel in their true element, the Waters of the Torah. The *coena pura* is the meal of the Sabbath, symbolic of the food of Paradise and the banquet of the bliss of the future life. Fish are eaten on the eve of the Seder.

Aphrodite took the form of a fish when she fled from Typhon, a natural shape for her to assume since she originally emerged from the foam of the sea. The fish is also her attribute as symbolic of love and fecundity. It also represents Poseidon/Neptune as the power of the oceans. Orpheus was also a Fisher of Men. But for the Greeks the fish also typified stupidity, though it appeared on ancient tombs as carrying the soul across the sea to the Isles of the Blest; the **Dolphin** was mainly used in this context. In Rome the fish maintains the same significance for Venus as for Aphrodite, but it has, too, a funerary aspect and depicts new life in the next world.

In Celtic lore salmon and trout are of great importance, connected with sacred wells and springs and symbolizing wisdom and the

Chinese pair of fishes

foreknowledge of the gods and the healing waters. Nodon was a Fisher God.

The Chinese word for fish is a homophone for 'abundance', hence the fish represents that state, also wealth, regeneration and harmony. A single fish portrays the lonely person, the orphan, widow or bachelor, but a pair of fishes depicts the married state, union, fertility. The fish is an emblem of Kwan-yin and the T'ang Dynasty. The **Carp** has a symbolism of its own, representing literary eminence and also perseverance against difficulties, since the carp struggles upstream to spawn. In Japan it is a homophone for 'love' and is also an attribute of Kwannon.

The Early Fathers of the Christian Church called the faithful *pisciculi*, and the Apostles were Fishers of Men. Christ was symbolized by the rebus ICHTHUS – *Iesous Christos Theou Huios Soter* – and the fish signified Christ in the Latin Church (but not in the Greek Orthodox Church). As immersed in water the fish signified baptism, and from the story of Jonah it derives the meaning of resurrection. In Christian art the disciples are often depicted as seated at a table with bread, wine and fish as a sacramental meal. Fish had a funerary significance for the Mandaeans and was eaten sacramentally at feasts of the dead.

The Bestiaries say that fish are symbolic of compassion and love as, when danger threatens, they open their mouths and draw in their young, then bring them out again unharmed when all is safe. They also portray purity as they do not cross-breed.

Certain fish, notably the shark, are held sacred in parts of Africa and in Polynesia. For the Ainu the world is supported on the back of a large fish; earthquakes are caused by its movement (here the fish takes on the role of the **Tortoise** in Chinese and Indian myth).

Fish-God of the Dahomey

The ebb and flow of the tides is caused by the fish sucking in and
sending out the waters.

In Heraldry a fish in horizontal position is *naiant*; in the
perpendicular it is *hauriant*.

See also **Carp**, **Dolphin**, **Salmon**, **Shark**, and **Whale**

Fish-hawk. Ainu myth says the fish-hawk came down from
heaven and therefore must be venerated, but it is hot-tempered so
must be handled with care.

The Five Animals. The Five Animals of Chinese myth are: **Fox**,
Weasel, **Snake**, **Hedgehog** and **Rat**. They were greatly dreaded as
the Five Great Families. They lie in wait on the road and bewitch
anyone who treads on them.

Flamingo. In Justinian's time flamingoes were depicted as the
blessed in Paradise; they were sacrificed to Gaia's Godhead
(Caligula). Pliny says the tongue and brain are a great delicacy. The

bird was believed to straddle the nest, leaving its legs dangling straight and unsupported on either side.

Flea.   A term of contempt; the most insignificant of living things, the smallest quantity. Referred to in the Old Testament in I Samuel 24: 14.

Fly.   Represents feebleness and insignificance but is also associated with evil gods and corruption. Beelzebub, the Phoenician Lord of the Flies, is the power and agent of putrefaction and destruction; he appears as God of the Dunghill with the Hebrews. In the *Avesta* the Death Demon takes the shape of a fly. In Christianity the fly symbolizes evil, sin, pestilence; it is depicted in Christian art with the **Goldfinch**, the latter representing the Saviour and the fly disease. Demons are frequently portrayed as flies.

The fly can also signify supernatural power. Among the Ashanti of Africa there is a fly-god, and the Kalmuks regard the fly as a soul creature, not to be killed.

Among the Amerindians Big Fly appears as a hero figure in Navajo myth.

Flying Fox.   The totem animal of the Bouganvilia tribe of Papua, New Guinea; in Samoa it was worshipped as the incarnation of the War God and omens were read from its flight.

The Number Four.   The Four Spiritual Creatures or Four Auspicious Animals of China are the **Dragon**, **Ky-lin**, **Tortoise** and **Phoenix**. They were attendants of P'an Ku, the First Man, a Creator; they also represent the four classes of animals – the Scaly, Hairy, Shell-covered and Feathered – and the four directions and four seasons. Originally the **Tiger** took the place of the Ky-lin.

The Four Beasts or Living Creatures represented the four great cosmic forces – earth, air, fire and water. In Ezekiel 1 they came out of the fire, having four faces: from the front the face of a man, the face of a lion on the right side and of an ox on the left side and the face of an eagle at the back. These appear in the New Testament as the Tetramorphs, with Matthew as the man representing the incarnation and the human nature of Christ; Mark as a winged lion depicting the dignity and royalty of Christ; Luke, a winged ox as his sacrifice, priesthood and the atonement, and John as his divine nature, the ascension, the eagle 'who can gaze on the sun'.

The Four Elements or Humours were symbolized by the Ape as Air, the Lamb as Water, the Pig as Earth and the Lion as Fire.

Fox.   In myth and fable the fox is credited with greater cunning and guile than any other animal; it is universally the epitome of craftiness, trickery and hypocrisy. There is, however, some difference in its significance between the East and West: while it is the **Trickster** figure of the West, in the East it has even greater strength and import, being not only a Trickster but having supernatural powers as a transformer and shape-shifter.

The fox's history as a Trickster goes back to Sumerian times, when it was associated with the Trickster God Enki; the fox revived him when he had eaten poisonous plants. In Zoroastrian myth the fox has supernatural powers and scares off demons.

Dionysos/Bacchus was associated with the fox: on the one hand he protects his vines from the 'little foxes' who spoiled them, on the other hand, in Thrace, the fox was the feminine counterpart to the Dionysian bull.

The theme of the little foxes spoiling the vines is repeated in the Bible. In the Old Testament the fox and **Jackal** are often interchangeable as symbolic of cunning and duplicity and in both Old and New Testaments the significance is one of deceit and guile. Herod is called 'that fox'. Christianity equates the fox with the Devil as deceiver; the manner in which it feigns death to trap its prey depicts the stratagems of Satan. This appears in the *Physiologus*, where it says that the fox buries itself in the earth as though dead, and then when ravens and other birds come to devour it leaps up and eats them – 'So the Devil deceives those who love the corrupt things of the flesh and lures them to their own destruction.' The fox also 'injures the earth by burrowing in it; the earth signifies man, who should bring forth the fruits of righteousness; sin is the hole which the Devil digs and thereby causes those to wither away.' In the Bestiaries the Fox, or *Vulpis*, is fraudulent and ingenious; 'it runs in tortuous windings and pretends to be dead and when birds light on him he grabs them. The Devil has the same nature.'

The *Physiologus* and the Bestiaries greatly influenced European literature in the Middle Ages, in which the Fox of the *Physiologus* changes to the much-quoted Renard, that crafty, stealing, hypocritical and sanctimonious creature. The association with the vine and vegetation continues and connects the animal with drunkenness, hence 'to be foxed', a popular phrase used by Pepys and others. There is a French and German saying that when a field of corn waves in the wind a fox or wolf is passing through, and children are frightened by this bogey. The fox is also suggested as lurking in the last sheaf of corn, which is thus reaped with the cry – '*Attention, le renard va sortir*', and in some parts it is said of a harvester who falls ill '*il a le renard*', while the harvest-home feast was called *renard*. To flail the corn was to strike the fox. In the European Epic *The Tales of Renard the Fox* the hypocritical, sanctimonious guile of the animal is depicted by foxes wearing monks' clothing as a disguise to catch the unwary. Foxes in cowls were portrayed to satirize the itinerant friars who wandered about disturbing the peace of the regular clergy by exposing established abuses and who themselves later deteriorated into professional begging vagrants.

The fox appears as a shape-shifter in Amerindian myth among the Innuits (Eskimo) and there are Algonquin and Susquahanna fox tribes and clans. Brer Fox is a well-known character in North American literature.

China and Japan have innumerable myths of fox spirits taking human form, usually as beautiful maidens, to cause trouble and bring disaster; alternatively they can take the shape of a holy man to deceive people into worshipping them. But the true nature of a fox can be revealed by its reflection in water or a mirror, or by meeting a dog or hearing it bark. Although the fox is the archetypal illusionist, shape-shifter and magician it is not entirely malefic as it can be induced to help and bring good fortune if shown appropriate attentions. It is an attribute of the Rice Deity Inari and also a 'spirit of rice' in Japan. There is also the myth of the fox spirit appearing as a beautiful maiden who married the Emperor Hansoku and caused the death of more than a thousand men. Fox spirits can compound the Elixir of Life, which can be stolen from them; they are also messengers between worlds. A black fox is good luck, a white fox calamity, and three foxes disaster. In China the fox can symbolize longevity, as well as the usual crafty qualities, and spirits of the dead can dwell in foxes. The fox is one of the **Five Animals** of Chinese lore.

The Ainu admire the fox for his cunning and fleetness, and keep fox skulls to use in divination; both fox and bird skulls are used by wizards. The fox rite is known as 'the ceremony of the light-footed person'. The fox and **Cat** are of the same family and rose out of the ashes of the Great Demon, which was defeated and burned by **Mole**. The fox is, again, a shape-shifter with demonic supernatural powers which can bewitch people, send them mad or make them ill.

Fox-fire (light without heat) applies in Japan to the will-o'-the-wisp or *ignus fatui*. In Scandinavia the aurora borealis is 'the light of the fox'.

The fox appears in Heraldry as a charge, a supporter, or a crest, but is often confused with the wolf in poor representations.

Frigate Bird.   Also known as the Man-of-War Bird and the Son of the Sun, this is a Melanesian totem animal, sometimes tamed as such.

Frog.   As a creature of the waters the frog is lunar, a rain-maker, bringing fertility and new life; rising from the waters and having a skin that is moist as opposed to the dryness of death it also symbolizes life and resurrection. Living in the primordial slime, which is the basis of matter, it is fecundity. The Great Frog is one of the traditional supporters of the universe. Frogs are widely considered to be rain-bringers.

Seti I making an offering to the Frog Goddess Hequat at Abydos

The ancient Egyptians had a Frog Goddess Hekt or Hequat who was the power of the waters, the midwife at the birth of the world, protectress of mothers and the new-born. Later the frog was also an emblem of Isis and Hathor as Great Mothers, goddesses of fertility and birth. The early Egyptian gods Hah, Kek, Nau and Amen were represented as frog-shaped. The Great Frog of the Nile signified new life, abundance, the prolific reproductive powers of nature; it also depicts strength in weakness. Like the **Scarabs**, frogs appear at the beginning of the rains, coming out of the ground in large numbers, hence they are symbolic of fertility and the fecundity of the waters. Small amulets of frogs were found in tombs from all periods in Egypt, representing and holding the spirit of the deity. Later Egyptian Christians used the frog as a symbol of new birth; a lamp was found decorated with a frog-figure surrounded by the words 'I am the resurrection', but the frog came to mean both the resurrection and the repulsiveness of sin, worldly pleasure, envy, greed and heretics. In the Old Testament the Second Plague of Egypt was brought about by the magician Aaron, who 'stretched out his hand over the waters of Egypt, and frogs came up and covered the land' (Exodus 8: 6). In the New Testament frogs are equated with unclean spirits (Revelations 16: 13).

The lunar *yin* principle is represented by the frog in Chinese symbolism, and the Frog Spirit Ch'ing-Wa Sheng is venerated both as a healer and for prosperity in business. A frog in a well depicts a person of limited understanding and vision.

In the *Rig Veda* (VII 103) frogs are invoked as deities; their croaking is the chanting of Brahmans performing the rites and praying for rain at a time of drought. The Great Frog supports the universe and

represents the dark, undifferentiated *prima materia*. In
Zoroastrianism the frog is evil and belongs to Ahriman. In Sri
Lankan myth the frog is the lowest supporter of the earth.

Graeco-Roman symbolism uses the frog to represent fertility and
also harmony between lovers; as an emblem of Aphrodite/Venus it
is also licentiousness. Plato calls it a rain-lover and a devotee of the
nymphs. Juvenal says that frog entrails were used as charms in
ancient times; they were also used as medicaments by mediaeval
quacks and were employed in magic and as an ingredient of witches'
brews. Frogs croak in the swamps of the underworld.

In magical rites frogs were whipped to produce rain, water being
their natural medium.

Celtic tradition has the frog as Lord of the Earth; it also represents
the healing waters.

For the Amerindian shaman the frog is a cleansing power, a rain-
bringer, refreshment, purification, the power of the waters and
initiation by water. The water deity of the Mayas and Aztecs was
a frog. In Huron mythology the Great Frog swallowed all the waters
of the earth but was slain by Ioskela, the White One. The frog is the
totem of the Hopi Water Clan and an ancestor of the Lillooet tribe.
Among the Hopi it is also associated with the maize cycle,
representing the necessary water. The frog is naturally associated
with Deluge myths, in which it is Lord of Waters, in both
Amerindian and Australian Aboriginal lore. It is also the totem
animal of an Aboriginal tribe.

According to the Ainu of Japan the frog originated from a woman
who behaved badly, killed husbands and generally displeased the
gods, who turned her into a frog. She gave birth to frogs from then
on.

Funereal Animals. Animals often appear on tombs, sarcophagi
and in catacombs, with varying symbolism. Fierce animals
devouring weaker depict the strong soul triumphing over the weaker
body. Figures on tombs, at the feet of effigies, at first represented
overcoming the evil powers and qualities of such animals as the lion
and the dragon. Later the lion at the feet of a man portrayed manly
strength and courage, and the dog at the feet of a woman
represented love and fidelity. Dogs at the feet can also typify faithful
friends and guardians.

Scenes depicting animals in funerary art are often those of pastoral
life and rural tranquillity, symbolizing the peace, plenty and idyllic
life beyond the grave; these appear particularly in Roman art. In
Christian art the theme of the Good Shepherd has the same
significance and such subjects also appeared on Christian
catacombs.

Swans denoted a happy death, as the 'swan-song' was symbolic of acceptance of death as good. Sarcophagi, both pagan and Christian, often depicted the goat-herd milking goats in paradisial scenes. Fish, symbolic of immortality, appear frequently. The eagle, as an apotheosis, was released at the funeral of a Roman Emperor. The lizard and butterfly as symbols of death and rebirth also appear in funerary art. The scarab was buried with Egyptian dead and vultures' plumes adorned the coffin in the funeral rites of Osiris.

G

Garuda. Possibly the oldest of the great sky-birds, the Persian **Simurgh**, the Arabian **Roc**, the Chinese Fei Lien and the **Gryphon**. It was so large it could darken the sky and blot out the sun, but unlike the other monster birds the Garuda was beneficent, the Bird of Life, the King of Birds. It is the vehicle of Vishnu and was represented as half-man, half-eagle, its face white, wings red and its body of golden lustre. The Garuda is the traditional enemy of the Nagas, the **Serpent**. Vinata, mother of Vishnu, was sister to the Queen of Serpents; the sisters were at enmity, hence the continuous war between the Garuda as eagle and the snake or naga. The Mahabharata says the parents of the Garuda gave it permission to devour bad men, but not Brahmans. There is also a traditional war between the Garuda and the Dwarfs, *Kirata*, a theme which appears again in Graeco-Roman myth as the war between the **Crane** and the Pygmies. The Garuda emerges fully grown from the egg and nests in the wish-fulfilling Tree of Life. The symbol of the winged man also appeared in pre-Buddhist Tibet.

Gazelle. In its symbolism the gazelle can change places with the **Antelope**, **Deer** and **Goat**; it has a varied significance, gentleness in one tradition and evil in another. As an animal of the desert it was associated in ancient Egypt with the oryx and goat as an attribute of Set in his typhonic aspect, and Horus trampling on the gazelle depicts victory over the typhonic powers. But for the Hebrews the gazelle represented peace, gentleness and fleetness (1 Chronicles 12: 8) also timidity (Isaiah 13: 14); it is clean meat for the Jews (Deuteronomy 12: 15–22), but was not used in sacrifice. Arabs sacrifice gazelles, but as a poor substitute for a sheep; gazelles are sacred in Mecca and in Islam; ibu Arabi likens them to spiritual states, 'My heart, a pasture for gazelles'. The animal was also sacrificed in Phoenicia.

In the Hindu Zodiac Capricorn is represented by a gazelle or antelope: it is also the vehicle of the Moon God Chandra and an attribute of Siva, whose chariot is drawn by antelopes. Two gazelles or deer are shown in Buddhist iconography: the Buddha preached his first sermon in the Deer Park at Benares.

The deer or gazelle is an attribute of the Moon Goddess and Huntress Diana in Greece and Rome and in Pompeii gazelles are pictured as driven by Cupids in light carts; but in Sumeria it is associated with Mullil, God of Storms, and is also an emblem of Astarte.

Christianity uses the gazelle or deer fleeing from some animal of prey to represent the soul fleeing from earthly passions.

Ghosts. There is a widespread belief in the ability of ghosts, apparitions or wandering spirits to take animal forms. In Chinese iconography this was depicted most usually as a man's head on a cock's body for a male and a woman's head on a hen's body for a female. There are innumerable headless horse ghosts, and the black dog myth is widespread in Europe. Tribal societies assume the ability of human and animal souls to change places, and any animal or bird may embody the soul of an ancestor or relative.

Giraffe or Cameleopard. Known to the Graeco-Roman world as the Cameleopard, Pliny says it has the neck of a horse, legs and feet of a bull, the head of a camel with a spotted skin like that of a leopard. Horace said it was a mongrel breed, half-camel, half-leopard. The giraffe is a cult animal and a vehicle of supernatural power among the African Bushmen; there are ritual giraffe dances.

Glutton. See **Wolverine**

Gnat. Gnats, mosquitoes and other insect pests, according to Ainu lore, rose from the ashes of a hobgoblin killed and burned by an Ainu hero. In the New Testament the gnat is used to represent the most insignificant of things (Matthew 23: 24).

Goat. Both sexes of the goat symbolize fertility, vitality and ceaseless energy. The he-goat is the epitome of masculine virility and creative energy, while the female typifies the feminine generative power and abundance. Symbolically the goat can be interchangeable with the **Gazelle** or the **Antelope**. The wild goat of the Old Testament and Arabic lore is the **Ibex**. The goat was probably, after the **Dog**, the earliest domesticated animal. Goats grazing or at rest, or being milked by a goat-herd, are frequent subjects for idyllic scenes, representing the paradisial state; as such they appear on both pagan and Christian sarcophagi.

There were many strange beliefs about goats. Oppian says they breathe through their horns, while Varro maintains they breathe through their ears; Pliny expresses a general belief that they are perpetually feverish. Goat skins were used for water and wine bottles when travelling and camping, and for parchment, goat hair

Goat-man

was woven and the animal provided food and milk. The goat, especially the kid, was a sacrificial animal and was used also as a sin-offering (the **Scapegoat**). The goat is lust personified, and a goat with a human head depicts depravity.

The Sumerian god Marduk often has a goat as an accompaniment, and it also appears with hunting goddesses. The wild goat was sacred to Artemis and is an attribute of Dionysos, who took this form when fleeing from Typhon, and of the satyrs, who are half-goats with goats' horns. Pan also has the legs, horns and beard of a goat. Zeus Dictynnos was suckled by the goat Amalthea, whose skin became the aegis and her horn the cornucopia – she thus represented the protector and preserver, abundance and plenty. The goat was sacrificed to Faunus, who guarded the woods, fields and shepherds of flocks; also to the other nature gods such as Silvanus and Pan. The goat was used as a draft animal and is depicted as such at Pompeii, with Dionysos/Bacchus reclining in a cart driven by Cupid and drawn by goats. The she-goat was sacrificed to Artemis at her Athenian festival of Munichia. Herodotus says that the goat skin or *aegis* was worn by the statues of Athene in the Lybrian sacrifices and rites. Goats and dogs were sacrificed at the Roman Lupercalia; the 'Lupercal' was naked but for a goat skin and he carried goat-skin thongs for the ritual fertility whipping of women in the crowds, who put themselves in his way to receive the fertility-magic. The goat, with the **Horse** and **Dog**, could not be touched by the Roman Priest of Jupiter, the *Flamen Dialis*.

The Semitic goat-god Azazel symbolized life and creative energy. The Hebrew Scapegoat was chosen from two goats, one of which was for the Lord. The other, the sin-bearer, was sent into the wilderness for Azazel (Leviticus 16: 7–10). The Hebrew *sa'ir*, goat, is rendered as *satyr* in the Old Testament (Isaiah 13: 21 and 34: 14) and is an object of worship of false gods (Leviticus 17: 7 and II Chronicles 11: 15). The goat symbolized lewdness. This tradition was carried over into Christianity, where the goat represents the Devil, lust, lubricity and the damned while the **Sheep** symbolizes the saved. Christ is portrayed as the Scapegoat taking away the sins of the world. But in the Bestiaries the goat, which climbs the highest peaks and possesses wonderful vision, depicts the highest perfection of searching and the gaze of Christ who sees all, past, present and future.

Arabic lore associates the stately march of the he-goat leading the herd with dignity of manner and bearing, but, as contrasted with the meek sheep, it also symbolizes lawlessness, independence and straying. It is a sacrificial animal.

The ram and the he-goat are attributes of the Vedic Agni, God of Fire and creative heat, who rides a he-goat.

Thor, Scandinavian God of Thunder and Fertility, has a chariot drawn by goats who are sacred to him; his goat Heidrun supplied the heavenly mead, the drink of the gods.

The Chinese Goat Spirit Yang Ching is the god of the star Fan-yin;

Goat climbing peaks (*from a Bestiary*)

he is the Transcendent Goat with white face, horns, a long beard
and a special head-dress. He is also a Mongolian god. In Chinese
the goat is a homophone of *yang* and so represents the solar,
masculine principle; it also signifies peace and the good.

Russia has a wood-spirit, the Leshi, which resembles Pan and the
Satyrs in having human shape with the horns, ears and legs of a
goat.

The goat is frequently used in Heraldry; with horns of a different
colour it is said to be 'armed'.

Goatsucker.   An evil and ill-omened bird, nocturnal and therefore
allied to the powers of darkness; said to drain milk from cows and
goats. Goatsuckers can embody the souls of people unable to rest
on account of crimes committed while in human form; their cries
are said to be the wailings of the ghosts expiating their sins.

Goldfinch.   In Christian art this bird is depicted with Christ or is
held in the Christ-child's hand; it represents the soul, the good. Its
red spot is the blood of Christ – at the crucifixion it drew a thorn
from his brow.

Goose.   The idea of the 'silly goose', symbolizing stupidity and
credulity, was a later European development. Ovid calls the goose
'wiser than the dog'; it is 'the protector of the house' and so
represents careful guardianship and was kept by the Greeks and
Romans. Tame geese were kept in temples and saved Rome by their
warnings when the Gauls attacked. In Greece the goose was an
attribute of Hera, Queen of Heaven, and signified love, watchfulness
and the good housewife; it was also associated with the solar Apollo,
with Hermes, the messenger, Ares as war, Eros as love and Peitho
as goddess of eloquence. This symbolism also appeared in Rome,
with Mars as war, Juno as Queen of Heaven and Priapus as fertility.

The Nile Goose, 'the Great Chatterer', was the creator of the world
in Egyptian mythology; it laid the Cosmic **Egg** from which the Sun
God Amon-Ra was hatched. It is also an attribute of Isis, Osiris and
Horus, and of Set, the earth god: again it symbolizes love.

The goose and **Swan**, both solar birds, are interchangeable in
symbolism, particularly in India where the Hamsa appears in either
form as a vehicle of Brahma and represents the creative principle,
self-existent being, freedom, the flight of the spirit, learning and
eloquence.

Although solar and *yang*, the wild goose is frequently associated
with the autumn moon in Chinese and Japanese art. It is 'the Bird
of Heaven', a messenger, bringing good tidings; it is swiftness, light,
inspiration, seasonal change; also conjugal happiness.

In the *Gallic Wars* Caesar says the goose was taboo as food for the
Britons, being a sacred bird. It was associated with both Celtic and

Teutonic war gods, who were accompanied by a **Horse** and a goose. In Gallic iconography Epona, the Divine Horse, is depicted riding on a horned goose. The Norse did not eat the goose.

The goose was a clean food for the Hebrews; probably the 'fowl' of Solomon's table.

In Christianity the bird typified vigilance and providence, and was associated with St Martin, who ordered an annoying goose to be killed and eaten; this gave rise to the great Goose Fair in France, held on his day, November 11. There was also a famous Goose Fair at Nottingham in England at Michaelmas and the bird was a traditional food at both Michaelmas and Christmas. The English tradition of a tenant giving the landlord a goose at Michaelmas was a relic of the ancient custom of placating the powers that be with a sacrifice or food.

The goose also symbolizes the wind, it is the 'breath bird' and a weather prophet. It is a lucky bird for sailors, as it floats rather than sinks. It was also associated with witches, and could carry them to the Sabbat.

Gorilla. In some African tribes the gorilla could incarnate the souls of the departed, in which case it was said to unite the intelligence of the man-spirit with the strength of the animal body.

See also **Ape**

Grampus or Orca. The killer; said to be the enemy of the **Whale**, which it hunts. Being smaller than the whale it hunts in packs. As it blows and spouts it typifies a person who puffs or breathes heavily.

Grasshopper. Aristotle says that the grasshopper is the only creature that has no mouth but a tongue-like formation which feeds on dew only.

In ancient Greece the golden grasshopper depicted nobility, a native aristocrat. This was carried over into European Heraldry where the symbol is used frequently; it is associated with the City of London.

The Chinese Pa Cha, the Spirit of Grasshoppers, protects against destructive insects and is depicted as having the head and claws of a bird of prey with ear-tufts. The grasshopper signifies good luck, summer abundance, many sons, virtue.

In Europe the **Ant** and the grasshopper are contrasted as industry and providence as against irresponsibility and improvidence, the one working all summer to lay up stores for the winter, the other singing all summer and starving in winter.

The Old Testament associates the grasshopper and **Locust** as permissible food for the Hebrews (Leviticus 11: 22), and also uses it to symbolize the insignificant (Numbers 13: 33).

Heraldic Griffin

Australian Aboriginal lore connects the grasshopper with lightning.

Grayling. The Tunguses Amerindians began their summer with the spawning of the grayling and their winter with catching the first good **Squirrel**.

Griffin, Griffon or Gryphon. A hybrid monster with the head and talons of an **Eagle** and the body of a **Lion**. Herodotus says it lives in the mountains of India and builds its nest out of gold; later, in the Middle Ages, Sir John Mandeville said it abounded in Bacharia and that it was 'more gret and more strong than eight lyouns and more gret and stronger than an hundred eagles'. It resembles the winged **Bull** of Assyria, the **Sphinx** of Egypt, the **Simurgh** of Persia, the **Garuda** of India, and the **Roc** of Arabia in that it was so huge it could blot out the sun. It appeared in Assyria and the East as the 'cloud-cleaving eagle' and the 'king of beasts'. In the East it shares the symbolism of the **Dragon**, representing wisdom and enlightenment. In ancient Greece, being solar, the griffin was sacred to Apollo, to Athene as wisdom and Nemesis as vengeance. In Roman art griffins draw the chariot of Nemesis. The Egyptian Set could be represented by the griffin.

   The griffin is a guardian creature, particularly as 'The Bird of

Gold' of the gold mines of Scythia and India. As gold it symbolizes the sun, the sky, the golden light of dawn. It also combines the powers of the earth and sky. As a guardian it furthermore depicts vigilance and vengeance.

Dante describes the griffin as 'the mystic shape that joins the two natures in one form', and Christianity uses these two natures to represent Christ as God and man, the union of the divine and human, and to represent the Pope as spiritual and temporal power; but also as evil, the Devil flying away with souls, or as the persecutors of Christians.

Griffin-headed bird (*from an 18th-century Tibetan woodblock*)

Used in Heraldry the griffin depicts strength and vigilance and is an emblem of the hero. In English heraldry the male is portrayed *sans* wings. The demi-griffin is often found as a crest.

Grouse or Hazel-hen. In Amerindian rites the Grouse Dance takes the form of the Sacred Spiral, symbol of birth, death and return, and of personal power.

The Ainu call it the 'bird of great sound', as it makes a noise in taking flight. It originated in parts of deer skins thrown away by a hunting god; having been touched by divinity the parts could not decay, so changed into birds which make a great sound like the crackling of dry skins.

Guanaco. The sacred animal of the Ona tribe of Tierra del Fuego. Chieftains wear a cap and robe of its fur. When hunting, the hunter wears a band of plaited guanaco sinew, a token of identification between the hunter and hunted.

Guardian Animals.   Mythical monsters and a wide variety of the fiercer animals have been employed universally in the guarding of treasures or sacred places. They perform a dual role, not merely acting as guardians but also symbolizing the dangerous aspect of the thing they guard, or, in the case of sacred buildings, of the power of the Presence within. Guardians of the threshold must be overcome before the sacred realm can be entered; they perform the function of preventing the would-be entrant from going too far too fast and encountering more than it is possible to bear or understand; the threshold being the meeting place of two realms, the outer and the inner, the profane and the sacred.

Treasures and the entrance to Temples, Churches and other sacred places are guarded by **Dragons**, **Lions**, winged **Bulls**, **Serpents**, scorpion-men, gargoyles and a great variety of fearsome creatures, all indicating the dangers of leaving one known state to confront the unknown and the esoteric.

The Dragon, Serpent or Naga is the most usual guardian and as such is generally depicted as guarding the most dangerous of all things, the Tree of Knowledge or the Tree of Life.

Fabulous monsters have their own specialized functions. The **Griffin** or Gryphon, being the Bird of Gold, naturally guards gold mines; the **Sphinx** guards esoteric knowledge, the **Eagle** watches over the two Gates of the World; **Scorpions** and Scorpion-men protected the gateway of the Sun and the Mountains of the East in Sumeria; a caged serpent guarded the Temple of Athene at Athens; Cerberus guarded the threshold of the underworld; **Nagas** in India frequently protect thresholds and treasures; the Bull, Winged-bull or Bull-man appeared frequently in Sumero-Semitic sculpture. In the East the Chinese Celestial Dragon T'ien Lung guards the mansions of the gods and prevents them from falling out of the heavens, while stone lions (which come alive at night) protect the law courts; the **Jaguar** protects temples and ceremonial sites in Central America, while the Eagle or **Thunderbird** is a powerful guardian in other regions.

Small animals can assume enormous proportions when acting as guardians. The Celtic-Irish Little **Cat** turned into a great flaming object and burned the approaching thief, while huge **Ants** guard treasures in Chinese, Persian, Indian, Greek and Celtic legend. The **Unicorn** is another animal which can appear in small or immense form.

Guardian animals can also be personal, in the form of **Amulets**, **Fetishes** or mascots. Houses in earlier times had symbolic figures buried under floors or thresholds, or placed on lintels or over windows. They were also carved on tombstones (in this case particularly the **Dog**), to protect the dead or help them on the journey to the other world.

Guinea Fowl. Kept at the Acropolis, guinea fowl were the metamorphosis of the sisters of Meleager. Sophocles mentions the birds weeping tears of amber, and they were associated with amber in Greek literature. Stratius says that they were among the presents thrown to the populace at the Saturnalia. They were sacrificed to Isis and to Gaius' Godhead (Caligula).

Gulon. A Scandinavian composite creature, a lion-hyena with sharp claws and a fox-tail: a symbol of gluttony.

H

Haddock. The dark spot on the haddock's skin represents the mark of St Peter's thumb when he took the fish which held the tribute money.

Halcyon. See **Kingfisher**

Hare. Essentially a lunar animal, the 'hare in the moon' is an almost universal myth, occurring from Mexico to South Africa and across Asia to China. The hare is always an attribute of lunar deities and acts as their messenger; like the moon it depicts periodic death and rebirth, rejuvenation, resurrection. The hare is also universally a fertility symbol; it also represents fleetness, timidity and craftiness. Like the **Hyena** it was supposed to change sexes, some said every year, though neither Aelian nor Pliny mentions this: Pliny says every hare is androgynous, a belief which occurred in ancient Egypt where both the hare and the moon were held to be androgynous – masculine when waxing and feminine when waning. This myth appears in mediaeval European literature. The Egyptians also believed that the hare was born with its eyes open and that it never blinked.

As an animal of the hunt the hare was shown on Assyrian reliefs and seals and on Egyptian wall paintings in hunting scenes and as being prepared as food. But for the Turks and Jews it was an unclean food, though the Arabs, who thought it chewed the cud, counted it among 'clean' animals. It was one of the chief animals hunted by the Romans; it was also a symbol of fertility and lasciviousness, and as such was let loose, with **Goats**, at the festival of the Floralia. It was an attribute of Aphrodite and Eros, and Cupids were often depicted with hares. As a messenger-animal the hare is also associated with Hermes/Mercury.

Caesar said that hares were important to the early Britons and as such were not eaten. Boadicia released one at the start of each campaign; her prophetic hare was kept and fed.

The lunar significance of the animal is prominent in the mythology of northern Europe. For the Celts it was an attribute of all moon deities and hunter gods, who were often depicted holding a hare. The Teutonic lunar goddess Oestra or Eostra (Anglo-Saxon) was hare-headed; it was she who gave the Easter festival its name. Her hare (sometimes incorrectly called the rabbit or Easter Bunny, the hare being a solitary, superior animal as opposed to the gregarious and proletarian **Rabbit**) represented the spring resurgence of life and fertility, resurrection and the rebirth of the moon. It was the hare that laid the Easter egg of new life. The Teutonic Holda, Harke or Harfa was also a Moon Goddess and was followed by a train of hares bearing torches. The Scandinavian Freyja also had attendant hares.

In China the Hare in the Moon epitomized the feminine *yin* power; it can be seen in the moon with pestle and mortar mixing the elixir of immortality and therefore also depicts longevity. It is the guardian of all wild animals and is the fourth of the symbolic animals of the Twelve Terrestrial Branches. The white hare represents divinity; the red, good fortune, peace and prosperity under good rulers; the black is also good fortune and a successful reign. Figures of hares or white rabbits were made at the Moon Festival. The idea of longevity is extended in Japanese myth to the fabulous age of one thousand years, the hare becoming white at five hundred years. The White Hare is a hero figure, and there is a hare deity of Inaba. In Buddhism the Hare in the Moon was put there by the Buddha and symbolizes total self-sacrifice, as when the Buddha was hungry and the hare offered to sacrifice itself and jumped into the fire. The Great Hare was one of the early incarnations of the Buddha. In Hinduism and Buddhism the hare appears with the crescent moon and the Hindu Chandras, a god in the moon, carries a hare.

Among the Ainu of Japan, hares came down from heaven where they were the hair of the skin of God's deer and were called deer, the fleetest being 'hare-deer'. They can also bewitch people and have the evil eye. Their tracks in snow must be scooped up and turned upside-down to avert evil and the evil eye.

The fear of the hare as a witch animal is prevalent in European legend; it is a witch's familiar and witches often take the form of a hare; such an animal can only be killed by a silver bullet. A hare crossing one's path was formerly regarded as so unlucky that even warriors were known to tremble before it.

In Christianity the animal plays a dual role; on the one hand it represents fecundity and lust, on the other hand a white hare at the feet of the Virgin Mary signifies triumph over passions. The Bestiaries say that the defencelessness of the hare typifies those who put their trust in Christ. Mediaeval lore said that the hare was a melancholy animal which transmitted that state to those who ate it.

The Great Hare, Manabozho, is an Amerindian creator and

transformer; he is a hero saviour and a member of the Council of Animals where, with the **Beaver**, **Spider** and **Otter**, he helped mankind to Recover the Light; he also founded the arts and crafts and slew the snake-fish which oppressed the people. He is the Hero of the Dawn and the Great Manitou, who lives in the moon with his grandmother and is 'provider of all waters, master of winds and brother of the snow'. The hare is one of the great **Trickster** figures of the Woodland regions. As such he symbolizes a nimble mind outwitting brute force. He stole the sun and fire for the people. The Winnebago hare was born of a deity and a human mother and was world-transformer. As Paul Radin says, the hare is only secondarily moral and superior: 'his attitude is ambivalent because he has as yet no understanding of the difference between good and evil'. The Snow-shoe Hare of the Alberta region is also a Trickster Culture Hero.

The Trickster Folk-hero occurs in West African lore, together with the Rabbit, and is a magic animal; his exploits and legends crossed the ocean to become the celebrated Brer Rabbit.

Harpy.   The Harpies were mythical creatures with the heads and breasts of women and the bodies of **Vultures**. Their claws and wings

Heraldic Harpy (*from the coat of arms of Nuremberg*)

were metallic and emitted a foul stench. They represented storms and whirlwinds and were regarded as ministers of sudden death; they also bore away the souls of the dead and were agents of divine wrath. They depict the feminine principle in its destructive aspect. Harpies appear in Heraldry, especially in Germany as the *Jungfraumadlor*.

Hart. The Hart and Hind of the Bible can apply either to **Deer** in general or to some particular species. They symbolize tender love (Proverbs 5: 19), swiftness, elegance, graceful movement and solitude; they are clean animals for the Hebrews. The hart was said to renew its life by finding a snake-hole and swallowing the snake, then hastening to find water and drink deeply, after which it would live for another fifty years. The Bestiaries, adapting this legend, said 'so must we hasten to the waters of baptism and enlightenment.' They also stated that the hart likes hilly regions and so typifies the contemplative life of the prophets and saints, and that the biblical phrase 'as the hart panteth after the water-brook' represents the soul being rejuvenated at the pure springs of salvation; it is also the catechumen thirsting after knowledge. The hart is at enmity with the **Dragon** or **Serpent** and this symbolizes Christ overcoming the power of evil.

See also **Deer**

Havfinc. Norwegian **Mermaids** of uncertain temper, they drive white cattle up before a storm.

Hawk. Having much the same significance as the **Eagle** and **Falcon**, the hawk is one of the great solar birds said to be able to fly up to the sun and gaze on it without flinching. Gods who are hawk-headed or accompanied by a hawk are Sun Gods, especially in ancient Egypt where it was the Bird of Khensu and Ra the Sun. Horus is usually depicted as hawk- or falcon-headed; other gods associated with the hawk are Ptah, Rehu, Sokar and Kebhsenuf. It is also an emblem of Amanti, Great Mother, Goddess of the West and the underworld. Hawk-divinities also symbolize keen-sightedness and detection. It was a royal bird, bearing the double red and white crown of ancient Egypt. The hawk-headed crocodile depicts Sebek-Ra.

In Greece the hawk was 'the swift messenger of Apollo' according to Homer. Pursuing its prey to the right was an omen of success, to the left, failure. It was an attribute of Circe. It is also a messenger in India and Gayatri, the hawk, was responsible for bringing soma from heaven. It is a vehicle of the Vedic Indra; an attribute of Ormuzd or Ahura Mazda as light in Zoroastrianism, and of Mithra as a Sun God.

Amerindian myth has the hawk as one of the creatures which

Hawk-headed Horus and Ibis-headed Thoth

helped create the world after the Flood and which, with **Coyote**, made the sun and set it alight. There is a hawk clan of the Iroquois tribe.

In northern Borneo the hawk is revered and is regarded as a prophetic bird; its feathers have healing powers. The Dyaks have a hawk god, Laki Neho, who is a god of omens. In Madagascar the bird is also prophetic. The Eagle-hawk is an Australian Aboriginal totem and deity. The hawk is regarded as lucky in Europe. Among the Ainu the hawk, though created by God, now serves a mountain demon and kills land- and sea-birds for him to eat. Hawks are reared in cages, worshipped and sacrificed.

Hedgehog or Urchin.   Aristotle says that hedgehogs can foretell a change of wind and accordingly 'shift the outlook of their earth-holes'. Pliny and Aelian go further, maintaining that hedgehogs have two holes, North and South, and block one or the other as the wind changes. Other beliefs were that the animal uses its spines to take the shock if it falls from a height, also that it collects grapes on its spines by rolling on them, then takes them home for winter storage. Plutarch says he had seen this done, the creature 'looking like a bunch of grapes shuffling along the ground, so thickly covered was the animal with its booty'. The Bestiaries used this belief to illustrate 'finding the True Vine of Christ', though the act of stealing the grapes was 'the Devil robbing men of their souls' – in general in

Christianity the hedgehog depicted the Evil One and evil-doing.

In early times the hedgehog was generally a symbol of the Great Mother, but in particular it was an emblem of the Sumerian Ishtar.

Irish lore associated the hedgehog with witches who could take its form to suck cows dry. In China it also had a sinister reputation as one of the **Five Animals**.

The hedgehog is called the Urcheon in Heraldry, and occurs in a number of coats of arms.

Helpful Animals.   The Hero or Heroine in myth, saga, legend and fairy tale is often accompanied by some animal which acts as a guide or mentor and symbolizes the instinctual and intuitive powers of nature as distinct from the rational human intellect and will; it also depicts the different aspects of the hero or heroine's own nature. Helpful animals are often born at the same time as the human they are to help, and play a significant part in his or her life, imparting wisdom and acting as guardians and guides. Examples include Ossian and his **Deer**, Finn and his **Dog**, and Cormac and his **Wolves**. The myth is prevalent world-wide.

Animals often foster gods or heroes, such as Zeus and Amalthea and the **Bees**; Romulus and Remus and the Wolf. Sometimes animals sacrifice themselves on behalf of the person, or the helpful animal is him- or herself an enchanted person who requires decapitation to regain human shape.

In cultures close to nature, such as the Amerindians, helpful animals can be an Elder Brother, having a greater wisdom with which to help and guide the human Younger Brother.

The function of the psychopomp is frequently assumed by an animal who conducts the soul to the next world and through the last rites, as does the Sag Dog in Zoroastrianism.

There is an endless variety of helpful animals, changing with the nation and environment, the most usual ones being the dog, **Horse**, **Cat**, **Fox**, wolf, deer, and **Dolphin** although **Whales**, **Snakes**, **Wolverine** and **Humming-birds** also assume this role.

Hen.   The hen appeared in Egypt in the 14th century BC and was domesticated about 3000 BC; and in the 6th century it had become common in Greece and Rome. In Rome hens were kept in the temple of Hebe and **Cocks** at the temple of Hercules. Romans used domestic hens for divination, noting whether they fed eagerly or ignored or came slowly to their food, the latter being a bad omen.

The Bible uses the hen as a symbol of maternal instinct and care (Matthew 23: 37) and the Bestiaries liken the hen with chicks to Christ and his flock and say that as well as vigilance and caring the hen depicts the call of Christ to the souls of men. The white hen is Christ, its chicks the Disciples; the black hen is Satanic, an agent of the Devil.

Mother Hen with Chicks (*from a Bestiary*)

The hen depicts procreation and providence in addition to maternal care and protection, but a crowing hen represents feminine dominance or a bold woman. The Greeks said that if a hen defeats a cock in battle it crows and assumes the plumage of a cock.

See also **Cock**

Heraldry. Heraldry 'is *par excellence* the science of symbols . . . it . . . insists on the observance of certain definite and easily understood rules, constituting it a science, by the observance of which anyone acquainted with heraldic language may from a concise written description (or *blazon*, as it is termed) reconstruct at any time the symbol or series of symbols intended and with perfect accuracy' (Vinycomb). The most frequent symbols are animals; they must be depicted in their best and noblest guise. Heraldic art insists on dignity throughout. Guillam says that the creatures 'must be interpreted in the best sense, that is, according to their most general and noble qualities . . . the fox is full of wit, and withal given wholly to filching for his prey. If then this be a charge of an escutcheon, we must conceive of quality represented to be his wit and cunning, but not his pilfering and stealing.'

It has been suggested that heraldry rose from having animals as totems and from using them as shields and banners to warn the foe of the fierce qualities they faced. Certainly men adapted for their crests symbols of the qualities they either admired or wished to emulate, such as the swiftness of some bird or beast, the courage of the lion, the power of the dragon or the wisdom of the owl. Alternatively, many of the mythical excesses of Heraldry may have arisen from, as Fox-Davies says, 'the desire to gratify the vanity of illustrious patrons'.

Heralds were non-combatant messengers who wore the coats of arms of the people they served; later they became officers serving the sovereign and formed an important part of noble and royal households. Armorial bearings were an indispensable part of a nobleman's equipment, necessary to identify him in combat.

Herding. Herdsmen usually lived on the products of their animals and did not kill them except for sacrifice, festivals or great celebrations. They were attached to their animals, who could also be revered as animal ancestors or incarnate souls of the dead, and mourned them when they died.

Heron. In symbolism and myth little distinction is made between the heron, **Stork** and **Crane**, they are all solar birds and also birds of the waters, they represent vigilance and are destroyers of reptiles; also they typify filial and parental affection and are weather prophets, beloved of men.

The heron is also a messenger bird, sent by Athene to Odysseus and Diomede as a favourable omen. It was an emblem of Athene and sacred to Aphrodite, but in Greek literature it was used to signify treachery, since when wading it reveals shallow waters which could then be forded by the enemy. It was deprived of the power of swimming by Neptune.

In China and Japan the white heron is associated with the black **Crow**; together they are the *yin-yang*, lunar-solar powers, one serious and silent, the other chattering and mischievous. In both countries and in Taoism and Buddhism the heron takes on the symbolism of the crane.

Ancient Egyptian myth had the heron as the first transformer of the soul after death; it also symbolizes the rising sun and the return of Osiris. It is regeneration as the bird of the flooding of the Nile and the renewal of life; the bird then leaves the river and flies over the fields.

The *Physiologus* calls it the *Henne* and says that it is the wisest of birds and the most discreet, never touching carrion and staying in one place where there is suitable food – 'So the righteous do not care for corrupt things of this world but abide in the simplicity of the faith of the Church.'

Heraldry, again, makes little distinction between the heron, stork or crane, except that the heron always has a tuft on its head.

Hippocampus. A fabulous creature which had the head and forelegs of a horse and the body of a fish. It was the mount of Neptune.

See also **Sea-horse**

Hippocerf. A fabulous creature, half-stag, half-horse; its two natures pulled it in opposite directions, hence it represented indecision.

Hippogripp or Hippogriffin.   The offspring of a mare by a **Griffin** or gryphon; it inhabited the mountain regions. A fabulous monster, it had a horse's body and the wings, beak and claws of the gryphon, which was itself half-eagle, half-lion. It featured largely in mediaeval legends. It was the uncontrollable mount of the Wizard Atlantis.

Hippopotamus.   Known to the Greeks and Romans as the Beast of the Nile, the Nile god being depicted riding on a hippopotamus or accompanied by one. The Great Mother Amenti, the 'bringer forth of the waters', is represented by the hippopotamus, as is also the Goddess Rerat who lived in the Nile and was one of the keepers of the gates which had to be passed by the soul of the deceased; it was necessary to know the names of the keepers. She is portrayed as a hippopotamus standing upright on her hind legs and is also a form of Ta-urt or Taueret, wife of Set. The red hippopotamus represents Set in his typhonic aspect. The thigh of the animal is the 'phallic leg of Set', symbolizing virility. When Ta-urt depicts vengeance or an avenging deity she is portrayed with the body of a hippopotamus and the head of a lioness. A pregnant hippopotamus typifies fecundity and childbirth. An ancient Egyptian myth recounts the victory of Horus over Set when the latter took the form of the red hippopotamus.

It is generally supposed that the Behemoth of the Old Testament refers to the hippopotamus, the largest animal known to the Jews.

Ho-ho.   The Japanese version of the **Phoenix** or the Chinese Fung-Huang, emblem of the Empress.

Hoopoe.   A solar bird with strong Arabic and Sufi mythological associations. According to *The Conference of the Birds* it is a messenger of the world invisible; its breast-mark shows it has entered the way of spiritual knowledge. An Arabic myth says that Solomon gave the bird its crest as a reward for giving him shade in the desert. It also brought him a special worm for cutting stones for the temple without using a metal hammer or axe. It is sacred to the

Arabs as *Al Hudhud*, the 'doctor bird', and is credited with the power of water-divining, finding hidden wells and springs. It is used as a charm. The bird symbolizes filial affection, as it was said to bring food to its parents when they were moulting and in their old age.

The hoopoe was also held in great reverence in Egypt as the 'Doctor Bird', and its head was used in magic. Its symbolism is, however, like that of the **Crocodile**, ambivalent. As against its good qualities it listens to whispers and betrays secrets. The ambivalence appears markedly in the Bestiaries. In one Bestiary it is called *Upupa* and is 'a filthy creature, [which] feeds on stinking excrement'. The blood of the bird causes 'nightmares about suffocating devils'. Yet in another version it is called *Epopus* and is a symbol of filial devotion and mutual kindness since it looks after its aged parents.

The hoopoe figures largely in African and South European mythology.

In one version of the Greek Tereus myth the gods changed him into either a hoopoe or **Hawk**.

Hornbill. An auspicious bird because it kills **Snakes** and **Lizards**. Its feathers and bill are used in ritual decoration.

Hornet. A sacred symbol of the Pharaohs and sometimes used as an alternative translation for the word **Bee** in Egyptian hieroglyphics, the bee being the emblem of the Kings of Lower Egypt.

In the Old Testament hornets are God's avengers against the Hivites, Canaanites and Hittites being used to drive them out (Exodus 23: 28, Deuteronomy 7: 20, Joshua 24: 12). They signify panic, alarm and vicious attack.

There was an ancient belief that hornets were generated from the bodies of dead horses, bees from dead oxen, drones from dead mules and **Wasps** from dead donkeys.

Horns. Horns are natural symbols of strength, vigour and the culminating point of power rising from the head. They depict supernatural power, divinity, royalty, protection and abundance – the horn of plenty. They represent both solar and lunar deities and powers and are attributes of sun gods but also represent the lunar crescent of the Great Mother, Queen of Heaven. The two often appear together in Egyptian iconography. Horns are the most frequent parts depicted with deities and appear on, or as, altars, often enclosing some sacred object. They are particularly prevalent in Cretan shrines.

Sometimes animals are represented with three horns or with horns ending in knobs (this has never been satisfactorily explained). This occurs in Celtic and pre-Celtic times, as does the horned **Serpent** which appears frequently with the Celtic Horned God. At La Tène (one of the most important archaeological sites of the Iron Age, situated on what is now Lake Neuchâtel) birds, swans and cormorants have horns, and there was a bird-stag.

There are also one-horned animals such as the **Unicorn**, which appears in practically every part of the world. One-horned animals are featured in Persepolis, Babylon and Nineveh, and symbolize undivided and unlimited sovereign power. Aelian says that only potentates hunt these animals and possess beakers made from their horns. The value of these drinking vessels was that the single horn had the property of both detecting and neutralizing poison in food or drink; it was also used to test the purity of water and in addition could be used to kill poisonous creatures such as the **Scorpion** or **Spider**.

The horns of sacrificial animals were often decorated and at the Hindu festival of Pongal the horns of the sacred cow are garlanded and painted.

Nature gods such as Pan are horned to depict virility and fertility; Pluto, God of Wealth has a horn of plenty, and the Cornucopia, the horn of Amalthea, symbolizes wealth and abundance. Dionysos can be portrayed with horns and his blowing of the horn-trumpet woke the gods from their winter death in the lower world and brought back life in spring.

Horns on helmets, such as those of the Vikings, represent power, virility, the warrior and protection. Deities with horns from which fell a long ribbon were Storm-Gods, as for example the Assyrian-Babylonian Adad. In these cases the symbolism can be of both good and evil.

Horned gods are Lords of the Animals; they variously have bulls', cows', rams' or goats' horns or antlers and are frequently accompanied by the horned serpent. The horns of cattle represent honour, dignity and power; those of rams and goats are fertility and generative power.

The Hebrew *shofar* is a symbol of God's mercy and forgiveness at the time of the substitute-sacrifice for Isaac. It is a trumpet made of the carved horn of a ram (in earlier times that of a wild goat), and is ritually sounded at the Day of Atonement (Yom Kippur) and other special occasions. It appeared as an early funerary symbol and on **Amulets** or tombs of the Roman period.

The power of the horn can be beneficent or malefic according to the context; on gods and warriors it is beneficent, but Christianity used it as evil, depicting the Devil with horns. The horn is also ambivalent as piercing and therefore masculine and phallic, but hollow and thus feminine and receptive.

Horse. Next to the **Dog** the horse is the closest associate of humans and has been used for domestic purposes, for pleasure and

racing and as a draft animal. In earlier times it was employed in war
and drew chariots. It was the mount of kings, nobles, warriors and
heroes. There are records of its domestication from about 1750 BC,
but little evidence before 2000 BC. It was a sign of wealth.

The symbolism of the horse is both solar and lunar. White, golden
or fiery horses are solar power on land and in the air, but the white
horse of the sea and the gods of the oceans is associated with the
watery, lunar element. It also appears with fertility gods and the
Vanir, or, again, it changes its significance when ridden by the Devil
or the Wild Huntsman or Erl-King and becomes destruction and
death. In general the horse represents dynamic power, fleetness,
wisdom and the intellect as well as the instinctive animal powers.
It is also a prophetic animal, with psychic and magic abilities.

The horse was one of the great sacrificial animals, the Vedic Horse
Sacrifice being possibly the most famous of all. The horse was highly
revered by the Aryans and the sacrifice was a royal function
performed in the presence of the King, four Queens and four
hundred attendants. The occasion was a spring and summer fertility
rite, with strong sexual aspects. Each part of the horse had a cosmic
significance.

Another of the famous sacrifices was the ancient Roman October
Horse festival, in which the main event was a two-horse chariot race.
The near horse of the winning team was sacrificed to Mars; its head
being cut off and decorated and taken to the sacred hearth of the
Regia.

Hindu symbolism depicts the horse as the bodily vehicle, with the
rider as the controlling spirit. Kalki, a white horse, is to be the last
incarnation of Vishnu when he appears for the tenth time and brings
salvation and peace to the world. Varuna, as God of the Waters, is
the Cosmic Horse born of the waters.

The white horse appears as particularly sacred; it was so regarded
in Persia, Greece, Rome and Scandinavia. In China the Cosmic
Cloud Horse is white and is an avatar of Kwan-yin; in Japan it is
the avatar of Kwannon, in Indian Buddhism of Avalokitesvara.
White horses draw the chariots of Apollo and of Mithra and the
Dioscuri ride white horses. In Iranian myth the chariot of Ardvisura
Anahita is drawn by four white horses representing wind, rain,
cloud and sleet.

While the white horse is solar, or an attribute of Poseidon/
Neptune's white horses of the sea, the black horse is the attribute
of Rain Gods; in Europe it can be the Devil, who can appear in that
form; it is also the mount of the Erl-King or Wild Huntsman as
death, or the mount of a witch.

Seven mares, of ruddy colour, drew the chariot of the Vedic Sun
God, Surya, and there is the Shining Sun Horse of the *Rig Veda* which
has its counterpart in The Skinfaxi or Hrimfax of the Edda: he

'draws the bright day – with his mane all-shining'. The horse with
the golden mane also occurs in Norway and in Iceland as Gullteppr,
ridden by the god to Balden's funeral. Cloud-horses carry the
Valkyrie through the air and over the seas.

The winged horse symbolized fame, eloquence, poetic ability and
swiftness and bears the soaring spirit through the realms of fancy.
Pegasus, the most famous, was captured by Bellerophon with the
help of Athene, who showed him how to tame him, and was ridden
by Bellerophon when he slew the **Chimera**. **Pegasus** ultimately
became a constellation. He was also sacred to the Carthaginians.

The horse was highly important in the Celtic world and was
frequently an attribute of deities such as the Celtic, Welsh, and Irish
war gods, and especially of the Gaulish Epona, the Divine Horse,
introduced into Britain and later adopted by the Romans. She is
depicted as riding a horse or accompanied by horses and foals and
sometimes is horse-headed. In Celtic lore horses appear in different
colours and are magical animals of the otherworld, carrying people
there. Sometimes there are monster horses, capable of carrying
fifteen people at a time. There are also magical water-horses which,
if mounted, plunge the rider beneath the waters. Magical horses
belonging to heroes can fly, cross seas, and become invisible. Many
Celtic solar deities could manifest as horses. The White Horse at
Uffington, in England, is associated with Celtic horse gods.

In Norse and Teutonic mythology the horse is sacred to
Odin/Woden, who had the eight-legged mare Sleipnir and no
obstacle could stand in his way. The white steed of the heavens also
appears in Norse symbolism and the horse and the Vanir are gods
of sun and rain, the fields and the forest. A horse can take the form
taken by the Icelandic Neeth, Kelpie or Water-Spirit: it appears as
a splendid horse on the sea-shore, but its hoofs are reversed; like
the Celtic water-horse it, too, carries any rider under the waters to
be seen no more. The theme of horses as water-spirits is widespread.

There is little of the horse in Egyptian symbolism, though Egypt
was famous for its horses and chariots and Solomon imported them
and sold them to the Hittites and Armenian Kings; they were sacred
to the Sun God (II Kings 23: 11). Horses were used as draft animals
but, in the Bible, were largely connected with war. Job 39: 19–25
gives a description of their war-like qualities. The terrain of the
country was mostly unsuitable for chariots, except in the plains, but
the Canaanites possessed many (Judges 4: 3).

In the Zoroastrian *Atharva Veda* (7.10.4) there is the serpent-killing
horse Pedu, guardian of the pure animals and the chief foe of
Ahriman.

For Muslims the horse is a 'god-sent' animal; the Prophet swore
by the horse and was carried to heaven by the steed Al Borak. It
prays for its owner from morning till afternoon and for itself for the

rest of the day. It is, again, a prophetic creature, foreseeing danger, also seeing the dead. It is also apotropaic and ornaments of horse-hair protect their wearers, while horse-shoes avert the evil eye. The horse attracts wealth and happiness and should not be used to pull a plough. One should be ritually clean before tending or riding a horse.

Depicted in the Christian catacombs, the horse represented the swift passage of life also the sun, courage and generosity. In the Middle Ages, however, it became synonymous with lust. In the Bestiaries the horse is the epitome of the spirited and exults in battle. The horse racing for victory is the Christian struggling for salvation; it races towards Christ, who is depicted as a monogram in front of the horse.

The horse as a magical animal is also a widespread myth; it is almost universally credited with psychic powers, as being prophetic and able to see the spirits of the dead; it can traffic between this world and the next, bearing messages, and has foreknowledge. St Columba's white horse knew of the saint's impending death and shed tears for him. There are innumerable horse-ghosts, particularly those of headless horses, and witches can adopt the horse as a disguise. There were Celtic horse-headed goblins, called Krops or Cops, who were of a savage and uncertain temper. In their magical and otherworld capacity horses are also associated with shamans, having the power, both physical and spiritual, which enables shamans to ascend to heaven. Horses were often killed at an Amerindian burial to carry the soul to the next world. Horses' bones are treated with great fear and respect. But among the South American Indians the horse can assume a demonical aspect and incarnate the soul of a sorcerer.

This magical connection appears also in China and Japan. The Chinese Taoist Immortals or *hsien* are associated with various animals, the horse among them; it is an attribute of the Immortal Ch'ang Kuo. The Horse King Ma-wang, the Celestial Charger, is the ancestor of all horses, he is the god of the star Fang and is depicted as either a king with his court or as a horse. The Ancestral Horse is accompanied by a **Dragon**, **Phoenix** and **Crane**. The Japanese *Sennin* are similar to the Taoist *hsien* and, again, are associated with various animals. Chokoro had a magic horse he could keep in a gourd and release when wanted.

The horse is a frequent figure in Heraldry, being used as a supporter or mount and often employed as a crest. Heads of horses are most usually called 'nag's' heads. The horse-shoe is a common charge.

Hraesvgl. A Norwegian **Eagle** who creates the winds.

Hsigo. A Chinese composite creature, having a man's face, a monkey's body, and wings.

Humbata. A Sumerian monster in the *Gilgamish Epic*, a **Guardian animal** with bull's horns, lion's paws and vulture's talons.

Hummingbird. The Bird of the Gods, the hummingbird is a natural symbol of beauty and harmony; it also represents joy, the vibration of pure joy. Hummingbird was created with magical qualities, different from other birds, hovering, flying backwards and forwards. His feathers have magic powers and are used as love charms, they 'open the heart' to taste the nectar.

In Mayan tradition Hummingbird is associated with the Black Sun and the Fifth World and is said to know the solution to the riddle of duality. In Amerindian myth it is connected with 'the Ghost Spirit religion which taught that a certain dance, done properly, would bring about the return of the animals and that the white people would disappear. Once again the Original People would know the joy of the old ways.' Both American and Basque lore say that the hummingbird always tells the truth. It was said to live on dew, to hibernate in a warm place from October to April and then revive; thus it is called the Revival Bird. Hummingbird of the Tlingit tribe was created by the culture hero **Raven** to give pleasure to men by its beauty as the **Robin** does by its song.

Among the South American Indians of Venezuela a hummingbird, mounted on a **Crow**, brought the first tobacco seeds from Trinidad. The hummingbird is also a **Helpful animal** and can act as a psychopomp.

The Aztec War God Huitzilopochtli's name means 'the hummingbird to the left' and had its feathers on his left leg; he is usually depicted with a crown of hummingbird feathers. The Blue Hummingbird was a messenger of Anasazi. The Mayan Quetzalcoatl was also a hummingbird deity and as the Feathered Serpent he wears the bird's plumes.

Hunting. Hunting plays an important part in mythology and symbolic art from the early cave paintings through to Egypt, Assyria, Babylon, India and China – where hunting was a symbol of royal or noble status indulged in by Pharaohs, Emperors and Kings, followed by their courts – to the simpler but more natural hunting of tribal people dependent on it for their food and clothing and the tools made from animal bones. In early and tribal hunting, rites and ceremonies, which generally include miming and dancing, precede hunting and fishing expeditions or seasons. It is suggested that the miming 'teaches' or predisposes the animal to let itself be caught, as a kind of sympathetic magic. In the same vein, shamans can imitate an animal and make its sounds – that is, they can speak its language in order to make it understand the situation and its necessity. Among hunters the chief animal hunted assumes an important part of their religion and rites; the hunted animals are revered, there is a special relationship between the slayer and the slain and a reconciliation must be brought about.

There are frequent hunting scenes in pagan and religious art, the basic symbolism being the idea of life found through death, the death of the self achieving greater life. This idea also stands behind the practice of sacrifice.

Hydra. The Lernean Hydra was a nine-headed fresh-water **Serpent**, or a beast with a dog-like body; if one head were cut off two appeared in its place. This monster was the offspring of **Echidna** by Typhon and was killed by Hercules as his second Labour; it was a guardian animal, defending the Golden Apples of the Hesperides. Mesopotamia had a seven-headed monster vanquished by a hero. There was a similar many-headed **Naga** in Hinduism. In Heraldry the Hydra appears as a **Dragon** with seven heads.

Hydrus. Not to be confused with the **Hydra** of Hercules; 'hydrus' was a Greek term for the Water-Snake. Pliny seems to identify it with the **Otter**, the *Enhydris*; Aelian also calls the Enhydris the otter. Confusion resulted in later accounts.

Hyena. Described by Diodorus Siculus as a cross between a **Dog** and a **Wolf**, and native to Ethiopia, the hyena was later described by Sir Walter Raleigh as a cross between a dog and a cat; it was therefore not included in Noah's Ark, being a mongrel. The Hyena was credited with strange and treacherous habits. Aristotle, Pliny and Aelian said that it learned to imitate the human voice in order to call men to their deaths; also that it imitated vomiting to lure dogs and kill them. To capture a hyena it must be approached on the left side, otherwise the hunter will go mad or fall off his horse; this also happens if the hyena turns round and follows a man's tracks. The skin of a male hyena, when inscribed with magical words, was a protection against rabies. The hyena, like the **Hare**, was supposed to change its sex. This was denied by Aristotle but accepted by Aelian and Oppian. The Epistle of Barnabas (9: 8) says 'Neither shalt thou eat of the hyena; that is again, be not an adulterer, nor a corrupter of others . . . and wherefore so? Because that creature every year changes its kind and is sometimes male and sometimes female.'

In the East the hyena is likely to be the reincarnation of a sorcerer. Arabic lore gives numerous instances of the evil deeds of wizards taking the form of hyenas. In this form they can steal their enemies' flocks. It is dreaded in Africa for its malign and magical powers, but it is also a West African **Trickster** character who is always outwitted by the Trickster **Rabbit**. In Africa souls of men can enter hyenas to attack or kill those who have injured them, or people can be turned into hyenas by witchcraft. Uganda has a hyena-god, Luisi among countless others associated with the elements and spirits. In one legend the hyena cut the cowskin rope which once joined heaven and earth, thus separating them. The hyena can be an animal ancestor in East Africa and is the sacred animal of a secret society. In earlier times several tribes exposed their dead to hyenas. The wizard cannot only change into a hyena but can use it as a messenger. In the Ewe tribes the hyena embodies a god or spirit, and it is a crime to kill one.

Generally regarded as one of the most unclean of animals, the hyena is a symbol of uncleanliness, a scavenger, a haunter of graveyards and an eater of corpses; as a desert animal it also signifies desolation, and typifies treachery, wantonness and avarice.

In the *Physiologus* and the Bestiaries it is 'This filthy beast'; quoting its habits of feeding on corpses, both mention the change of sex. The Bestiaries, calling it the *Yena* or *Hyaena*, say 'Its nature is that at one moment it is masculine and at another moment feminine and hence it is a dirty brute'. In art the hyena is usually depicted as preying on a corpse and symbolizes vice battening on corruption and the embodiment of evil.

Hyrax.   The Rock Hyrax is the '**Coney**' of the Bible.
  See **Rabbit**

Hyrcinian Birds.   These are birds having feathers which light up in the dark and show the road even on a dark night. Pliny says they inhabit the Hercynian forest of Germany and that their feathers shine like fire.

I

Ibex. The Nubian Ibex is the Wild **Goat** of the Bible and a clean animal for the Hebrews. It is an Arabic symbol of beauty: 'more beautiful than a wild goat'. Ibex horns are a frequent motif of Mesopotamian art and in the northern steppes of Asia. Pliny remarks on the great speed of the ibex and says that it hurls itself from heights and lands on its horns, which are elastic and can take the shock; thus it can bounce.

In Heraldry the ibex resembles the heraldic **Antelope** except for the position of its horns.

Ibis (*from a Bestiary*)

Ibis. Pliny says the ibis is the Egyptian bird *par excellence*. It was sacred to the lunar deities Isis and Thoth, symbolizing the moon (with the **Hawk** representing the sun). The ibis, being heart-shaped, represents the heart under the protection of Thoth/Hermes, god of Wisdom, Learning and Writing. Hermes changed himself into an ibis when fleeing from Typhon. The Moon god Aah, associated with Thoth, is sometimes ibis-headed. The white ibis appears in Lower Egypt at the time of the inundation. Black-and-white ibises suggest female and male, darkness and light, etc. The ibis, the Blessed Spirit, is in conflict with the winged **Serpent**, and snakes are terrified and paralysed by an ibis. The bird was said to enjoy freedom from sickness. An indolent or rapacious man was depicted as a **Crocodile** crowned with ibis feathers.

In the Bestiaries the ibis feeding on dead fish is the Christian who indulges in vile appetites and lacks chastity, one who 'goes in for deadly dealings as if they were good spiritual food'.

The ibis is sometimes depicted with the crescent moon on its head. In Christian art this represents devotion, aspiration and perseverance.

Ichneumon.   Also referred to as the Egyptian **Rat**, the ichneumon was said to be a carnivorous animal resembling the Indian mongoose or a **Weasel**. It was reputed to be the deadly enemy of the **Crocodile** and the **Asp** or aspis, but authorities differed: Aristotle says it fights only with the asp, but Pliny, Strabo, Aelian, Oppian and Solinus say it is the enemy of both the asp and the crocodile. Strabo says it was worshipped at Herakleopolis as the destroyer of crocodiles, while Martial says the ichneumon was tamed and kept as a pet in Rome and that it is depicted in Pompeii as attacking a snake.

To attack the crocodile the ichneumon was said to wallow in mud and dry itself in the sun, forming a hard crust; it would then dart into the open mouth of the crocodile, devour its entrails, and emerge again when the crocodile was dead. It was also said to attack the asp in this manner, but some maintained that it only destroyed the asp's eggs. Pliny, Aelian and Plutarch all relate its heroic crocodile-destroying feat, but this exploit is also told of the **Otter** and the **Hydrus** (or Water Snake). There is considerable confusion among these ancient authorities between the ichneumon and these other creatures; their legends have become inextricably mixed in connection with the conflict with both the crocodile and the asp.

In Egyptian hieroglyphics the ichneumon is strength in unity; it was said to combine and attack the asp in numbers.

The *Physiologus*, following Pliny, makes the ichneumon the enemy of the asp only, crediting the otter with the bowel-destroying killing of the crocodile.

The Bestiaries use the legend as symbolic of 'the Saviour, having put on the flesh, descended into hell and brought forth all that dwell therein . . . so Our Lord rose again on the third day.' It was also taken to represent the triumph of God incarnate over Satan.

The ichneumon appears frequently in ancient classical literature, but less often in the Middle Ages or later.

Ichthycentaur.   A horse-fish creature associated with Pan as a fertility symbol.

Ihuaivulu.   A South American seven-headed fire monster associated with volcanoes.

J

Hawk-headed Horus and Jackal-headed Anubis

Jackal. As reputedly haunting burial grounds the jackal is associated with the dead and is a psychopomp, guiding souls from this world to the next. In this context it is connected with the Egyptian Anubis, the Pathfinder, the Opener of the Way. One of the oldest deities, he can be depicted as jackal-headed or as a black jackal. He received the dead in the Judgement Hall and weighed the soul on the scales of the Judgement of Osiris. The jackal-headed Ap-Uat or Upuat was a variant of Anubis.

In the Old Testament the jackal is a symbol of desolation – 'a dwelling place of jackals, a desolation for ever', and, 'I will make Jerusalem heaps, a dwelling place of jackals.' (Jeremiah 49: 33; 9: 11).

It is also an unclean scavenger. It is sometimes interchangeable with the **Fox** in translations.

Buddhism uses the jackal as representing a person rooted in evil, incapable of following the Dharma, and in Hinduism jackals and ravens as scavengers accompany the Black Kali in her aspect as destroyer. In Zoroastrianism the jackal is an animal of Ahriman and thus is evil.

The jackal appears among African tribes in ceremonial dances and rites, in which its movements and cries are mimed and imitated.

In the West the jackal symbolizes one who toad-eats or does the dirty work for another.

Jackdaw. Symbolizes sociability, a chatterer and mimic, vain assumption, a talkative nuisance. It is a weather prophet and a sign of rain; it uses laurel as a medicine and it can be caught in a dish of oil in which, in its vanity, it will look at its own reflection.

Jaguar. The third largest cat in the world and the largest spotted one, the jaguar is held in considerable fear; it is a magical and were-animal and is a power symbol, although symbolically somewhat ambivalent, like the Chinese Tiger which represents male creative power and the fierce warrior but also the powers of darkness, the female earth and destructive forces, and is associated with the cave, symbol of the womb, and with the Western regions.

The jaguar is an outstanding animal of Central and Southern American myth and symbol. It is the animal of the Shaman and a cult figure. In Mayan rites jaguar-skin tunics and head-dresses appear in depictions of sacrificial ceremonies, and offerings were made to the Jaguar God, who could take anthropomorphic form. Shamans can be possessed by ferocious animals, such as the jaguar and **Cayman**, and in this state can travel through time and space. Peter Furst says: 'Shamans and jaguars are not merely equivalent, but each is, at the same time, the other.' The ceremonial carved stool of the Shaman is often in the shape of the animal and the jaguar mask plays an important symbolic part. The jaguar is sometimes called the Dog of the Shaman. After death a Shaman may turn into a jaguar.

In an Amerindian myth the Jaguar Woman marries a male Anaconda; and in another the jaguar, the Master of Animals, marries a human wife from whom fire is stolen. In Aztec lore the God of Warriors, Tezcatlipoca, is depicted as a jaguar; he was knocked from the sky by the Feathered Serpent and became a great jaguar when he fell into the sea. Jaguars were founders of the Mayan Quiche lineage. In Toltec symbolism the jaguar and **Eagle** flanking a figure symbolize night and day. The jaguar is also identified with thunder and rain; his voice is the thunder, but his yellow skin is the sun.

The jaguar and eagle devouring hearts symbolized the warrior class in Aztec society and there were military orders of Jaguars, Eagles and **Coyotes**.

As darkness and earth, the jaguar, like the Chinese Celestial **Dog**, swallows the sun at eclipses. The Sun God on his daily round becomes a fearsome jaguar when he goes underground at night. There is a belief among some Jaguar tribes that the world will end by jaguars devouring the sun and moon.

A jaguar roaring can be the reappearance of a dead person. Black jaguars become demons after death.

Jaina. In Jainism the twenty-four Jaina or *Tirthankaras* are in most cases symbolized by animals such as the **Bull**, **Elephant**, **Horse**, **Monkey**, Curlew, **Dolphin**, **Rhinoceros**, **Buffalo**, **Boar**, **Bear**, **Deer**, **Tortoise**, **Serpent**, **Lion**, **Goat**, or **Fish**. Jains show an extreme reverence for all forms of life and no animal, bird or insect may be destroyed.

Jay. A chatterer; it represents garrulity and imitation. It can be caught with a bait of olives. The jay is prominent in Amerindian myth, especially the Blue Jay, who is a creator and one of the creatures responsible for bringing up the first mud from the flood waters to make the earth. Blue Jay is also one of the **Tricksters** and is a supernatural being among tribes of the North-west Coast and the Chinooks. Among the Hudson Bay Indians he gives warning of the approach of the enemy. In some tribes there were Blue Jay shamans who identified with the bird and perched on rafters in dance houses during ceremonies. Blue Jay is also a guardian spirit. The Jaybird features frequently in the plantation-tales of the southern United States; it is not seen on Fridays as it takes sticks to the Devil in hell that day; it is the Devil's messenger. The blue feather is a reviver of the spirit and an awakener.

Among the Ainu of Japan the jay is classed with the **Kingfisher**, and their feathers are highly prized **Fetishes**.

Jinshinlewo. The **Fish** which supports Japan and whose lashing tail causes earthquakes.

Jormungander. The Scandinavian Midgard **Serpent** encircling the earth, a child of Loki.

K

Kangaroo. The Red Kangaroo Kolakola, in Australian Aboriginal myth, was the First Beast of its species to make the creative and supernatural Dream Journey across the land. The kangaroo is a tribal totem animal and ancestor; it gave man the first spear-thrower. There is a Kangaroo Dance; such mimetic dances give the dancers power over a particular animal.

Kappa. A Japanese river creature with a monkey's head, tortoise's body and scaly limbs. Treated with courtesy it is harmless; otherwise it preys on humans.

Kar-fish. Encircles the Zoroastrian Tree of Life and keeps the **Lizard** of Ahriman at bay.

Kelpie. See **Water-horse**

Kestrel. In Australian Aboriginal myth a bird rose from the ashes of a bloody tribal fight which ended in a bush fire; this was the kestrel, which keeps watch for ever to protect the spirit of the warrior against further attack.

Kid. The rites of sacrificing a kid was one of the religious customs of early pastoral peoples. The Phrygian Mysteries had a formula for initiates: 'A kid, I have fallen into the milk.' The Mosaic Law said: 'Thou shalt not seethe a kid in his mother's milk.' In Dionysian rites the kid represented Dionysos and its death was a preliminary to rebirth; it was sacrificed to him by the Meniads. Kids were also sacrificed to Silvanus and Faunus.

Kingfisher or Halcyon. The Halcyon Days, which were the seven days before and seven days after the winter solstice, took their name and symbolism from the myth of the kingfisher, which was reputed to make its nest either on the sea-shore or actually on the sea; from the time the eggs were laid until the young flew the sea was stilled and remained calm.

Basil writes: 'The Halcyon is a sea-bird. For it breeds along the shores depositing its eggs on the sand itself. And it builds about the middle of winter when the sea is dashed upon the land by many violent winds. But nevertheless all the winds are lulled and the ocean wave is calm when the halcyon broods during the seven days, for only in so many days does it hatch its young. And since these have need of sustenance, Providence, beautiful to the smallest thing, provides seven more days for the development of the young ones.' Accounts vary as to the length of time, one says eleven, another nine, but most quote seven days. They also differ as to the situation of the nest: Oppian says it is 'along side the waves and though their breasts are wet the tails are dry', while classical and Eastern myth has the nest actually floating on the sea.

In Greek mythology Alcyone, daughter of the Wind God, Aeolus, found her husband drowned and threw herself into the sea; the gods, to reward her love, turned her into a kingfisher. Aeolus then forbade the winds to blow during the period when the eggs were laid and the young in the nest. This association with the Wind God appears to be the reason for a custom which once existed, of using a mummified kingfisher, with extended wings, as a weather-vane. Professor D'Arcy Thompson suggests that the symbolism is stellar, associated with the appearance of the Pleiades. Suidas says that the Pleiades were called 'halcyones'.

The kingfisher was believed to breed at four months old and to lay five eggs and hatch them in anything from seven to eleven days. They are 'birds of calm who sit brooding on the charmed waves'. Aelian says the females carry the old males on their backs. Kingfishers are beloved of sea-nymphs and associated with Pallas, Hera and Thetys. The dead body of a kingfisher turns aside thunderbolts and gives peace; its bill points in the direction of the coming wind.

A mediaeval myth said that the kingfisher was originally grey but that after the Flood it flew straight up to heaven to survey the waters; it flew so near the sun that its breast was scorched red and its back took on the colour of the sky.

The Bestiaries call the bird the *Halcyon* or *Altion* and say that the bird lays its eggs at the edge of the sea rather than the classical version of on the sea itself.

In China the bird symbolizes calm beauty, a retiring nature and fine raiment. The Ainu of Japan class the kingfisher with the **Jay** and the feathers of both birds are highly prized **Fetishes**. In Madagascar the kingfisher is greatly revered as a **Helpful animal** and messenger.

Kite. Diodorus Siculus said that the Egyptian book of religious laws was brought to Thebes by a kite and that the scribes wore a red cap with a kite's feather. The bird is referred to in Greek myth as a robber and it robs men in the market place. The appearance of the kite heralded the time of shearing. The kite detests pomegranates and will never alight on the tree. A stick from its nest is a cure for headache.

Kokoburra. In Australian Aboriginal mythology the kokoburra was created to awaken the people, announcing that the sun was rising.

Koori and Bueu. The two **Birds** which enable the Shamans of Siberia to travel to the Spirit world.

Kraken. A Scandinavian monster of the deep.

Ky-lin. A Chinese fabulous creature which embodies the *yin-yang* balance, with the Ky as the masculine and the Lin as the feminine. It is also an incarnation of the five elements of the five virtues and has in its composition the five colours; it has the head of a dragon, with a single horn, the mane of a lion, the body of a stag and the tail of an ox. Having only one horn represents the unity of the world under one great ruler and the Ky-lin was said to appear during the reigns of virtuous monarchs and to herald the birth of famous people such as Confucius. The one horn also gives it the name of the Chinese **Unicorn**.

The Ky-lin is an animal of exceptional gentleness and does not strike with its horn, thus it symbolizes benevolence and good will; it is also a fertility symbol. It appears in Chinese art in company with sages and immortals and to be mounted on a Ky-lin denotes a person of great qualities or fame, hence the term 'to ride a Ky-lin' is to rise to fame; a particularly clever child is 'the son of Ky-lin'.

The Japanese Ki-rin is simply a borrowing from the Chinese.

L

Ladybird. Called the Bird of Our Lady as it performed good works in destroying pests. If a ladybird alights on one's hand this is said to be a sign of good luck.

Lamb. The lamb is pre-eminently a sacrificial animal as representing purity, innocence and the unblemished. Lambs also denote neophytes and mystic rebirth. Evil and sorcerers are powerless against its innocence.

At the Hebrew Passover the unblemished paschal lamb was sacrificed and its blood smeared on lintels – a widespread custom for repelling evil powers; the Lamb Without Blemish was the coming Messiah; Christianity adopted the sacrifice without blemish as that of Christ dying for the sins of the world. The lamb with the Cross depicts the crucifixion in Christian art, while Christ carrying the lamb represents the Good Shepherd caring for his flock; the lamb with a pennant or flag portrays the triumphant resurrection. The Lamb of the Apocalypse has seven horns signifying the seven gifts of the spirit, also omnipotence. Cyril of Alexandria says that the lamb with the **Dove** depicts the body and soul of Christ, his human and divine natures. The lamb lying down with the **Lion** portrays the state of Paradise, the Golden Age.

In Heraldry the lamb is often represented as 'pastoral'; it is a frequent charge in Welsh coats of arms.

Lamia. A cruel queen turned into a beast with the head and breasts of a woman and an animal's body with claws on the forefeet and hoofs on the hind feet, she was equated with the **Sirens** and **Harpies**. In an ancient Bestiary the hooves of the hind feet are cloven and the body has a flowing tail. The creature is suggested as the Hebrew Lilith, the Night Monster (Isaiah 4: 14), who was also a female demon in Babylonian lore.

The lamia was said to be the swiftest of all creatures, very cruel and treacherous. The Greeks and Romans used it as a bogey to frighten children, whom it was said to devour.

Language of Animals. There is a widespread and ancient tradition that in the Golden Age animals and humans spoke the same language but that this ended with the Fall, after which time only certain people could understand the language of the animals and birds. The saying 'a little bird told me' is based on the belief that birds could either use human language or that humans understood bird language in certain circumstances. In the Old Testament Elijah says: 'a bird of the air . . . shall tell the matter,' and in mythology prophets, shamans and magicians can obtain information in this way. Also the language of animals is often a gift bestowed in return for saving the life of some creature, but it always carries a prohibition against revealing the secret to anyone on pain of death or loss of all possessions. This theme occurs in Serbian and West African myth particularly. The hero or heroine is often accompanied and guided by an animal and knows its language.

Josephus says that the Jews believed that all animals spoke before the Fall. The Qu'ran says that Solomon understood the language of the birds and also says: 'oh men we have been taught the language of the birds and all favours have been showered upon us' (27: 15). Porphyry says that Melampus and Apollorius were among the philosophers who understood the language of animals.

The Norse Sigurd and the Teutonic Siegfried understood the language of birds because the former accidentally tasted the blood of the Fafnir monster and the latter the blood of the dragon.

In Christianity St Columba was reputed to know the language of the birds once he had turned a queen and her handmaid into cranes for irreverence; he was called 'the Crane-cleric'.

Lapwing or Peewit. As the lapwing was said to divert attention from its nest it was a symbol of pretence and treachery, but this also makes it symbolic of parental care. It also represents forwardness, as its young were reputed to be in such a hurry to be hatched that they ran from the nest with the shell still on their heads.

In Greek mythology the cruel king Tereus of Thrace was transformed into a 'crested bird' which was taken to be either the lapwing or the **Hoopoe**, this again bringing in the symbolism of treachery. But Solomon chose the peewit, with the **Cock** and hoopoe, as favourite birds for their ability to find water under the earth. According to the Qu'ran the lapwing was the means of introducing Solomon to the Queen of Sheba. In the Old Testament in Leviticus and Deuteronomy the same bird is variously called the lapwing (Authorized Version) and the hoopoe (Revised Version). Being crested it is a solar bird.

The lapwing is ill-omened in Scotland.

Lark. Having a crest the lark is a solar bird; it also soars towards the sun. It symbolizes cheerfulness. It was reputed to use oak leaves and grass as a protection and to be killed by eating mustard seed.

Leech. 'The cruel leech' is a symbol of a blood-sucker and a treacherous hanger-on.

Lemers. The lemers is a Norwegian mouse-like animal which appears from thunder clouds and devours everything green.

Lemming. The lemming's habit of mass migration and suicide makes it a symbol of self-destruction and mass-mortality.

Leogryph. A fabulous monster, a combination of a lion and serpent or gryphon, symbolizing *maya*, or illusion.

Leopard. The Leo-pard was thought to be the offspring of a lioness and **Panther**. Pliny says the **Lion** lies with a female pard, or the pard with a lioness; as this is a form of adultery it symbolizes sin. The leopard also represents ferocity, aggression and courage; the Arabic name for it, *Nimir*, is given to boys as it means courage and boldness combined with grace. The leopard is referred to in the Old Testament for its swiftness, cunning, strength and perseverance; it is also used to represent the extreme of fierceness in the quote '[in the coming millenium] the leopard shall lie down with the kid' (Isaiah 11: 6). In Hosea (13: 7) it depicts watchfulness and Jeremiah (13: 23) is the source of the well-known saying 'can the leopard change his spots . . .?'

In Egypt the leopard was an emblem of Osiris and his priests are often depicted wearing leopard skins. The animal is closely associated with Dionysos in Greek mythology; it is his traditional mount, and at other times leopards draw his chariot or are seen accompanying him as playmates; they also appear with Dionysos and Ariadne.

Chinese symbolism represents the leopard as bravery and warlike ferocity.

It is in Africa that the leopard holds a most dominant position and is frequently a cult animal. In Benin in West Africa it is sacred to the royal family; it is also a Ewe totem animal. On the Gold Coast it can be the abode of spirits of the dead. It is a vehicle of the Storm God and priests are often portrayed wearing leopard skins; a leopard skin or girdle confers immunity from all danger and can render a wizard invisible. Among the Ibo the leopard is particularly sacred and is associated with fertility; there are leopard societies and shrines and the Chief can take on leopard-powers. The soul can be sent out in leopard form. If a leopard or **Crocodile** is seen when out hunting it must not be named; nor may the flesh be eaten, as these animals helped the ancestors.

Christianity represents the leopard as the Devil and his duplicity, the Antichrist and in art the leopard depicts the Beast of the Apocalypse.

The leopard is also the *Lybbard* of Heraldry, appearing on European coats of arms, and those of the Kings of England, as a *lion passant*. French heraldry calls a *lion passant* a leopard, or when rampant a *léoparde lionné*, and it symbolizes brave and generous warriors having performed some bold undertaking. It also represents boldness, rashness and impetuosity.

Because its spots resemble eyes the leopard is also called the Great Watcher.

Leviathan. The Leviathan is a monster **Fish**, the primordial creature of the ocean; it is chaos and the serpent-power of the deeps, with **Behemoth** as the land and **Ziz** the air power. It is 'that crooked serpent' of the Old Testament (Isaiah 27: 1), also the 'piercing serpent', and as such it could be the Great Python or Rock Snake formerly known in Egypt. It also appears as the Islamic *Nun*.

Lice. In the Old Testament the Third Plague of Egypt came in the form of dust turned into lice by the magician Aaron, who smote the dust with his rod so that 'all the dust of the earth shall become lice' (Exodus 8: 17 and Psalms 105: 31). The presence of lice immediately rendered the Egyptian priests ceremonially unclean; they ritually shaved their heads every third day to keep themselves clean when performing rites.

Lindworm. The Lindworm is an heraldic dragon *sans* wings, or the **Wyvern**, or the Lindorm snake, which ate cattle and bodies and invaded churchyards; it symbolized war and pestilence.

Linnet. See **Acanthis**

Lion. Although the lion is obviously solar, being the sun sign, the power of the sun, the fiery principle, strength, might, and the King of Beasts, the lioness can be lunar, associated with the Great Mother goddesses and drawing their chariots, and representative of the nocturnal instinct of the earth. These goddesses are widespread, appearing in Crete, Mycenae, Phrygia, Thrace, Syria, Lycia and Sparta, Sumeria, and also in India and Tibet as an attribute of Tara. Macrobius says that lions are emblematic of the Earth, 'Mother of the Gods'.

Lions were found extensively in the Middle East, Palestine and Egypt in ancient times; they were trained to help in hunting. Lion hunting was practised in Babylon and Assyria. In Egypt in the 3rd century BC a procession in honour of Dionysos had twenty-four lions along with **Leopards** and **Cheetahs**. Rameses II had a tame lion accompanying him into battle. Plutarch says: 'The lion was worshipped by the Egyptians who ornamented their doors with the gaping mouth of that animal because the Nile began to rise when the sun was in Leo.' Horapollo says lions were placed before the gates

Horned Lion (*from a stone carving in an Indian temple*)

of temples as symbols of watchfulness and protection and were represented in Nile inundation, while Aelian says: 'The people of the great city of Heliopolis kept lions in the vestibules or areas of the temple of their God, the Sun, considering them to partake of a certain divine influence . . . and temples are even dedicated to this animal.' He also says that the Egyptian held the lion sacred to Vulcan, 'attributing the fore part of the animal to fire and the hinder part to water'. A lion guarded the tunnel through which the sun passed at night. With the solar disc the lion represents Ra, the Sun God, with the crescent, Osiris. Two lions back-to-back depict past and present, yesterday and tomorrow. The lioness is an attribute of the Mother Goddess Sekmet, symbolizing both maternity and vengeance.

The Babylonian Mother Goddess Ishtar is depicted standing on a lion or accompanied by two lions and the Sumerian Sun God, Marduk, has the lion as an emblem of sovereignty, strength and courage. The Chaldean Nergal, God of War and Death, is portrayed as a lion in the hostile aspect of the scorching, destructive power of the summer sun. The Weather God of the Hittites had a lion-drawn chariot and the Great Mother rides a lioness; a lion is often depicted standing below the pedestal of a deity.

In Hinduism the lion was the fourth avatar of Vishnu, sometimes half-man, half-lion. The lion is the Guardian of the North and represents Durga as destroyer of demons and is an attribute of Devi. A lion and lioness together symbolize the shakta-shakti, with the lion as the Supreme Lord and the lioness as the power of the uttered Word.

Buddhism has the lion as the Defender of the Law and the Buddha is sometimes seated on a throne supported by lions, while a lion with a cub under its paw represents the Buddha ruling the world with compassion, the lion's roar being his fearless teaching of the Dharma. Buddha was called the Lion of the Shakya clan. The lion also represents wisdom, spiritual zeal, advancement and an enlightened one; the newly initiated Bodhisattva can be portrayed as a lion cub. The Chinese *hsien* or Immortal Ch'iu-Shou was a lion which took human form and fought in wars. He was captured and ordered to resume his lion form, after which he became a mount for the Buddha Wen Shu. Stone lions guarded the *yamens* – courts of justice – and came to life at night and roamed about. In China the lion represents strength, with the horse as speed, and signifies the man in marriage symbolism; it is vigour, valour, energy. The 'lion with the ball' portrays either the sun or the Cosmic **Egg** and dualism in nature. There is a Lion Dance at the Feast of Lanterns. In Japan the lion ball depicts emptiness. The lion is the King of Beasts, with the peony as Queen of Flowers.

Roman funerary art uses the lion as a symbol of the devouring power of death and its conquest by man; representations of lion-hunts on sarcophagi thus symbolize triumph over death. A lion devouring its prey also represents the ravages of death. Hercules defeating the Nemean Lion is another instance of triumph over death and the powers of evil. Androcles and the Lion is symbolic of gratitude and friendship. Lions draw the chariot of Cybele and that of Cybele and Attis.

The lion is mentioned 135 times in the Old Testament and features in myths such as those of David and Goliath and Samson. The lion died out in Palestine at the time of the Crusades. The winged lion represents the South and the Lion of Judah. It is a symbol of dignity and strength, also royalty, but in Christianity it becomes ambivalent, having both the royal significance of Christ's kingly nature, power and might, and an evil import: Christ delivers the faithful from the lion's mouth, which is the Devil, a 'roaring lion . . . seeking whom he may devour'. The lion was an emblem of St Mark, who emphasized the royalty and majesty of Christ.

It was believed that the lion slept with its eyes open, also that lion cubs were born dead, remained so for three days, and then were given the breath of life by their sire. Another belief was that the lion always wiped out its tracks with its tail. The Bestiaries used these myths for their symbolic moralizing: 'As the lion wipes out its tracks with its tail, so the Saviour, Lion of Judah, conceded his Godhead on descending to earth. As the lion sleeps with its eyes open so Christ slept in his body on the Cross but woke at the right hand of the Father. As the lioness brings forth dead whelps and watches over them for three days until the lion comes and howls over them and revivifies them with his breath, so the Almighty Father recalled our Lord Jesus Christ from the dead and will raise us all to eternal life.' The three-day death is a frequently-used symbol of resurrection. Sleeping with the eyes open makes the lion an appropriate **Guardian animal** at the doors of churches and sanctuaries, but in this position it can also represent Satan subdued by the Church. The Bestiaries also say that as David throttled the lion and the bear which took the lamb out of the flock, 'so Christ throttled them when he descended into hell and delivered captive spirits out of their jaws'. In the *Physiologus* the lion's open jaws are often depicted devouring heads; these are the jaws of hell.

Among Arabian deities there was a lion-god, Yaghuth. In Islam the lion protects against evil. In parts of Africa the lion can embody souls of the dead or be a form taken by wizards.

The lion is the most important animal in heraldic art. It is usually depicted *rampant*, other positions being later developments. The heraldic lion can have more than one body or head. The *Lyon-poisson* is the heraldic lion-fish.

Lion-dog. The lion-dog with a ball underfoot symbolizes duality: the animated and undefined contrasted with the static and defined.

Liver. The liver was a sea-bird similar to a cormorant in shape which lived in a pool near present-day Liverpool and thus gave the city its name.

Lizard. As a creature of the humid principle the lizard is lunar. It was believed to be tongueless and to live on dew, and so typified silence.

Egyptian and Greek myth represented the lizard as wisdom and good fortune and it was an emblem of Hermes and Serapis, but in Zoroastrianism it was evil and belongs to Ahriman and is kept away from the Tree of Life by the **Kar-fish**.

It was believed by the Romans that the lizard slept all winter and reappeared in the spring, hence it was a symbol of death and rebirth; as such it appears with the **Butterfly** and is depicted with sleeping cupids in Roman art; it also appears in funerary art. It is apotropaic on the Votive Hand of Sabazius and is one of his attributes. Lizards could sometimes take the place of snakes as the guardians or genii of a house; when they lived under the foundations they were given crumbs and milk and wine and were greeted with delight if they appeared, this being a good omen.

Mahomet would not eat lizards because they were the offspring
of a tribe of Israelites who had metamorphosed into lizards. They
are also said to be despised and persecuted in Islam since they
'mimic the attitude of the Faithful at prayer'.

The Lizard or Tree Lizard of the Amazon Indian is a manifestation
of Desana, Master of Animals and Fish. He is generally represented
as a dwarf who is covered in the juices of magical plants, and he
dominates the forests and rivers. The shaman must negotiate with
him before any game animals can be taken in return for human souls,
who then reincarnate as game animals. Desana can manifest as a
lizard, **Jaguar**, **Squirrel** or **Fish**. The lizard is a messenger of God,
who told men they must die. The tail of the lizard contains magic
splinters and thorns which it can shoot out to cause sickness; it is
dangerous to pregnant and menstruating women but not to men.
Among Amerindian desert tribes the lizard is the Spirit or Master of
the species and is a totem animal. It also appears in Africa as a totem,
but can be sinister and unlucky if used in 'evil medicine'. It is also a
shape-shifter, in East Africa it is believed it can transform itself into
a **Hyena**, in West Africa that it can become a **Leopard** or **Lion**.

The lizard occupies an important place in Polynesian myth. The
lizard cult is widespread, and the Green Lizard particularly
prevalent. Moko, King of the Lizards, is generally revered as a god
in his own right and is venerated as a protector of fishing. Hawaii
had lizard gods who were regarded as animal ancestors; the lizard
could be the form taken by a god or tutelary deity. In Tahiti a temple
was dedicated to such a deity, who was represented by a stone lizard.
There were different forms of lizards representing different aspects
of deities. In the Sandwich Islands lizards are part of the food of
souls after death. In Malaysia there was a small flying lizard who
was a messenger of the great flying lizard, a guardian of souls in the
body. Maori myth says that it was the lizard who drew the first of
their race out of the waters at the creation.

Tarrotarro, the lizard, is an Australian Aboriginal culture hero who
separated the sexes and taught the people tattooing and other arts.
It can also be a symbol of disobedience since the lizard was
originally a man changed into a lizard for his disobedience.

In Europe the lizard is generally regarded as sinister, but it can
be a love charm. It is the **Scapegoat** at the Eastertime festival of the
Gypsies, during which a lizard or snake corpse is placed with herbs
in a wooden vessel, carried from place to place, exorcized, then
thrown into running water.

The *Physiologus* says the lizard goes blind in old age, creeps into
a wall and faces the sun. 'So must man seek the wall of help and
watch until the sun of righteousness removes spiritual blindness.'
The lizard also symbolizes regenerative power and the illumination
of the Gospel.

The lizard appears occasionally in Heraldry, more often in Ireland than elsewhere. It is the personification of Logic in the Liberal Arts.

Llama. The llama is a sacred animal having supernatural powers and particular *mana*; souls of the dead can enter llamas. They are sacrificial animals, the sacrifice being a two-fold rite propitiating the Sun God and giving him strength to help the people and provide them with warmth and fertility. The fat and blood of the animal are a particularly potent offering to the gods. The gentle humming sound the llama makes is likened to prayer. A llama foetus was one of the sacrificial objects buried under new buildings in Peru to ensure their stability. Llamas are used as workers, for meat and for their wool or 'fibre'. A white llama is especially sacred.

Lobster. Generally held sacred in ancient Greece, the lobster was dear to Perseus. It is taboo in parts of Madagascar.

Locust. The locust is shown on carvings of the 8th century BC as food for a banquet of Asurbanipal. Diodorus of Sicily in the 2nd century BC, as well as other historians, refer to the locust-eaters of Ethiopia. Locusts, being entirely vegetarian, were also clean food for Jews and Moslems. The locust is the most frequently mentioned insect in the Bible; it is a symbol of destruction and wasting – 'the year that the locust hath eaten' (Joel 2: 25) – and of helplessness, as tossed by the wind (Psalms 109: 23). It is also quoted as an instrument of punishment (Deuteronomy 28: 42) and represents a greedy and devouring person. It is furthermore associated with multiplying powers, with drought, pestilence and calamity. It was food for John the Baptist (Matthew 3: 4).

African tribes eat locusts and preserve them by drying them, as do the nomads of North Africa.

The Chinese Ma-Cha Shen, Goddess of Locusts, was struck by lightning, a sign of divine favour. A prayer says: 'O Locust Goddess, O Locust Goddess, eat all our neighbour's crops but don't touch ours!' Liu-Meng, one of the gods of agriculture, is also a Protecting Spirit against locusts and **Grasshoppers**.

Lokapala. In Tantric mythology the eight Lokapalas who support the world ride on **Elephants** which have horns and wings.

Loon. The loon is regarded by the Amerindian as one of the creatures which brought up mud from below the flood waters to create the earth. For the Algonquins loons are messengers of the great hero Glooscap, or Kuloskap, who taught the loons their characteristic cry. The bird is also a conductor of the dead in the Slave tribe; it took them across a great lake to the next world, helped by the **Otter**.

Lybbarde. In Heraldry the Lybbarde is a cross between a **Lion** and a **Panther** and symbolizes wildness.

Lycanthropy. There is a world-wide belief in the ability of sorcerers, shamans, magicians and others to turn themselves into animals. The term 'Lycanthropy' should, strictly speaking, apply to the **Wolf** (*Lycos*), but it is used to include other fierce beasts. On Mount Lykaios, in Arcadia, Pan shared sovereignty with Zeus Lykaios, a totally different god from the Homeric Zeus. His festival required human sacrifice; the human entrails were mixed with those of sacrificial beasts and the whole given to the devotees to taste. Anyone getting a taste of the human parts was immediately transformed into a wolf. Plato quotes this myth in the *Republic* and Pliny says that werewolves were members of this Arcadian clan who claimed descent from Zeus Lykaios and who had the power to change into wolves. He also said that the family of Antaeus cast lots annually for one of them to be changed into a wolf, staying in that form for nine years. Herodotus said the Neuri had the power of lycanthropy once each year. Varro and Virgil both believed in lycanthropy.

Tigers, **Leopards**, **Hyenas**, **Foxes** and **Badgers** are also capable of shape-shifting. There are were-**jaguars** in Central and South America and were-leopards in Africa; Malay has a particularly dangerous were-tiger. Shamans in particular take animal shape to travel in this and the spirit world; they then take on the powers of the animals whose shapes they assume. In some societies the power of shape-shifting was believed to be hereditary, elsewhere it could be exercised by sorcerers, magicians and witches, or it could be the result of a spell or enchantment, or even of being bitten by the particular animal. The usual manifestation of these powers occurred at the full moon. This demonstrates a belief in cosmic and psychic forces which can be manipulated, that different forms can be taken at will, but lycanthropy is not the same as **Metempsychosis** in that it is a pathological condition while metempsychosis is the transformation of the soul after death.

The belief in lycanthropy was especially prevalent among Slavonic people, who were said to be 'possessed' and thus went mad and craved flesh to eat. Norse mythology is full of were-wolves. Wolf skins were kept and donned at night by men who roamed the forest as wolves. In Iceland the 'Fylgia', as a dog or bird, acted as a person's double.

In China and Japan the **fox** takes the place of the wolf, but there are also were-tigers, -**dogs**, -badgers, -**monkeys**, -**birds**, -**hares** and -**cats**.

While in Africa the leopard holds the most important place, the **Lizard** can also change into a hyena, leopard or **Lion**.

Witches change themselves into **Cats**, dogs, **Hares** and **Horses** and, in Scandinavian mythology, into **Magpies**.

Lympago. In Heraldry the Lympago is a man-tiger or man-lion, taking on the qualities of both.

Lynx. The lynx symbolizes suspicious vigilance and keenness of sight ('lynx-eyed'). It was believed to be able to see through walls. The name was also applied to the fabulous animal, half-dog, half-panther, which was also credited with exceptional sight. Both appear in Heraldry, usually as supporters and mostly as blazoned *coward* (tail between legs). It depicts keen eyesight and prudence, and the ability to profit from both.

According to the Bestiaries the lynx, or *Lincis*, is 'a kind of wolf distinguished by spots on the back like a pard, but he looks just like a wolf. Its urine hardens into precious stones, the Ligurius.' Isadore says this is the carbuncle.

For the Amerindians the lynx signifies the secret; it is a keeper of secrets and occult knowledge, it unravels mysteries, it is the powerful and silent.

M

Macaw. The macaw is the totem bird of the Amerindian Zuni clan. For the Hopi Indians the macaw is both the God of Death and the Fire of Life which bursts from volcanoes. In Columbia it is the Fire Bird. As a totem the medicine-man can assume its form in order to fly to the spirit world. Rites are performed in its honour and its feathers have a magical quality.

Magic. Grimm wrote that primitive man endowed the animals of the wild with magical or demonic powers and that the animals incarnated forces which could be beneficent or malignant and therefore required propitiation. One of the chief methods of this propitiation was to avoid naming – always a dangerous feature in magic as it can attract the creature – and thus contradictory or complimentary terms were used instead, especially for fierce animals or any associated with sorcery, such as the **Lion**, **Tiger**, **Bear**, **Wolf**, or **Fox**. All sorts of titles were employed, such as 'Lord', 'Grandfather', 'hairy face', 'striped one' or 'old man'. Hunters, fishermen and sailors were to be particularly careful in this respect. But animals as well as humans often needed protection against evil powers or the evil eye and **Amulets** were used for the purpose, for example, horse brasses.

Magic-making medicines may be obtained from animals, birds, reptiles and insects, especially those that have *mana* or, again, are associated with sorcerers, such as the cock's egg of the **Cockatrice**, which was the chief ingredient for the ointment used by witches to transform themselves into animals. Mutton fat could be smeared on people or figures to produce fertility, or could be put on the fire to make an enemy or offender 'perish as the mutton fat has perished'. Burying fierce animals or figures of them in the foundations of buildings frightened off evil powers. Grasping the horns of a fertile **Cow** 'fills the house with descendants'.

Grimm's 'primitives' are not the only people to subscribe to magic: amulets, lucky black cats, wishing on white horses or counting magpies are still prevalent superstitions.

Magpie. The magpie's significance is ambivalent: as the Bird of Joy and good fortune in the East where its chattering signifies good news and the arrival of guests it was an imperial symbol under the Manchu rule in China; but in the West the same chattering means trouble between husband and wife and it is a bird of ill omen which can bring disaster (this, however, can be averted by spitting at the bird or doffing one's hat; an onion in one's pocket protects against its evil powers). A magpie landing on a roof is a sign of a death in the house.

Called the *Picae* in the Bestiaries it represents unseemly chatter and Christianity uses it as a symbol of the Devil, vanity and dissipation. There are various folk-rhymes that refer to seeing it in numbers . . . 'One for sorrow, two for mirth,' etc. In Norse mythology it is associated with witchcraft and is a form taken by witches.

One legend says that the magpie was not allowed into the Ark because it chattered so incessantly, but had instead to perch on the roof.

In Amerindian lore the magpie is one of the **Trickster** figures.

Makara. The makara is a huge Hindu sea-monster depicted in various composite forms as sea-elephant, **Crocodile**, **Naga**, **Shark**, **Dolphin**, or half-antelope, half-fish. It is a vehicle of Varuna, who rides it as God of the Deeps, it also represents the dual nature of good and evil. It is the sign of Capricorn in the Hindu Zodiac.

Manatee. Known as the 'Madonna of the Sea', the manatee is thought to be the origin of the **Mermaid** myth, a half-woman, half-fish sea-creature. Amerindians grind the bones as a cure for asthma and earache. The manatee is a sacred animal among West Africans; if accidentally killed rites of propitiation and purification must be performed, as it is considered to have once been a human being.

Mantis. Mantis, or Kaggen, is a hero-god among the Bushmen of Africa and can symbolize the Great Spirit; he is also a **Trickster** and, as such, treated with due respect. His secret name must not be pronounced. His adventures are full of caricature, mockery and comedy. Modern anthropologists have found little evidence of the cult in the present day, though Laurens van der Post vouches for it. In Egypt, Mantis could act as a psychopomp in place of the Wolf- or Jackal-god Ap-Uat, to conduct the dead through all the gates that must be passed.

Marabou. The marabou **Stork** is a sacred bird in Arabia; it is a hermit.

Marakihau. The marakihau is a Maori sea-monster with a human head and body and the tail of a fish; it has a long tubular tongue and is of such gigantic size that it can draw canoes into its huge mouth.

Marten. In Ainu myth the marten and **Racoon** were created to act as servants to **Bears**; their black faces indicate that they are cooks. Both are offered in sacrifice.

In the Dance House ritual of the Whaling Festival of the Bering Straits Innuits (Eskimos) the marten (made up as a mechanical device), along with a mechanical bird, is a figure of central importance.

Marticoras. The marticoras is a lion-like monster having a man's head and a scorpion's tail. It is capable of shooting barbs from its tail. Vermilion in colour, with blue eyes, it is derived from the Persian *Mardkhora*, a man-slayer.

Martin. An heraldic bird associated with St Martin.
See also **Martlet**

Heraldic Martlet

Martlet, or Merlot. In Heraldry the martlet represents the **Swallow** or House Martin. It was popularly believed that these birds had no feet and thus in heraldry are never depicted with feet (the legs end in feathers); some heraldic books also state that they have no beaks. They are a common heraldic device. Sylvanos Morgon says that having no feet signifies that 'as that bird seldom lights on land, so younger brothers have little land to rest on but the wings of their own endeavour, who, like the swallows, become the travellers in their seasons.' The martlet is an emblem of swiftness.

Masks. Masks are frequently used in festivals and ritual dances, often representing the spirits of the dead. These masks are frequently fashioned in the form of animals, especially those of fierce appearance likely to frighten off evil spirits. Wearing the animal or bird mask establishes communion and restores the paradisial state of one-ness between animal and human; it also signifies the instinctual wisdom of the animal or bird from which humans can learn, in addition it can depict the animal nature with which people must come to terms.

Memnonides.   Birds of Memnon, a mythical king of Ethiopia, who
helped Priam, his uncle, in the Trojan War and was killed by Achilles.
His companions were turned into birds who flock annually to his
tomb and fight over it. Pliny and Aelian record this, but Aelian adds
that half the birds are killed and the others fly away. Professor
D'Arcy Thompson suggests that the legend refers to the combats
and killings of Ruffs.

Heraldic Mermaid

Mermaid.   The mermaid has the body of a beautiful woman and
the tail of a fish; she is usually depicted holding a mirror and a comb.
The mermaid represents a divinity of the waters and was said to
appear mainly in the sea but also in inland waters. One was reputed
to be captured in Holland in 1404, taken to Haarlem, taught to spin
and converted to the Catholic faith. There were also mermen; both
they and mermaids were seen off coasts.

Tritons appear in the form of half-men, half-fish as escorts of
Neptune and Galatea. The merman also resembles the Babylonian
Ea-Oannes the man-fish or goat-fish.

Ovid quotes the legend that mermaids rose from the burning
galleys of the Trojans, the timbers turning to the flesh and blood of
the 'green daughters of the sea'.

The Melusine of fairy tale has two tails and occurs in German
heraldry. The Japanese mermaid Ningyo is a fish with a human
head. In Polynesian myth Vatea, Creator God, was half-human,
half-porpoise.

Metempsychosis.   There is a widespread belief that at death the
soul can pass into some other body, either that of another human

or of some animal, bird or insect. This belief is particularly prevalent among cultures living close to nature, death being simply a change of form which is capable of infinite variety, since form is itself regarded as impermanent.

Ancient Egypt held that in transmigration a soul could enter any form it pleased and remain there as long as it liked, so that it could become a **Crocodile, Heron**, golden **Hawk** and so on, travelling in the air, on land or in the water according to the form adopted.

Nor is it necessarily at death that the soul can transmigrate: Plutarch says that in the war between Typhon and the Gods the latter took refuge in the bodies of animals and there are endless legends of gods transforming themselves into animals. Plato and Pausanias said that men tasting the blood of a human sacrifice were changed into wolves, but this last is **Lycanthropy** rather than metempsychosis, which is a change of the habitat of the soul, whereas lycanthropy is a purely bodily condition. Shamans and sorcerers when they enter animal bodies to visit the spirit world exemplify temporary metempsychosis of a kind which appears to involve two souls occupying one body, in that the animal has its own soul before being taken over by the spirit of the shaman or magician. Or, it has been suggested, the sorcerer may send only part of his own soul into the animal body. This is not regarded as strange by cults such as those of some Amerindians, who believe that each person has two souls of an animal-human nature.

Religions which teach the doctrine of reincarnation, for instance Hinduism and Buddhism, assume that souls can progress upwards or downwards in accordance with the quality of the life led; an evil human may descend into an appropriate type of animal, while a noble animal can be born into human form.

Karsten, working among the South American Indians, wrote that: 'According to the Indian theory all animals – quadrupeds, birds, reptiles, insects – possess a spirit or soul which in essence is the same kind as that animating man, and which survives the destruction of the body. All animals have once been men or all men animals.' Or, as Sir Everard Thurm said: 'other animals differ from men only in bodily form and in their various degrees of strength, and they differ in spirit not at all.' In such cultures there is not necessarily a moral cause for the change, as there is for reincarnation; it may be undertaken for some temporary purpose, as with the Shaman.

Celtic mythology also assumes the constant interchanging of souls which can pass from one body to another. Finn's two dogs were actually his nephews. In Polynesia animals such as the **Lizard**, **Shark**, or particularly a nocturnal bird can reincarnate the souls of relatives or ancestors. The same applies to Australian Aboriginal myth. Death is never an extinction of life, merely a transition from one form to another; the soul dwells only temporarily in the physical state, whether human or animal, and is involved in a cyclic process of death and rebirth.

Mimik-dog. Said to be able to mimic anything, the mimik-dog was used as a servant in Egypt in Ptolemy's time; it had an ape-like body and hedgehog face.

Mink. The mink features in the mythology of the Amerindian Kwakiutl tribe and is the **Trickster** Culture Hero of the North West coast. He is among the favourite Tricksters and has much in common with Raven and, like him, is a solar symbol. Mink was conceived when the Sun's rays struck the Hero's mother, who gave birth to him as Born-to-be-the-Sun. His visit to his Sun-Father and its disastrous results have much in common with the Phaeton myth of ancient Greece.

Minotaur. A monster, part man, part bull, born of Pasiphae by the Minoan Bull and killed by Theseus. In combines the solar bull and the humid principle, as the miasma slain by the sun, the solar hero Theseus; it is also suggested as symbolizing the savage passions of nature.
See also **Bull**

Mixcoatl. An Aztec cloud-serpent or **Dragon**, a Storm God and huntsman.

Moa. A flying moa carried the Maori Pou-Rangahua on his journey to obtain Kumara, which revolutionized the diet of the people.

Mockingbird. A figure in North Amerindian Shasta tribe myth. The dead travel eastward along the Milky Way to the land of the Mockingbird.

Mole. In the West the mole symbolizes blindness, obtuseness and a misanthrope; as an underground dweller it is in touch with the powers of darkness. The term 'mole' is, in modern times, applied to traitors, spies or providers of secret information.
 The mole is, among Amerindians, a totem of a Hopi clan; with the Zuni it is a Guardian and Master of the Lower Regions and is 'stout of heart and strong of will'. For the Ainu of Japan the mole was originally an earth deity who came down from heaven and defeated the Great Demon in a contest, finally rolling him into the fire where he was burned to ashes, but as these ashes were the remains of a supernatural being they still had life in them and so were changed into **Foxes** and **Cats** who are of the same family and have demonic natures.

Monkey. Hinduism has a monkey-god Hanuman, son of Vayu. A wind god, he has divine power and is noted for bravery, speed and

The Indian Monkey-god Hanuman carrying the gods Siva and Parvati in his heart

strength and is the epitome of a useful companion and servant. At
the Ram Lila festival little boys dress as monkeys to commemorate
the help given by Hanuman when the demon Ravana abducted Sita.
Hanuman bestows longevity and is remembered on Hindu
birthdays. He can also be depicted as monkey-headed with a human
body and the tail of a cow, usually green-coloured. In Buddhism the
monkey was one of the early incarnations of the Buddha, but also
one of the Three Senseless Creatures, representing greed while the
Tiger symbolizes anger and the **Deer** love-sickness. Monkey is the
hero of the classic story of the *Journey to the Western Paradise*, in
which he symbolizes unregenerate human nature. The monkey is
the ninth animal of the Twelve Terrestrial Branches. He has powers
of transformation and is apotropaic, but also represents trickery and
ugliness. In Japan the monkey is revered and the Three Mystic
Monkeys of Japanese myth are *Mizaru* – its hands covering its eyes,
Kikazaru – hands over its ears, and *Iwazaru* – hands covering its
mouth, as seen in depictions of the phrase 'see no evil, hear no evil,
speak no evil'.

The monkey is capable of speech but refuses to use this ability lest he be set to work.

Monkeys and mythical monsters guard the doorways of shrines in Cambodia and monkeys were trained to guard against thieves in markets there.

In Rome, monkeys were recorded as pets in the 3rd century BC, and were used as performers and entertainers.

The Mayan God of the North Star is portrayed with a monkey's head and there were monkey deities depicted in ancient Peruvian art, sometimes with human characteristics or limbs.

In Christianity the monkey represents trickery, vanity and luxury; it can also be the Devil and is represented as such in the Bestiaries, typifying cunning and hypocrisy, mischievousness and conceit.

Among West African tribes monkeys are known as Servants of Ogugu and are sacred and left unmolested. Certain monkeys can embody the spirits of the departed.

Monoceros. Pliny says the monoceros has a stag's head with a single horn, elephant's feet, boar's tail and the body of a horse. In the Bestiaries it is represented in this manner but the horn sticks out from the middle of the forehead; it has a horrible howl. It is not possible to capture it alive, but it can be killed.

See also **Unicorn**

Monsters. Monsters and freaks occur in all traditions and in early times were accepted by people of learning and intellect and seldom queried. In some cases they were believed to be the special works of the Creator sent for some particular purpose, in others they could be regarded as misbegotten hybrids. They were also frequently taken as omens or portents of divine displeasure: just as comets and eclipses presaged disaster, so did freak animals. There were monsters of every element – animals, birds, reptiles and insects of land, sea and air.

Berosus wrote, 'there was a time they say when all was water and darkness and these gave birth and habitation to monstrous animals of mixed form and species. For there were men with two wings, others with four, and some again with double faces. Some had the horns of goats, some their legs, and some the legs of horses and the fore-parts of men, like the Hippocentaurs. There were bulls with human heads, dogs with four bodies ending in fishes, horses with dog's heads, and men and other creatures with the heads and bodies of horses with the tails of fishes and a number of animals whose bodies were a monstrous compound of the dissimilar parts of beasts of various kinds. Together these were fishes, reptiles, serpents and other creatures which, by a reciprocal translation of the parts of one another, became all portentously deformed.'

See also **Composite Animals**

Moose. In Amerindian myth the moose represents the Northern Region, the direction of wisdom; it is the balance between gentleness and strength, also self-esteem.

Mosquito. There is a Siberian festival at the time of the arrival of mosquitoes when a sacrifice is made to the One on High so that the mosquitoes do not scatter the herds. In Ainu lore mosquitoes, gnats and all insect pests rose from the ashes of a hobgoblin killed and burned by an Ainu hero.

In China the mosquito represents rebellion and wickedness.

Moth. In the New Testament the moth is used as an agent of corruption (Matthew 6: 19); it also represents fragility and impermanence. A Malagasy myth traces the descent of the people from a moth. In Maori lore it is a form taken by a spirit.

Mountain Lion. Among Zuni Indians the mountain lion is 'stout of heart and strong of will' and is Guardian and Master of the Northern World. It represents leadership and its related powers and responsibilities and is a balance of physical grace and strength.

See also **Lion**

Mouse. In Greece the cult of Apollo Smitheus developed from the early cult of the mouse and it was an attribute of Zeus/Sabazios and Apollo – it is suggested that mice were associated with these gods because they were used as food for the gods' snakes.

As underground dwellers mice are chthonic and in touch with the powers of darkness, but they are also one of the 'soul' animals; a soul can take the form of a mouse on leaving the body.

In the Old Testament mice are among the unclean animals and Christianity equates them with the Devil as devourer; a mouse is depicted in Christian art as gnawing at the root of the Tree of Life.

Aesop's fable of the **Lion** and the mouse symbolizes strength in weakness and weakness in strength. This symbolism is also found among the Amerindians, where the mouse represents both great power and great weakness, also scrutiny, orderliness and method. In Dakota the waning moon is nibbled by mice. Ainu lore says the mouse and **Rat** are one family created on the earth together. If venerated they do no harm; if ignored they wreak havoc and destruction.

Mule. The mule was said to have the strength of a **Horse** and the surefootedness and patience of an **Ass**; it was used from early times as a transport animal and for ploughing; it was the Roman pack animal *par excellence*. It symbolizes obstinacy, stubbornness and, according to Aristotle, tameness – 'Man and the mule are always tame'. Mules were imported by the Hebrews, as it was forbidden to cross-breed animals, but the mule is later mentioned in the time of

David as a mount for his sons, and Solomon rode on one.

In folklore the mule can play the part of a **Helpful animal** and may be the form taken by an enchanted human. There was an ancient belief that drones were generated from the carcass of a mule, bees from oxen, hornets from horses and wasps from donkeys; the maggots turning into these insects.

Mullet. One of the taboo foods in Greece at the Women's festival of the Haloa. According to the Bestiaries Red Mullet, or *Mullus*, cools lust but dulls the eyesight.

Mushrush. See **Sirrush**

Mushussu. The Sumerian three-headed **Dragon** serving Tiamat; identified with the constellation Hydra.

Musimon. A fabulous hybrid ram and goat, also called the Tityron. It has four horns, two of them straight (for the goat) and two curved (for the ram).

Muskrat. The muskrat features in the Amerindian Manabozho cycle. In Algonquin myth it is one of the creatures which brought up mud from the bottom of the primaeval waters to create the earth.

N

Naga. In Hindu mythology the Nagas are depicted as human-headed snakes, as monsters, or more usually as snakes, particularly the cobra. They have semi-divine power and occur frequently in Indian art, depicting cosmic power and the Shakti. They sprung from Kadru, wife of Kasyapa, to people in the underworld or underwaters where they reign in splendour from fabulous palaces. Nagas also dwell under Mount Meru, the World Centre. Their palaces are bejewelled and full of flowers; they dance and sing; some of the female nagas marry mortals. Like **Dragons** they can control the rain-clouds. They are at enmity with the **Garuda** Bird. Sometimes nagas are depicted as many-headed; Sesha, King of the Nagas and having one thousand heads, is dressed in purple. The naga is the serpent on which Vishnu slept at the creation of the world and which will destroy the world by fire at the end of the cycle. The two intertwined nagas of Vishnu represent the already-fertilized waters, the life-force of the waters. Nagas are guardians of treasures, both material and those of esoteric knowledge.

See also **Serpent**

Narwhal. The sea-unicorn; its tusk was said to project from its forehead. The narwhal tusk was frequently accepted as the 'Alicorn' and used for making drinking vessels.

See also **Unicorn**

Nependis. An heraldic beast, half-ape, half-swine, suggesting the qualities of both.

Newt or Efeta. A harmful creature, to be regarded with aversion. Ceres transformed a youth who mocked her into a newt.

Nidhogg. In Scandinavian myth the *Nidhogg*, the Dread Biter, lives at the root of the *Yggdrasil*, the Cosmic Tree, and gnaws at the roots, symbolizing malefic power.

Nightingale. In the Greek myth of Tereus, Philomela and Procne, Philomela was turned into a nightingale and Procne into a **Swallow**.

Nightingales and swallows are also connected with the Rites of Adonis and Attis, the 'melancholy song' being suggested as appropriate to the rites of the dying year. In Greek authors Philomel is the name of the swallow and Procne the nightingale: Latin authors reverse this. Philomela is associated with grief, loneliness, the love-lorn, forlornness; it is the bird of the Muses. In ancient Greece a bad poet was 'enough to give the nightingale the shivers'.

Eastern myth has the nightingale in love with the rose. It is the *bulbul* of Persian literature which presses its breast against the rose thorn to kill the love pain in its heart. Pliny says it often dies with its singing and has a special 'variety of song of long continuance' until it dies of the love of music. Aristotle and Plutarch say that the nightingale teaches its young to sing and that those reared in captivity never sing so well.

In the Bestiaries the nightingale is called *Lucina*; it is said to herald the dawn and symbolizes a woman constantly working for her brood but who lightens her burden with sweet song. They also say that the bird singing in the night and increasing its song with the coming of light depicts the holy soul in the darkness of night awaiting the arrival of the Lord of Light with such joy that the soul cannot remain silent.

Nightjar. The totem of an Australian Aboriginal tribe.

Night Raven. This bird is sometimes identified with the **Owl**, but Aristotle says it differs in that 'the eared owl is like an ordinary owl, only that it has feathers about its ears'. The *Septuagint* uses the same word for both birds.

Nuckalavea. An Irish sea-monster of **Centaur** type; it had no skin and its breath brought the plague.

Nunyanune. A huge bird of the Northern Amerindians, which preys on humans. It appears to have affinities with the Arabian **Roc** and the Persian **Simurgh**.

O

Ocelot. An important cult and totem animal of the ancient Peruvians. As living and hunting near water and streams it was associated with the **Otter** and the two were sometimes combined in iconography.

Octopus or Polypus. A frequent subject in Aegean art, depicted on Cretan jars. Like the **Chameleon** it was a symbol of inconstancy and faithlessness as it changes colour under stress. This was stated by Aristotle, Pliny and Aelian and quoted by mediaeval writers, who said it matches its surroundings to deceive its prey. It takes on the symbolism of the spiral in Mediterranean art, but in Celtic and Scandinavian art its arms are depicted as straight. As the spiral it is associated with thunder and the phases of the moon. In the **Zodiac** it is connected with the sign of Cancer, the waters of the deep, the summer Solstice and the descent into the *Janua inferni*. It also has affinities with the **Dragon** and **Spider** in spiral symbolism.

In Polynesian myth the octopus rose from the primordial waters and had two children, Fire and Water, who were thereafter involved in a conflict which ended in the destruction of the world by flood. The octopus was the sole survivor from this earlier world. As a food it and the turtle are restricted to the gods. It is sacred in Samoa, but in Hawaii it is a miscreator, having made an untimely attempt at creating man and then leading a revolt against the gods it was cast into the lower regions. The octopus is most important in the Society Islands as a creator figure; signifying the number eight, it determined political divisions. Like the **Shark** and **Turtle** it embodies sacred beings and powers.

Odontotyrannus. A huge amphibious beast with three horns, living in the Ganges. It attacked men, whom it hated, and ate twenty-six of Alexander the Great's soldiers.

O Goncho. In Japanese myth the O Goncho appeared as a white dragon which could turn into a golden bird every fifty years; its cry was an omen of famine.

Onager.   The Wild Ass of Central Asia, which drew chariots.
   See **Ass**

On Niont.   A huge **Serpent** of Huron Indian myth; it had a sharp
horn which could pierce mountains. It was never seen.

Heraldic Opinicus

Opinicus.   In Heraldry the Opinicus is a variation of the **Griffin**,
having four legs instead of two; it has the wings and neck of an eagle
and a camel's tail.

Opossum.   In Amerindian lore the opossum depicts strategy,
diversion, playing dead when threatened and excreting the odour
of death; it is a warrior strategy.

Orc.   According to Pliny a huge creature 'armed with teeth', the
Grampus or Killer Whale.
   See **Whale**

Oryx.   Both Aristotle and Pliny believed that the Oryx was the
Unicorn. Aelian says that ancient hunters kept any captured oryxes
as presents for Kings. It was revered and used as an emblem by the
Egyptians and was a sacrificial animal. It could represent

Capricornus in the Zodiac. The oryx was a clean animal for the Hebrews; the desert oryx of the Old Testament was the only one seen outside Africa, in Palestine, Syria, Iraq and Arabia. It is now rare, having been hunted almost to extinction.

Osprey. Pliny gives the osprey the same qualities as the true **Eagle**. Albertus Magnus says that it had one webbed foot, with which it swam, and one with talons, with which it captured fish. It was believed that, like the eagle, it made its young fly up to the sun to test them and killed any failures. Mediaeval lore said that it terrified, turned over and immobilized any fish it flew over. It is called the sea eagle in Heraldry and is always depicted as a white eagle.

Ostrich. The symbolism of the ostrich is ambivalent, being beneficent in some cultures and demonic in others. In Semitic mythology it is a demon and can represent a dragon, and in Babylon in the Marduk-versus-Tiamat conflict the hero could be depicted as an eagle with the ostrich as Tiamat and evil. But in Egypt the ostrich feather is an attribute of Maat, Goddess of Truth and Justice – the feathers all being exactly equal – and it is the feather against which the heart of the deceased is weighed in the Judgement Hall of Osiris. The bird is also an emblem of Ament, Goddess of the West and the Dead, and of Shu as air and space. The feather is worn on the heads of divinities, being Masters of Truth.

In Zoroastrianism the ostrich is a divine storm bird.

There are many strange myths associated with the ostrich, its eggs and its digestive powers. Pliny says that it can eat and digest everything. Aelian and Albertus say it eats stones and one version of the *Physiologus* maintains it even swallows iron and fiery coals, which are good for its cold stomach. Aelian also says that the stones are a medicine for its eyes. The well-known 'head in the sand' story is affirmed by Pliny and Oppian, but Pliny also says that it can hide its head in a bush. Diodorus maintains that hiding its head is not a matter of stupidity, as most assume, but is for protection as the head is the 'tenderest Part of the Body'.

The hatching of ostrich eggs is also the subject of different myths. The *Physiologus* says that, like the **Tortoise**, the ostrich hatches her eggs by the heat of her gaze only; if the gaze were removed the eggs became addled and broken. In the Old Testament, however, 'she leaveth her eggs on the earth and warmeth them in the dust and forgetteth that the foot may crush them . . . she is hardened against her young ones' (Job 39: 14/16), and so becomes a symbol of cruelty to the young. Aelian, on the other hand, maintains that the ostrich shows solicitude for her eggs. The belief in her neglect was used to show that 'God will break evil-doers as the ostrich her worthless eggs.' In contrary symbolism, the ostrich egg suspended in Coptic Churches, Temples and Mosques, and sometimes over tombs, depicts creation, life, resurrection and vigilance.

Arabs prize the ostrich highly both as food and for its eggs, feathers and skin, but it is regarded as stupid. It is the product of a camel and a bird and can be a form taken by a djinn.

In the Bestiaries it is also the *Assida*; it lays its eggs when the Pleiades appear and leaves its eggs to hatch in the warmth of heaven and 'disregarding earthly things, cleaves to the heavenly ones – even to forgetting its own offspring . . . so should man strive after the reward of the starry calling.'

Ostrich eggs are one of the vehicles of supernatural power among the African Kung Bushmen, and for the Dogons the ostrich signifies both light and water, the latter being typified by the bird's erratic and undulating movements. It is an African cult bird and there are ritual ostrich dances.

Among South American Indians the ostrich is the bird of festivals of the dead. Processions are headed by ostrich-men representing the dead, and the men eat ostrich meat, while the women eat that of the armadillo, as the ostrich is a male incarnation of the female **Armadillo**. An ostrich dance is performed to prevent the dead from doing any harm.

The ostrich is frequently met in Heraldry, though not commonly as a charge; it usually holds a horseshoe, key, or piece of iron in its beak, perpetuating the digestion legend. The head alone is sometimes used as a crest. Ostrich feathers play a large part in armory.

Otter. Pliny and Aelian call the otter the *Enhydris* – meaning aquatic – and identify it with the water-snake or **Hydra**, transferring the legend of the destruction of the **Crocodile** to it when it is actually the **Ichneumon** which is the real enemy of the crocodile.

In Zoroastrianism the otter is one of the clean animals belonging to Ormuzd; to kill it is a great sin.

The otter was an important cult animal in ancient Peru and was associated with the **Ocelot** as living near streams and water; the two can be combined in iconography. For the Amerindians it represents the feminine energy and the power of the earth and waters; it is a creature of grace and playfulness. It is one of the North American **Tricksters**. When caught Otter pleads not to be thrown into the water and drowned and then, being thrown in, swims away laughing. Otter is the buffoon of the Woodlands Cree tribe. Assisted by the **Loon** he helps the dead cross the lake to the next world. A chieftain's otter-skin head-dress signifies wisdom.

In Celtic art Cernunnos, as Lord of Animals, is depicted as accompanied by an otter, **bear** and **wolf**.

The Bestiaries, following Pliny, also confuse the otter with the ichneumon in the crocodile-killing legend, which they use as a symbol of God incarnate triumphing over Satan: 'The Saviour, having put on the flesh, descended into Hell and brought forth all that dwell therein. The otter emerges safely from the belly of the crocodile, so Our Lord rose uninjured on the third day.'

For the Ainu the otter is not a high deity. He was told to create foxes and make them red, but he forgot and made them white. The foxes complained, so the otter rubbed them with salmon roe and made them red. The otter is forgetful and wasteful since he takes a bite out of a fish, leaves it and forgets it. A forgetful person is an 'otter-head'. Loss of memory results from being possessed by an otter. If eating otter flesh, or fish killed by an otter, a band must be tied round the head to prevent the otter entering the brain. The dried heart is a specific against cholera.

Ouzel or Merle. According to the *Physiologus* the sweetness of this bird's song typifies the grace of God.

See also **Thrush**

Owl. The owl has a dual symbolism as wisdom and as a bird of

The Owl: darkness as evil attacked by diurnal birds *(from a Bestiary)*

darkness and death. In ancient Greece it was sacred to Athene as she represented wisdom and was in her earlier character a Goddess of Night. The owl appeared on Athenian coins as an emblem of the city and to 'send owls to Athens' was the equivalent of the modern English saying 'sending coals to Newcastle'. The owl was also sacred to Demeter. In most places the hooting of an owl presages death or misfortune; it is a prophetic bird. The death of Dido was foretold by an owl. Several Roman emperors' deaths were foretold by the omen of owls alighting on their homes; it could also be a vampire. The owl was an attribute of the Etruscan God of Darkness and Night.

In Hebrew symbolism it represents both blindness and desolation 'the owl and the raven shall dwell therein' (Isaiah 34: 11; Job 50: 39). It is an unclean bird.

The owl is prominent in Celtic lore, being a sacred, magic bird; it appears in early times as an owl-goddess and is depicted frequently in La Tène figures, preceding the cult of Athene. It is chthonic, the 'night hag' and 'corpse bird', and is an attribute of Gwyan or Gwynn, God of the Underworld, who ruled over the souls of warriors slain in battle.

Yama, the Vedic God of the Dead, sometimes sent an owl as his messenger instead of his two dogs; the bird is one of his emblems. In Buddhism the owl and the **Crow** are mortal enemies, as the owl kills the crow's young in the nest at night; so the Buddhist devotee must kill ignorance; he must also, like the owl, seek seclusion.

In the Middle East the owl is a bird of ill-omen and an evil spirit can take its form to carry off children at night. In China and Japan it also carries the symbolism of evil, death and ill-omen; in the former it also signifies crime and ungrateful children.

The Bestiaries call the owl the *Noctua* and it symbolizes the Jews who rejected Christ and therefore value darkness more than light. Christianity equates the bird with Satan, the powers of darkness, desolation and bad news; its call is the 'song of death'. It is depicted with a human face and with birds of the daytime attacking it.

The death-warning of its hoot also obtains among the Amerindians, where it is also called the Night Eagle. Its silent flight represents deception and silent observation; it is a bird of sorcerers. The Pueblos will not enter a house where there is the body or feathers of an owl. The Kwakiutls say that when a slave dies he goes to the home of the owls. For the Navajo owls are ghosts of the dead and messengers of the otherworld, but on the contrary the Cherokee of the South-east Woodlands hold the owl and the **Cougar** sacred since their ability to see in the dark gives them an advantage over others. For the Pawnee it is the Chief of the Night and gives protection.

Among West African tribes the owl's head can be used by wizards preparing evil spells; again, the owl's cry presages evil, especially for pregnant women. The owl is a messenger for sorcerers according to Yoruba and Zulu lore.

Although among the Ainu of Japan the owl is generally evil, brings misfortune and is not to be trusted, the Eagle Owl is beneficent and

trusted as it warns people of approaching evil; it is worshipped as
a divinity and mediates between God and humanity. Eagle Owls
were kept in cages and venerated but finally sacrificed to take
messages and requests to the heavens. The Screech Owl warns
against danger and confers success in hunting, but the Horned Owl
is a bringer of trouble and is ill-omened. It is a misfortune to have
one fly in front of one, but total disaster to see it fly across the face
of the moon. In the first case evil can be avoided by spitting, but
in the second the situation is so serious that the only remedy is to
change one's name. The Barn Owl is also demonic and feared and
must not be imitated.

Australian Aboriginal myth says the owl is a messenger of the evil
deity Muurup; he eats children and destroys people. The bird is a
bringer of ill-luck among the Maoris, but it is a sacred emblem in
Samoa.

The owl is a favourite bird in Heraldry, always depicted *face
affronté*.

Ox. A multi-purpose animal but pre-eminently a worker, it is
depicted ploughing, reaping, threshing, carrying loads, drawing
carts and hauling barges. Large ox wagons are used for family
transport. A Christian catacomb painting shows Jacob and his sons
arriving in Egypt in carts drawn by oxen. At Pompeii Bacchus and
Ariadne are portrayed in their triumphant car drawn by oxen.

The ox symbolizes strength, patient toil, wealth and sacrifice, and
can be symbolically interchangeable with the **Bull** though, being
castrated, it cannot share the Bull's fertility significance.

According to Varro it was a capital offence to kill an ox in Attica
and Peloponnesia; it was killed only as a sacrifice and even then this
act was treated as murder and a scapegoat was found, or
alternatively the knife used in the killing was execrated and thrown
away.

The Bestiaries equate the sacrificed ox with the true sacrifice of
Christ; it also symbolizes the yoke of Christ, patience, strength and
gentleness.

There was a Hebrew ban on oxen and asses being yoked together
for ploughing (Deuteronomy 22: 10).

Many of the features of the ox are taken on by the **Yak** in Tibet
and the water **Buffalo** in China. The ox takes the place of the bull
in Chinese spring and fertility rites and symbolism. It is the second
of the Twelve Animals of the Terrestrial Branches. The white ox is
contemplative wisdom in Buddhism and the Taoist-Buddhist 'Ten
Ox-herding Pictures' represent the ox as unregenerate nature,
dangerous when untamed and undisciplined but useful when
brought under control. The ox, first depicted as black and wild,
gradually becomes white and tame until it finally disappears

completely as its unregenerate conditions are transcended. Niu Wang, God of Oxen, the golden-haired Buffalo, protects against epidemics affecting oxen and is also the spirit of the star T'ien-wen. His image is placed in stables for protection.

Oyster.   Represents the womb, the creative power of the feminine watery principle and cosmic life; it is the power of the waters, lunar – 'the sacredness of the moon' – and in Chinese symbolism the *yin* and fertility.

Its closed form makes it a natural symbol of secrecy – 'as close as an oyster'. In Christianity it represents the Old and New Testaments joined in the Bible, creating pure pearls of divine truth. The Bestiaries say that the oyster is tricked by the crab, which inserts a pebble in the oyster when open and thus cheats the oyster's innocence, just as the Devil does with people.

Oyster Catcher.   Among the Gaels this bird is an emblem of St Bride, who carried one in each hand. It bears the form of a cross on its plumage as it once covered Christ with sea-weed when his enemies pursued him.

P

Pajur. A Romanian bird which killed its ungrateful young, then, repenting, opened its breast and revived them with its blood. A **Pelican**-type myth.

Panther Demon of Tibet

Panther. The panther was said to be a friend to all animals except the dragon, but there was a well-established belief that it killed its prey with its sweet breath. This is quoted by Aristotle, Pliny and Aelian, and used by them as a symbol of treachery; but the *Physiologus* says that after feeding it sleeps for three days then gives a roar and emits a sweet perfume which attracts other animals, who then follow it about – 'so is the Lord God and so the hope of salvation which he gives – that is a noble fragrance'. While its sweet breath attracts most animals it is offensive to the dragon, who flees from it. 'In like manner did Our Lord Jesus Christ draw all nations through his sweet savour,' and 'Christ like the panther, makes that old serpent the devil flee.' The panther is often depicted as routing the **Dragon**, with numerous beasts following it and divided into two groups: the Jews and the Gentiles. The skin of the panther is beautiful and of many colours like Joseph's coat. Late Bestiaries derive the word 'panther' from 'pan' – all, implying that Christ came to save the whole world. Later in Christianity the panther became associated with evil. There was an ancient tradition that the real father of Christ was a Roman Centurion named 'Panthera'.

The Underground Panther lived in the evil underworld of the Algonquins and Ojibwas of the Amerindians, but it was sacred to the South-eastern Cherokee tribe; the panther or **Cougar** and the **Owl** having the special power of being able to see in the dark.

In Polynesia there is a sacred panther which has flames emerging from its head, back and legs.

Heraldic Panther

The heraldic panther often has the tail of the lion, forelegs and talons of an eagle and horns on its head, with flames issuing from its mouth, but later the flames are depicted as coming from every opening on its head, denoting savagery, fury and remorselessness. It is always borne *guardant*.

Para.   A cat-spirit which steals milk, cream, butter and honey from its owner. It appears in Sweden as the *Bjära* and in Finland as the cream-cat, *Smierragatta*.

Pard.   According to the Bestiaries this is 'a parti-coloured species, very swift and strongly inclined to bloodshed.'
See also **Leopard**

Parrot.   Aelian writes of the wisdom of the parrot and of its vocal powers and says that the Brahmins regard it as sacred on this account. In Hinduism it is an attribute of Kama, God of Love, and is a prophetic and rain-bringing bird. It is a natural symbol of imitation and mockery and can also represent unintelligent repetition.

Ovid mentions that the parrot was a fashionable cult in ancient Rome and was carried in Ptolemy's procession at Alexandria.

The Parrot Clan is next in importance to the Bear Clan in the four leading Amerindian Hopi clans. It symbolizes the fruitful South and fertility; the parrot is the mother of the Hopi clans. It is an oracular bird.

In **Heraldry** the parrot is called the Popinjay and is usually depicted naturally.

Partridge.   The partridge was sacred to Aphrodite (she representing fertility), to the Cretan Zeus and Latona, also to the Sun God, Talos; it was used in fighting and sometimes kept as a pet.

The bird was prevalent in Palestine and was a clean food. It was used as a decoy bird – 'the snare of the falcon', and David hunted like a partridge. Also 'as the partridge that gathereth young which she hath not brought forth, so is he that getteth riches and not by right' (Jeremiah 17: 11) is based on the ancient belief that the partridge stole the eggs of other birds and therefore depicts deceitfulness and cunning. This assumption was used in the *Physiologus*, which says the bird desires large broods, but when the young are mature they recognize their own mothers and fly to them, so the partridge typifies the Devil who gathers the children of men to himself who, when they grow in wisdom and strength and learn the truth, forsake him and flee to their natural mother, the Church. In Christian art the bird is portrayed alone in her nest with the young flying away above her. The Bestiaries call the partridge the *Perdix*, representing cunning, perversion and the Devil trying to steal the faithful.

The Redwing Partridge is one of the vehicles of supernatural power among the African Kung Bushmen.

Peacock. Ovid calls the peacock 'Juno's bird who carries the stars in its tail'; the circular tail is the vault of the heavens and the eyes the stars, it thus symbolizes the heavens, to which the dead ascend, and immortality. The immortality symbol was also derived from the belief that the bird's flesh did not decay. The peacock is Juno's emblem, with the **Eagle** that of Jupiter; together they became symbols of the apotheosis of the Roman Empress and Emperor and hence were carved on tombs and funeral lamps.

The peacock was kept in Babylon and there was a Peacock Throne. This also appears in Persia, where the peacock denotes royalty. Peacocks stand on either side of the Tree of Life, signifying duality in man and nature. In Egyptian art the peacock sometimes accompanies Isis. In China and Japan it is a sacred bird and has been depicted in art from ancient times; it represents dignity, rank and beauty; the peacock's feather was awarded as conferring imperial favour and high official rank. It was an emblem of the Ming Dynasty. In Buddhism the peacock's feather is an attribute of Avalokitesvara, who also appears as the goddess Kwan-yin, and the Amitabha Buddha as signifying compassion. It is also a symbol of marital fidelity, as it was believed that if one died the other either died of grief or remained celibate.

There is a Hindu saying that the peacock has angel's feathers, the devil's voice and the walk of a thief. It is ashamed of its ugly black legs and screams when it sees them. The Vedic Sarasvati, Goddess of Wisdom, Learning and Music, is depicted riding on a peacock or a lotus; it is sometimes the mount of Brahma, also of Lakshmi. When ridden by Kama, God of Love, it portrays impatient desire.

Christianity uses the peacock's symbolism of resurrection by referring to both the incorruptibility of its flesh and the renewal of its plumage. The 'hundred eyes' are the all-seeing Church and the saints, as its tail forms a halo. Surmounting an orb it signifies rising above worldly things. The peacock is mentioned in the Old Testament in connection with the treasures and freight of Solomon (I Kings 10: 22). The peacock is the *Pavo* of the Bestiaries, which also emphasize its incorruptibility; they also say that a man devoid of prudence is like a peacock that has lost its tail and draws attention to its showy plumage, hiding its ugly feet, walk and cry. The *Physiologus* says its cry in the night signals fear of losing its beauty and is like the soul in the night of the world fearing to lose the gifts of the grace of God.

The peacock foretells rain by dancing. It is said to hate gold and will not alight near it. It was the largest game bird in the old world. It is frequently used in Heraldry, usually represented with its tail displayed, this is termed 'in his pride'; it is not often used on a shield.

Peewit.   See **Lapwing**

Pegais.   Said by Pliny to be the fabulous horse-headed birds of Scythia.

Pegasus.   The Greek winged **Horse** born from the blood of Medusa's head when Poseidon mixed this blood with sea-sand. Athene taught Bellerophon how to tame the steed; he then mounted it and overcame the **Chimera**. In trying to reach Olympus, however, Bellerophon offended Zeus, who sent a gadfly to sting Pegasus and make him throw his rider. Pegasus was later transformed into a constellation.

Peist.   An Irish dragon caught and imprisoned by St Patrick.

Pelican.   The Greeks said the pelican was hostile to the **Quail**, and Martial alludes to it as a symbol of gluttony. It is a bird of ill-omen for the Hebrews and represented the desolation of the wilderness (Psalms 102: 6). It is unclean food (Leviticus 11: 18).

The symbolism of the pelican's maternal devotion and self-sacrifice does not appear in early classical writers, but is in the *Physiologus* and was developed under Christian influence. It was said that the young were killed by the mother, smothered in an excess of love; another myth said that the young struck the parents who struck back and killed them, but the outcome in either case was that the mother mourned them for three days then brought them back to life by stabbing her breast and feeding them with her blood; this depicts sacrifice, charity and piety, 'piety' meaning filial devotion. Dante called Christ *nostro Pelicano* who gave his blood for the sins of the many at the crucifixion.

The Bestiaries say: 'The holy man loves solitude like the Pelican in the wilderness'. It is the *Pelicanus*, quoted as at first devoted to its young but later killing them when the young flap their wings and hit them, then repenting and after three days resuscitating them by the mother opening her breast and feeding them with her blood. This represents Christ, 'who begets us and calls us into being out of nothing'. It is also Christ pierced on the cross, Christ buffeted, beaten and shedding his blood to give us eternal life.

Both the pelican and **Phoenix** were used by mediaeval poets to illustrate the power of heavenly and earthly love.

In Heraldry the pelican is usually portrayed with the head and body of an eagle, wings elevated, neck *embowed*, pecking with its beak at its breast: this is *vulning* itself and depicts maternal solicitude. The 'Pelican in her Piety' is a common symbol on monuments and brasses. Both the pelican and the eagle are used in Christian churches as lecterns.

Pheasant. Aelian refers to pheasants as being reared by Indian kings. In China it is a *yang* bird symbolizing light, virtue, prosperity, good-fortune and literary refinement. It was an emblem of the Emperor Yü. In Japan it represents maternal love and protection. It is also a symbol of thunder.

Pheng. A Japanese fabulous bird like the **Roc**, so large it could eclipse the sun and swallow a camel.

Phoenix. The earliest reference to the phoenix is by Hesiod in the 8th century BC. Ovid, Pliny and Tacitus all write about it, but Aristotle does not mention it. Herodotus and Pliny call it 'The Arabian Bird', but in the classics it appears to be of Egyptian origin. In one legend the bird flew to Heliopolis and was immolated on the altar fire; in another it builds a nest of spices which is ignited by the sun, the bird fanning the flames with its wings. In either case it is a fabulous bird which dies by self-immolation. It remains dead for three days – symbolizing the dark of the moon – then rises again from its own ashes. The symbolism is ambivalent, lunar in its associations with the moon but also solar, being a fire-bird. The bird is the epitome of gentleness as it kills nothing, feeding only on dew and crushing nothing it touches. It is of great size and there is only one in existence. There are varying accounts as to its age, some say it lives 1000 years, Pliny says it lives 660 years, Herodotus 540, Seneca 500 and Albertus 350. Ovid says that its tears are of incense and its blood of balsam. The Talmud version is that after 1000 years it shrivels to the size of an egg and then emerges again.

In Egyptian tradition the phoenix is equated with the Bennu, the Sun Bird, emblem of the Sun God, Ra, and symbol of resurrection and immortality as associated with both Ra and Osiris.

The phoenix is of outstanding importance in Chinese myth and symbolism. It is one of the Four Spiritually Endowed or Sacred Creatures. Like the dragon and the **Ky-lin** it is a fabulous creation and shares with them the quality of combining the *yin-yang* powers. It is the Feng-huang, the *feng* being *yang* and solar, the fire-bird, the *huang* as the *yin* and lunar. With the **Dragon** as the Emperor the phoenix represents the Empress and in this context becomes *yin* and represents beauty, delicacy and peace. It is also a bridal symbol of 'inseparable fellowship' for the couple personally but also for the *yin-yang* balance and harmony in the universe. Again, like the dragon and Ky-lin, it is a composite creature composed of different elements and symbolizing the entire cosmos, having the head of the solar cock, the back of the swallow as the lunar crescent, its wings as the wind, its tail representing trees and flowers and its feet the earth. It has the five colours of the five virtues. An ancient manual of rites said: 'Its colour delights the eye, its comb expresses righteousness, its tongue utters sincerity, its voice chants melody, its ear enjoys music, its heart conforms to regulations, its breast contains the treasures of literature and its spurs are powerful against transgressors.' Again like the Ky-lin its appearance was highly auspicious and heralded peace, good government and the coming of a great ruler or sage. A pair of phoenixes depicted the combination of Emperor and Sage.

The Ho-ho is the phoenix of Japanese myth. It appears on earth in different ages to accomplish a new era, after which it ascends to heaven until it comes again to establish the next cycle. It represents the sun, justice, fidelity and obedience. It is also associated with the Empress.

The Greek words for palm-tree and phoenix are the same, as the tree was said to die and rise again, and the bird and the tree can appear together. The Romans also used the phoenix to represent rebirth and also as the imperishable existence of the Empire. Tacitus says the phoenix is consecrated to the sun and is distinguished by its rich appearance and variegated colours, symbolizing those in Paradise enjoying eternal youth and pleasure. At a great age it makes a nest of rare spices which is ignited by the heat of the sun and the fanning of the bird's wings; from the ashes it rises again.

The Old Testament says: 'I shall die in my nest, and shall multiply my days like the phoenix' (Job 29: 18). Christianity adopted the bird as a symbol of resurrection, of Christ consumed in the fires of the passion and rising again on the third day, triumphant over death. In the Bestiaries the *Fenix* also carries the same significance. The *Physiologus* says that the phoenix is a native of India and Arabia and, when 500 years old, flies to Lebanon, fills its wings with fragrant gum, then hastens to Heliopolis in Egypt where it burns itself on the high altar of the temple of the sun. The priest comes next day to remove the ashes and finds a small worm of exceedingly sweet odour, which in three days develops into a young bird and on the fourth day attains full plumage, then, greeting the priest, it returns home. 'This symbolizes our Saviour who said "I have power to lay down my life and I have power to take it again." ' The perfume denotes 'the sweetness of divine grace diffused in the Old and New Testaments'. Coins of the early Christian emperors often bore the image of the phoenix as an ancient emblem of the solar cult; it also appeared on Roman cinerary urns and from this passed to the Christian tombs. Christianity maintained that the phoenix alone of all birds did not share in the sin of Eve when she ate the forbidden fruit.

The symbolism of the phoenix is used extensively in literature. In Heraldry the bird usually appears as a crest, depicted as a demi-eagle rising from the flames. It is also an Alchemical symbol of burning and regeneration, the *magnum opus*.

The Physiologus. The *Physiologus*, a Greek work of early Christian times (*c.* AD 140), was translated into every language. *Physiologus* was a term for the Naturalist, but over the years the phrase 'but the *Physiologus* says . . .', that is, the naturalist says . . . became, through ignorant copyists, a person called *Physiologus*, and thus is frequently referred to as such.

Based mainly on the Egyptian *Book of the Dead* and the Bible, there were many versions, the Latin version being responsible for the translation into European common languages which introduced it to the people in general, becoming common property and passing into general literature. It was constantly quoted by all mediaeval writers and used in ecclesiastical symbolism.

As E. P. Evans writes, in explaining the importance and influence of the *Physiologus* and the Bestiaries: 'Indeed, without such guidance it would be difficult for us at the present day to understand what the builders of a mediaeval church, or an embroiderer of sacerdotal vestments meant by adorning them with seemingly incongruous representations of lions, eagles, phoenixes, pelicans, ravens, doves, partridges, panthers, harts, foxes, hedgehogs, ferrets, ichneumons, lizards, serpents, tortoises, whales, elephants, ibises, crocodiles, unicorns, salamanders and other real or mythical animals, or to conjecture what conceivable relation they could bear to Christian theology or Christian worship.'

The symbolism now appears strained and the moralizing obscure and far-fetched, but the *Physiologus* and the Bestiaries were widely used in sermons, discourses and literature of the Middle Ages. In those times an illiterate population relied largely upon these art-symbols for their instruction in, and understanding of, the Church's teaching; they were, as St Bernard said, 'the books of the laity', and they provide a record of human thoughts and beliefs at a certain stage of civilization. Their strange information was accepted by most of the highly intelligent and learned Fathers of the Church as well as by the mainly illiterate lower orders of the priesthood recruited largely from the poorer members of society and the peasant classes. For this we have the famous criterion of Tertullian – *Credo quia absurdum*. Not everyone accepted these works, however: St Nilus said it was 'puerile to amuse the eyes of the faithful in this manner', and St Bernard reproved the clergy for letting 'wild cats and lions rank with the Saints' in the House of God. St Augustine said it was not for us to find out if the marvellous stories were true or false but rather to give heed to their spiritual significance, and Roger Bacon reiterated this in the Middle Ages.

In later editions each article in the *Physiologus* or the Bestiaries began with a quotation from Scripture followed by the formula – 'But the *Physiologus* says . . .', and then followed a description of the major traits, real or fancied, of some animal, capped by a moral deduction and the lesson to be learned from it. Thus, as said above, the whole collection became regarded as the work of one person, and various authors were suggested such as St Basil, Chrysostom, Isadore, or an Alexandrian Greek.

A great many errors arose as a result of poor translations made by semi-literate scribes with an imperfect knowledge of the language. Also travellers' tales were added to the reports of the naturalists.

Pig. See **Swine**

Pigeon. See **Dove**

Pike. In the Bestiaries the pike is called **Lupus** for its wolfish greed.

Ping-feng. A Chinese black pig with a human head at each end.

Poison. Various animals, or parts of them, were believed to be able to detect poisons in any food or drink. Chief among these were the alicorn, the unicorn's and rhinoceros' horns; snakes' tongues, the cerastes, the jewel in the toad's head, the griffin's, vulture's or raven's claw, wolves' tusks, and parrots.

Ponaturi. A horrible Maori sea-creature which fears sunshine and light and only comes ashore at night, at which time it is dangerous.

Porcupine. Aristotle and Pliny state that the porcupine shoots out its quills like arrows at its enemies, while Aelian adds that it can aim them to hit its pursuers. In Amerindian lore the porcupine represents the South region; it symbolizes innocence, faith and trust; it is gentle and non-aggressive unless attacked.

Poua-kai. A Maori fabulous eagle-type bird which preyed on the people of the plains; it kept constant watch on them from its eyrie but was finally killed by a band of warriors, or, in another version of the myth, by a red-headed man.

Ptarmigan. This bird is the Rai-Cho of Japan, a thunder-bird sacred to the God of Thunder. Among the Innuits (Eskimos) the autumn festival is a tug-of-war between the Ptarmigans (that is, those born in winter) and the **Ducks** (those born in summer); if the Ducks win it will be a good winter, but a hard one if the Ptarmigans are victorious.

Puk. A small four-footed dragon which in Baltic myth brings treasures to the household.

Puma. Largely associated or identified with the **Jaguar**, the puma is a power symbol. The Shaman or medicine-man can incarnate in the animal to contact the spirit world. There is a Puma Clan among the Sierra Nevada Indians.

Puppy. A puppy and a **Sheep** were sacrificed at the Roman festival of the Robigalia to protect the crops from the Spirit of Mildew.

In modern times a puppy symbolizes conceit.

Pyong. The Chinese **Roc**.

Q

Qiqlon. An Innuit (Eskimo) **Dog**, hairless except for its mouth, feet and the tip of its tail, it causes fits in men and dogs, but is easily frightened off by being named.

Quail. The quail mythology and symbolism covers a wide geographical range, from Ireland to China and Japan, Northern Europe to the Cape of Good Hope and Central America. Although a night bird it is also associated with the **Phoenix**, as fire, and represented spring and good luck in some parts and summer in others. It is generally regarded as extremely amorous in character, so its symbolism is often phallic and erotic. It can depict the courtesan in this context; it was also a lover's gift. The quail was, and is, a fighting bird and so for the Romans represented courage and victory in battle. In Roman times the birds were also kept as pets and playthings for children and the term 'quail' was one of endearment. A quail in a cage was a symbol of the soul imprisoned in the body and longing to escape.

There are various myths connected with the quail. Pliny says that like the **Crane** it posts sentries who stand on one foot with a stone in the other so that if it falls asleep the dropping of the stone wakes it; alternatively it fills its throat with sand for the same purpose. He also said that quails carry three stones each on migration in order to hear, by dropping them, whether they are over the sea. They landed on ships in such numbers, in this migration, that they sank them. It was believed that quails were immune from poisons and that they could eat the poisonous hemlock with impunity. Aristotle says: 'Henbane and hellebore are harmful to men but food for quails', and Lucretius asserts that these poisonous plants fatten quails and goats. The quail's brain was a specific for epilepsy.

In Greek legend the jealous Hero turned Leta into a quail. She was the mother of Apollo and Artemis in Delos, so the bird is also associated with them; it is also an emblem of Asteria, who was changed into a quail. It is connected with Hercules as the slayer of Typhon.

The Phoenicians sacrificed the quail to Melkarth after his defeat of Typhon, or Sephon, as darkness; it was a feature of the spring festival commemorating the resurrection of Hercules. It was also sacrificed to the Tyrian Baal. Eating it was forbidden. For the Hebrews it was a clean food and was a source of miraculous nourishment in the desert (Exodus 16: 11–12), but it was also the food of wrath and lust.

In Hinduism the quail is a solar emblem of the returning sun. The Asvins, as day and night, light and darkness, revive the quail, which has been swallowed by the **Wolf** of darkness, symbolizing the quail leaving in winter but returning in spring.

The quail appears in Russian myth as solar, with the **Hare** as lunar; they are the sun and moon found by the Dawn Maiden. In imperial times the bird was an emblem of the Tsars.

Chinese tradition associated the quail with the phoenix as a bird of fire. Shen Kua, of the 11th century AD, says: 'The Scarlet Bird of the Astronomers is a symbol based on the Quail.' The Taoist Ho-Kuan Tzu (4th century BC) says: 'The Phoenix is the bird of the "quail's heart", it is the essence of the principle *yang*.' It represents the element of fire and the season of summer. Shen Kua also says that the Red Quail 'alighting on a tree is as fire lighting on wood, wood being the Element of Spring and Fire of Summer'.

In Ainu lore the quail was made on earth and did not descend from heaven as did most birds. It is a maker of riches, being well-nourished and clothing itself. If killed it must be eaten by the killer.

The Bestiaries call the quail the **Coturnix**; it is 'the only animal which suffers from the falling sickness like man'.

The quail was one of the sacrificial animals of the Mayan gods. It is the totem of an Australian Aboriginal tribe. It can also be a witch's animal.

R

Rabbit. The rabbit and **Hare** are both essentially lunar animals, living in the moon and associated with Lunar Goddesses and Earth Mothers. The rabbit symbolizes fecundity and lust, but wearing rabbit skins in rites represents humility and docility. In Christian art the rabbit depicted at the feet of the Virgin Mary signifies victory over passions.

The rabbit is the archetypal **Trickster**; in West Africa he is an artful character who always outwits the treacherous hyena. He is the origin of Brer Rabbit, the myth which migrated with the African slaves to Jamaica and the United States as Brer Rabby, passing into New World legend. The Rabbit appears in Algonquin customs as a Hero and Trickster and is a favourite of the Woodland tribes as Trickster and one of the Fire Theft heroes, but it can symbolize fear; it attracts the things it fears and is a breaker of friendships.

There was an Aztec Man-rabbit. The Sun threw a rabbit at the face of the Moon, which darkened the moon so it is not as bright as the sun.

In China figures of white rabbits are a feature of the Moon Festival.

In English Heraldry the rabbit appears as the Coney.

See also **Hare**

Racoon. A **Trickster** figure of the North Amerindian Abnaki tribe. In Ainu myth the Raccoon and **Marten** were created to act as servants to the **Bears**: their black faces indicate that they are cooks. The racoon is also a deity, the Cook of the God of the Mountain. Both racoon and marten are offered in sacrifice.

Rainbow Serpent. See **Serpent**

Ram. The ram is a natural symbol for masculine virility and the generative force; it is solar, procreative power and is associated with Sky Gods. It is one of the chief sacrificial animals. Although the animal is solar its horns (forming a spiral) connect it with thunder and the moon deities. But solar gods such as the Phoenician Baal/Hamon are depicted with rams' horns on their heads; Rashap

The Soul of Osiris incarnate in a Ram

also has horns and his throne is supported by rams. The ram's head on a column personifies Ea-Oannes, Babylonian God of the Deeps and Destiny (said to have risen from the sea as part-man, part-fish); it also personifies the god-fish of the Zodiacal Capricorn, representing renewed solar power.

Amon-Ra, the Egyptian Sun God, is addressed as 'Ra . . . thou ram, mightiest of created things.' He is the creative heat, the renewal of energy and procreation. The ram-headed Khnemu, who later became Khnemu-Ra, was an ancient cosmic deity identified with other Niletic ram-headed gods; his horns are long and heavy, while those of Amon-Ra were curved. The Sacred Ram of Mendes embodied the souls of the gods Ra, Osiris, Khepera and Shu. At Thebes a ram was sacrificed to Amon and the death was bewailed; the image of the god was then clothed in its skin. At the Feast of Oppet his boat was adorned with rams' heads fore and aft.

In Greece the ram was sacred to Zeus/Sabazios as the ram god of fertility, it was also sacred to Dionysos as generator. Devotees of Attis were bathed in the blood of a ram and a ram carried Phrixus and Helle across the sea with the Golden Fleece. The Ram of Mendes was sacred to Pan. In Cyprus the ram was associated with Aphrodite. In Rome a ram was sacrificed to the domestic Lar in the rites of purification. The ram is frequently associated with the hearth.

The Hebrew ritual horn, the *shofar*, which is blown as festivals and special occasions, is made from a ram's horn. The ram represents the substitute sacrifice. The inner covering of the Tabernacle was of rams' skins dyed red (Exodus 26: 14). Christianity uses the ram that was substituted for Isaac to represent the sacrifice of Christ, and Christ is also the leader of the flock. In the Bestiaries it symbolizes spiritual leadership.

The ram is the chief of the sacrificial animals of Islam.

Sacred to the Vedic God of Fire, Agni, the ram represents the sacred fire in Hinduism. In Tibetan Buddhism the ram's head is the *dorje* (sacred mace of Tibet, the rod of the Dalai Lama) Lak-pa.

Contrary to its Egyptian and Indo-European symbolism the ram appears as chthonic in Celtic tradition. It accompanies Horned Gods but has both fertilizing and death associations; it is also an attribute of war gods. There are ram-headed serpents and geese, and rams with human heads. Supernatural rams and sheep are found in Celtic lore and later in the stories of Christian saints. Rams were connected with the sacred hearth, the entrance to the underworld, and among Celtic remains there were found near the hearth andirons of clay decorated with a ram's head. Fire-dogs were also made in ram effigy, rams were depicted on Gaulish tombs, and heads of rams appeared on monuments to Gallic gods of the underworld. The Great God of the Gauls was Belin, the ram, and his material and earthly manifestation was Bélisama, his consort, wife and sister. The ram was a Celtic and Gaulish sacrificial animal.

Ramora. In Latin the ramora was known as the *Delaya*, in Greek *Echeneis* (the Ship Holder). It was a little **Fish** which could keep a ship anchored in the strongest wind or fiercest storm. Pliny uses the strength of this little fish 'not above half a foot long' as an example of the vanity of man, who is helpless in the face of the power of a small creature. He also extols the great strength of the ramora, which decided the battle of Actium by clinging to Anthony's galley and preventing it from going into action. Aelian gives a similar account. A number of these fish also saved three hundred children from being murdered by Periander by halting his vessel.

The Ramona is sometimes called *Serra*, but the latter is usually a griffin-like, fire-breathing monster.

In the Bestiaries the ramora is called *Essinus* and is confused with the **Sea-urchin**. It is described as a fish of the Indian Ocean, about a foot long, which can keep a ship from moving by fastening on to the keel. This symbolizes Our Saviour, the sea being the world and the ship man, buffeted by the waves of temptation.

Rat. Associated largely with death, decay and the plague, the wider significance of the rat is ambivalent. In Hinduism it symbolizes prudence and foresight and is the most powerful of the demons. As such it is the steed of Ganesha, the elephant-headed

God of Wisdom, Prosperity and Successful endeavours, and is an object of veneration.

A white rat accompanies the Japanese God of Happiness and is an emblem of the God of Wealth, Daikoru, and is often depicted emerging from a bale of rice or wielding the Mallet. On the other hand, in China the rat represents meanness and timidity. It is one of the **Five Animals**. It is also the first of the animals of the Twelve Terrestrial Branches.

Rats were sacred to the Phrygians and in Egypt they were ambivalent: destructive but also symbolizing wisdom as they always choose the best.

The Ainu say that the rat was created by God to punish the Devil. In an argument God put his hand behind his back and produced a rat, which bit off the Devil's tongue. The Devil was so enraged that he caused rats to increase until they became a plague and God had to create cats.

The rat is an Australian Aboriginal totem animal and among moieties a Rat must marry an Emu.

There was an Irish belief that rats could be killed by reciting rhyming spells.

Sailors believed that rats deserted a doomed ship; this is also said of a house that is destined to fall.

Rattlesnake. The crested rattlesnake appears in Mexican figurines in conjunction with a priest or shaman wearing a Jaguar mask. It is the totem animal of a South Amerindian tribe.

Raven. As the raven is a talking bird it is connected with prophecy and hence wisdom, but as black and a carrion-feeder it represents darkness, destructiveness and evil and, with the wolf, it often appears with gods of the dead. It can be a solar symbol, as in Mithraism and in China, or it can depict death and the Devil as it does in the West.

There was a legend that there were never more than two ravens in Egypt, but the bird signified destruction and malevolence. It had the same symbolism for the Hebrews, who considered it unclean and for whom it typified the impure, mortification, destruction and deceit. It is the first bird specified in the Old Testament and, with the **Owl**, represented desolation. It was said to have been cursed by Noah at the Flood. On the other hand it was a protector of Prophets and showed God's providence by feeding Elijah. There were also Christian saints, such as Paul the Hermit, fed by ravens – the raven, signifying solitude, represented the hermit. St Cuthbert was helped by them and St Bernard's raven prevented him from eating a poisonous loaf, but ravens were also thought to incarnate the souls of wicked priests and the damned, or those denied Christian burial, and to be the familiars of witches.

It was said in the Bestiaries that ravens do not feed their broods properly until they show black and in the *Physiologus* it is stated that the young are hatched without feathers and remain so for a long time, during which their parents ignore them. They cry to God in distress and he sends manna from heaven; then, as the Psalmist says, 'He giveth food to the young ravens that cry.' After twelve days the feathers grow and the parents recognize and feed their young. 'So man, who lost resemblance to his Creator, when grown in grace into divine likeness is recognized by God and nurtured through the Church.' When feeding on carrion the raven first eats the eye, so 'confession and penance are the ravens which pull out the eyes of covetousness or sin.'

There are many legends, world-wide, which describe the raven as having been white originally. Ovid says it was formerly silver but grew black from its chattering tongue and its desire to be the first to bring evil news. As prophets, ravens foretold the deaths of Plato, Tiberius and Cicero among others, and they could also find lost property – this has been known as 'Ravens' knowledge'.

The beneficent aspect of the raven appears in Zoroastrianism, where it is a 'pure' bird since it removes pollution. This is carried over into Mithraism, where the first grade of initiation is the Raven, the servant of the sun. It is also solar in Greek myth as a messenger of the Sun God Helios/Apollo and as an attribute of Athene, Cronos and Aesculapius. It is also a symbol of fertility and as such is invoked at weddings, but in Orphic art the raven depicts death and appears with the pine cone and torch of life and light, representing death and rebirth.

In China the raven is again solar; the three-legged raven lives in the sun, representing the three phases of rising, noon and setting. It is one of the creatures of the Twelve Terrestrial Branches and symbolizes power. In Indian myth Brahma appeared as a raven in one of his incarnations.

The raven was an emblem of the Danes and Vikings and two ravens were the messengers of Odin/Woden. They sat on his shoulders, and one was called *Hugin*, 'thought' and the other *Munin*, 'memory'. They ranged over all the land reporting what they had seen. In both Norse and Celtic lore the raven is associated with deities of war and features as a helper and protector of warriors and heroes. It is an important Celtic figure but is ambivalent as helper on the one hand and connected with death and the Raven-Crow goddesses on the other; it can be ill-omened but also represents wisdom, intelligence and prophetic power. The Raven-Crow goddess, 'The Blessed Raven', had a three-fold function as war, procreator and prophecy. The raven is also associated with the **Wren** in prophecy and divination, appears with the **Swan** in solar symbolism, and is connected with the dove-cote as a house-symbol, this probably being pre-Celtic. The Raven of Battle, the Goddess Badb, symbolizes war, bloodshed, and malevolence. Morrigon as a raven goddess watched over battles. Bran has a raven, and Lugh or Lugos, who had two magic ravens, is an all-purpose and wise raven-god like the Teutonic/Scandinavian Woden/Odin. The Welsh hero Owein had an army of ravens which had magic powers and fought King Arthur's men. When all black the raven is malefic, with a white feather it becomes beneficent.

Of all the Amerindian Trickster-Heroes Raven is the most widely distributed; he is the archetypal Trickster but also appears as a creator and Raven Man. He is The Big Grandfather, the Outer One, he steals the sun and is one of the creatures which recreated the land after the Flood, a culture hero and demiurge who created night and day, also a shape-shifter. He is the subject of myth from Alaska and the Innuits (Eskimo) to the Plains, Woods and Pueblos Indians. He is also a messenger of the Great Spirit.

Among Palaeo-Siberians the raven is a creator deity who flew down from the heavens to create the world.

The raven appears frequently in Heraldry, said to have originated as a Danish device. No difference is made in depicting the Raven, Crow, Rook or Chough.

Redpoll. An Amerindian hero who brought fire to the people, having stolen it from a ferocious bear in the northern regions. Its colour commemorates this feat.

Reem. A huge wild **Ox** of which there are only two in the world, one living in the Far East, the other in the West. They meet to mate every seventy years, then they die after the female has given birth to male-female twins. They were too big to get into the Ark so Noah had them tied to the stern; they swam in the waters and so were saved from the Flood. The word *Re'em* is also used in the Old Testament for the **Unicorn**.

Reindeer. Tartars take the names of such animals as the reindeer and **elk** but do not necessarily make them a cult object. The spirit of a Shaman can take the form of a reindeer, or can mount on one and run on the earth (or can take the form of a bird to fly through the air). Palaeo-Siberian people have a Lord of Reindeer who watches over the herds. The Lapps made reindeer sacrifices to bring good luck to the herds. The lives of the Tsaatang nomads of Mongolia are totally bound up with the reindeer. In Labrador there was a belief in a Great Reindeer, Lord of them All. The reindeer was also sacred to the Scandinavian Great Mother Isa or Disa.

Rhinoceros. The rhinoceros as a symbol of power and sovereignty was often kept by Eastern potentates. Its horn, like that of the **Unicorn**, was said to detect poison. It also cured convulsions, smallpox, epilepsy, worms, vertigo, and stomach ache, and was a specific against fevers. In the Buddhist Sutta-Nipata the animal is used to depict the Sage's retirement and chastity.

The rhinoceros was known to the Greeks and Romans; it appeared in the Roman arenas and was portrayed in mosaics.

The animal was frequently confused with the unicorn and referred to in the same terms and Arabian sources often describe the one as the other, but the Romans, who knew the rhinoceros, believed the unicorn to be a different creature. In early Christianity the comparison between Christ and the rhinoceros 'Christus assimilatus rhinocerate' was due to this confusion with the unicorn. St Jerome and Tertullian, calling it the monoceros, or 'one-horned', held that the two were identical.

The horn, as well as thought to be capable of curing diseases and detecting poison, was (and still is in the Middle and Far East) regarded as a powerful aphrodisiac and cure for impotence.

Rinjin. A Japanese Dragon-king living in a palace under the sea.

Robin. Early mythology connected the robin with fire, a Promethean legend. It brought fire from the underworld and this associated it with death, so it is unlucky for it to enter a house; otherwise it can be a lucky bird. It is also a weather prophet.

In Christian tradition the robin got its red breast trying to take the nails out of the cross at the crucifixion. Another myth said it scorched its breast taking drops of water to souls in hell; it was thus a symbol of piety and also represents trust and confidence.

Soaked toast was offered to robins at Christmas wassailing ceremonies. There was a saying: 'The Robin and the Wren are God's cock and hen.'

In Scandinavia the robin is a form of the storm-cloud bird and sacred to Thor, the Fire and Thunder God.

The Amerindian Tlingit tribe have Robin as a culture-hero. **Raven** created Robin to give pleasure to the people with his song.

Roc or Rukh. A mythological bird of Arabia, the Roc was so huge it blotted out the sun and fed its young on elephants. It has the same characteristics as the Persian **Simurgh** and the Indian **Garuda**. It is a storm bird – the wind is the rush of its wings and lightning is its flight. According to tradition it never lands on earth except on Mount Qaf, the *axis mundi*. Its huge, luminous egg is the sun. It is the Rook in the game of chess.

Rompo. An African and Indian composite creature, it has a hare's head, man's ears, a long body and tail, badger's feet in front and bear's feet behind. It is a scavenger.

S

Sacrifice. Sacrifice is based on the belief that the deity, to whom the offering is made, wants, appreciates or is influenced by the sacrifice and therefore has much the same emotions and appetites as do the devotees; it unites the divinity and the people. Another form of sacrifice occurs when the victim acts as a medium between gods and people, taking petitions or messages, or, in the case of the **Scapegoat**, bearing and purging the sins of the people. The killer of the sacrifice can, in some cases, become unclean and therefore himself a scapegoat and rejected. Sacrifice often averts the wrath of a god.

There is also a magical aspect in sacrifice, in the energy released by contact with supernatural beings, and also in some cases the victim itself may have inherent magical qualities, or be a sacred animal which can impart magical powers. The magical power of blood is also an element of this ritual.

Sacrifice was practised not only to propitiate deities but also to ward off evil powers. The foundation stones of buildings, particularly those of a sacred nature, required blood sacrifice; in early times this was human, later animals were used. The sacrifice provided the 'genius' of the place, or, on the other hand, the existing genius or spirit of the place might itself need a sacrifice, just as some rivers are said to require a heart each year. The soul of the sacrifice passes into the place or object, becoming the soul of that place or object and acting as a guardian. A Hindu text says: 'The sacrifice is the chariot of the gods and the gods derive power from it.' The blood was believed to restore the vital force. In many agricultural communities it was believed that the life and blood of a sacrificial animal was necessary for the growth of the crops. Sacrifice could also be made to sacred places such as springs and wells.

Sacred sacrificial animals were often treated as kin and addressed as such, for example in the **Bear** Sacrifice of the Ainu, and it was believed that the sacrifice benefited and was acceptable to the victim since the ritual enabled the victim to return it to its ancestors where it is provided with a feast of good things; it also benefits in the next incarnation.

Spirits of the dead were often thought to require sacrifices, either to help them in the next world or, if they were feared, to ward them off.

On the higher level the symbolism of sacrifice is that of the birth, death and rebirth cycle – all of creation implying sacrifice.

Salamander. Generally depicted as a small wingless lizard, dragon, or dog-like lizard either surrounded by fire or breathing out fire, the salamander is 'ugly and venomous'. Aristotle writes: 'This creature, so the story goes, not only walks through fire but puts it out in doing so.' Pliny, Aelian and later Bacon all record this, but Pliny adds that it is the most venomous creature in the world and that it 'seeks the hottest fire to breed in, but quenches it with the extreme frigidity of its body'. It is born of a fire that has been burning for seven years. Aelian says salamanders haunt blacksmiths' forges but that the smiths take no notice unless the salamanders put the fire out, then the smiths kill them and the fire burns again.

The *Physiologus* says that the salamander extinguishes the fire, but with the later development of the Bestiaries the idea evolved that it lives continually in the fire. The *Physiologus* represents the creature as 'the righteous man who is not consumed by the fire of luxury and lust, but extinguishes them. As Isaiah says of the righteous, "When thou walkest through fire thou shalt not be burned." Shadrach, Mesach and Abednego were examples in the Fiery Furnace.' The Bestiaries say it is the most poisonous and strongest of all creatures, its venom even penetrates trees and makes their fruit poisonous and it infects wells and drinking water.

The salamander appears frequently in literature, representing the element of Fire with the **Eagle** as Air, the **Lion** as Earth and the **Dolphin** as Water. It is Fire personified. It was thought to be sexless, so signifies chastity.

In Heraldry the salamander signifies generous courage that cannot be destroyed by the fire of affliction.

Salmon. Believed to be one of the oldest creatures in the world, the salmon was particularly sacred to the Celts and was a form for **Metempsychosis** and associated with the sacred wells. It was consulted for its wisdom and foreknowledge. In Celtic lore eating the salmon of wisdom conferred supreme knowledge, as in the case of Finn. The five salmon in the well into which the hazel nuts dropped from the sacred hazels, with five sweet streams flowing from the well, symbolize the five senses which give knowledge. The salmon is an attribute of the god Nodons. It takes the place of the **Serpent** of other traditions in being the means of contact with otherworld powers and wisdom.

In Scandinavian myth the evil Loki took the form of a salmon when escaping from the wrath of Thor, but was caught and chained to a rock where he remains until Ragnarok, Doomsday.

For the North Amerindians the salmon is a spirit being and is sacred. It is a lunar symbol of death and rebirth and is also a guardian spirit. The First Salmon Festival rites are an important occasion. When the salmon is killed and prepared ceremoniously it is addressed as a chief of high rank.

The Ainu call the salmon 'The Great Thing', or the 'Chief Food'.

Papal Ass (*from the Cathedral of Como*). The Ass's head represents servitude, the elephant's trunk elephantiasis, the eagle's claw rapacity and the ox's hoof suppression

Satire. Animals are frequently used in literature and art to satirize human failings and foibles, particularly in Europe in the Middle Ages, though earlier the comedies of Aristophanes and the fables of Aesop are two of the best-known examples of animal-human satire. In other parts of the world the Trickster-Hero of African and Amerindian tribes showed the same characteristics of burlesque and mockery.

In Europe, as E. P. Evans says, animals which were taken from the *Physiologus* and the Bestiaries were originally employed as symbols of natural or divine wonders or to illustrate moral teaching and theological dogma, but as the Papacy and clergy became corrupt and the vices of the mendicant friars a bye-word, the same animal symbols were used to satirize and caricature them in such forms as the Papal Ass, or *Papstesel*. Asses were taken braying into churches, wolves represented the clergy's ravening and preying on the people, wily foxes – employing every cunning trick, hogs and goats – taking their stench, all were portrayed and used in satirical festivals or processions and in art. Foxes were depicted in cowls, apes acted as acolytes, a horse appeared as a sexton and an ass held a rosary in its mouth. Nor was this mockery confined to being used by the people: the dignitaries of the Church did not hesitate to use satire, caricaturing both themselves and their office. One bishop had an ape decked in episcopal robes used on his official seal and another an ape with a cowl and crosier.

Centaurs were used in early Christian art to depict the lower passions and impulses, but were employed later to satirize the degenerate clergy, monks and nuns.

The scepticism prevalent at the Renaissance robbed many ancient devils and monsters of their horror and they were satirized in comical and grotesque forms, making them a source of laughter rather than fear.

Satyr and Sileni. Satyrs were of a semi-animal form, having human heads, with horns and a goat's beard, human hands and arms but goats' bodies from the waist downwards. They are followers of nature gods such as Silvanus, Pan, Faunus and Dionysos/Bacchus, and represent male spirits of a lustful, untamed and profane nature. Their attributes are the ivy-crown and thyrsos of Dionysos, also bunches of grapes, baskets of fruit, pitchers of wine, the cornucopia and the snake. Their female counterparts were the Maenads.

In the Old Testament satyrs are a symbol of desolation and destruction (Isaiah 13: 21).

The Sileni were similar except that they had horses' rather than goats' bodies. Nonnus said that 'the shaggy satyrs are by blood of centaur stock.' Aelian said that there were certain sea-monsters resembling satyrs.

Satyr-fish. A winged heraldic monster, having a satyr's head, a fish body and wings.

Scapegoat. The use of a scapegoat to bear the sins of the entire community is a universal custom, appearing from the rites of ancient Babylon to those of modern-day Japan. The name is derived from the Hebrew ceremonies of the Day of Atonement (Yom Kippur), when a goat was used to carry away the sins of the people into the wilderness, thus freeing them from the consequences. The scapegoat is delegated guilt and escape from the consequences of sin.

Almost anything could be employed as a scapegoat, but it was more usually a human, animal or bird. The Greek *Pharmaicos* was a criminal or some 'ignoble or useless person', but animals and birds were more often used at festivals involving scapegoat ceremonies. In addition to the transference of sins there were rites for transmitting illness to a bird, which then flew away with the disease, or, as in the Old Testament, a leper could be cured by 'the blood of the guilt offering' (Leviticus 14: 27). In Christianity the scapegoat is used as symbolic of Christ suffering for and bearing the sins of the world.

Scarab or Scarabaeus. The Scarab, or Dung Beetle, rolling its dung-ball across the earth was used as a solar symbol. Symbolic of the path of the sun, it also represented self-creative power (life emerging from the dung) and was associated with Khepera, God of Creation and Immortality – the Sun God rising daily. Scarabs were believed to be all males; they were one of the most common Egyptian amulets and were buried with the dead to help restore the heart in the next world, being associated with vitality and new life. These beetles appear about the beginning of the wet season and were therefore connected with the rising of the Nile and the fertility brought by the river. The beetles disappear when the rains are over.

Scarabs were found on the seals of Palestinian Jews BC.

In the African Congo the beetle becomes lunar but is still a symbol of eternal renewal.

Scorpion. A natural symbol of death and destruction and, as living underground, of darkness; it also represents envy and hatred.

In Sumeria scorpions or scorpion-men were guardians of the Gateway of the Sun, the Mountains of the East and the Twin Gates; they were associated with Ishtar or Nina and with the Phrygian Sabazius.

For the ancient Egyptians the scorpion was an incarnation of evil. The child Horus was stung by one (the god Set took the form of a scorpion for this attempt at murder), but Isis prayed to Ra who sent Thoth to cure the young god. As a desert animal the scorpion was associated with Set. There was a scorpion goddess Selket or Selquet who is portrayed wearing a scorpion on her head, or as a scorpion with a woman's head; she is a protector of the dead. Seven scorpions accompanied Isis on her search for Osiris. A dead crocodile could turn into a scorpion.

Zoroastrianism relegates the scorpion to the realm of Ahriman as evil. It is permitted to kill it.

Mithraism has the Dadophori, the twins with upward- and downward-pointing torches, as the Bull and the Scorpion, representing life and death, the rising and setting sun.

In the Old Testament the scorpion signifies the wilderness, drought, desolation, danger and torment, a dreadful scourge (I Kings 12: 11).

Pliny says that the scorpion provides the remedy to its own sting;

a roasted and powdered scorpion drunk in wine is the only cure.

Orion was killed by a huge scorpion, sent to prevent him from killing all the animals, as he had boasted he could.

Buddhist teaching says that as the scorpion erects the sting in its tail, so devotees should wield the sword of knowledge.

It was said that to be stung by a scorpion and survive was to be immune from hornet, wasp and bee stings.

Sea-Buddhist Priest. The Chinese Sea Monk Hai Ho Shang is dangerous and aggressive and can capsize junks; it can be warded off by burning feathers. It has the shaven head of a monk and a large fish body.

See also **Bishop Fish**

Heraldic Sea-dog

Sea-dog. An heraldic animal depicted as a talbot but with scales, webbed feet and a beaver's tail. It is at enmity with the **Sea-hare**.

Sea-eagle. The white-tailed Sea-eagle is the emblem of the Orkney Islands; it is also a Melanesian totem bird. A Melanesian clan may, however, kill or eat the eagle, but not the pigeon, with which it is associated, for the latter was once a living man.

Sea-griffin. The heraldic Gryphos-marine, the fore part being an eagle, but sometimes depicted without wings, and the lower part a fish.

Sea-hare. The Sea-hare is a mollusc the colour of a hare and having a hare-like head with fins behind its ears, a fish body and hare's feet. It is said to be venomous and was used as a poison by the ancients. Nero and Domitian were reputed to have used its poison on their enemies. It is bold in the sea but timid on land. It is the enemy of the **Sea-dog**.

Heraldic Sea-horse

Sea-horse. The steed of Poseidon/Neptune, drawing his chariot. It has the head and neck of a horse and tail of a fish, or sometimes legs with webbed paws; a fin can be depicted on the back of its neck. Used in Heraldry it generally symbolizes some laudable action at sea, or it can occur in the arms of a seaport to suggest the overseas commerce of that port, for example as depicted in the arms of the city of Belfast.

Sea-lion. A mythical creature frequently used in Heraldry, emblematic of bold action on the high seas. It has the upper part of a lion and the tail of a fish. It is depicted with the Menorah on the Arch of Titus.

The Ainu venerate the sea-lion and it is given divine honours.

Sea-scolopendra. An annelid worm, also called the **Centipede**. Aristotle says that when caught on a hook the worm turns itself inside out until the hook is ejected, then resumes its correct shape. Aelian says it is the greatest of all marine creatures and that it swims with its many legs. It has long bristles projecting from its nostrils. Oppian says it stings like the sea-nettle (anemone) and that no fish will go near it.

Sea-serpent. Reported world-wide as a huge snake-like form in the seas, sometimes it is said to have a crest. It slides through the waters or lies on the surface and can attack ships and whales.

Sea-stag. The sea-stag has the body of a stag ending in a fish-tail. It appears frequently in German Heraldry.

Sea-urchin. Called **Echinns** in the Bestiaries, the sea-urchin is said to foretell the coming of a storm by taking on a stone as an anchor. It is a poor, blind creature and a symbol of God caring for the weakest. Celtic tradition calls it the 'serpent's egg'; it represents the seed, latent force, life.

Seal. Pliny says that there was a belief that the seal was the only animal never struck by lightning and that 'no living creature sleepeth more soundly.' The Romans believed that seal-skins protected against thunder storms.

In European myth and fairy tale seals, like swan maidens, can change into humans as Selchies and can mate with humans. The seal is one of the animal ancestors. If the skin of the seal is stolen while it is in human form the seal cannot return to the sea. In the Faroes there is a legend that seals cast their skins every ninth night, appearing and dancing on land as mortals until dawn.

The Innuits (Eskimos) have a Bearded Seal Festival in the autumn with a ritual killing and propitiatory rites in which the bladders of all seals caught must be returned to the sea. These rites are the last of the festival, which requires a month's preparation.

Sefert. A fabulous Egyptian creature with the head of a hawk and the body of a lion and wings, he was keeper of the parts of the body of Osiris.

Seps. A tiny snake which Lucan says destroys bones and bodies with its poison – hence the word 'septic'.

Serpent. There is no cult more universal or ambivalent than that of the serpent and few creatures have been regarded with more awe, reverence and fear than the snake with its strange sinuous movement, the rapidity with which it can strike a death-dealing blow, either through strength or venom, its underground dwelling which puts it in touch with the powers of the underworld and its ability to cast its skin with apparent renewal of life. Associated with graves it was frequently accepted as a form of the dead returned to the upperworld.

The Aztec double serpent, Huitzilopochtli

The symbolism of the serpent is polyvalent: it can be male, female or self-created; it is solar and lunar, life and death, good and evil, healing and poison. It embodies all potentialities, both material and physical; it is masculine and phallic 'the husband of all women' but accompanies the Great Mother deities as intuitional wisdom, the secret and the enigmatic. It is a mediator between the three worlds, the sky in that it resembles solar rays and lightning, the earth and the primordial waters, from which all creation emerges, and the underworld, in which it lives. It is often depicted as encircling the world – the Ouroboros. As Joseph Campbell says: 'Serpents seem to incarnate the elementary mystery of life wherever apparent opposites are conjoined.'

The serpent and the **Dragon** are often interchangeable, while in China and Japan the dragon largely takes the place of the serpent and has the same significance. In Sumero-Semitic myth the Serpent of Darkness, the 'footless' Tiamat is depicted as a dragon and represents chaos, the undifferentiated, guile and evil and is overcome by the Sun God Marduk. Lakhmu and Lakhamu are serpents of the sea and give birth to the male and female principles of heaven and earth. Ishtar the Great Mother Goddess and Nidaba the Corn Goddess are accompanied by serpents or have them springing from their shoulders; this is also seen with the Dying God Son. The snake is a form of the Canaanite Bel and the serpent set on a pole was a symbol of healing in Canaan and Philistia. The Phrygian Sabazius has a serpent as his chief attribute and it appears on his votive hand; in worship his priestess held a golden snake which she dropped through her robes from her bosom to represent 'God through the bosom'.

As elsewhere, the serpent is ambivalent in Egypt. There are many references to serpents in the sacred books and in myths, but most of them are accepted as different aspects of the monster-serpent Apop, Apep or Apopis, symbolic of all that is evil; he is Set in his typhonic aspect, the demon of darkness, of thunderstorms, lightning and whirlwinds, who tried to prevent the sun from rising by obstructing the barque of the Sun God Ra. Apop is depicted in company with a demon in crocodile form whose tail ends in the shape of a serpent's head. In other cases the serpent is wisdom and a power for good. There was a huge speckled serpent Kheti, known as the Spitting Serpent, with seven undulations; through its open mouth it belches fire at the faces of the enemies of Ra. There are also twelve small serpents who pour fire out of their bodies to light Ra on his way and the serpents depicted at the side of the sun disc represent the goddesses who, as royal serpents, drove out the enemies of Ra. The royal serpent is the *uraeus*, the cobra, worn on the head of Ra to represent the supreme divine, royal power and wisdom. The snake goddess Buto also takes the form of a cobra. A lion-headed serpent protects against evil. The asp was also venerated.

In Mithraism the snake is beneficent; with the dog it is portrayed lapping up the life-blood of the sacrificial Bull and it is also depicted as travelling beside the God's horse to protect him. In Zoroastrianism it is again evil and a symbol of Ahriman, 'the Fiendish Snake', the antagonist of all moral order, depicted as the tyrant king Azhi Dahaka who has serpents springing from his shoulders.

Pet snakes were kept and encouraged in Greek, Roman and Cretan households. They were associated with the deities of healing and fertility and with the Mystery Cult Saviour divinities, they also represented the beneficent spirits of the dead or were incarnations of the dead. The serpent is prominent in medicine, being an attribute of Asclepios, son of Apollo and God of Medicine. He took the form of a serpent when he appeared in Rome during the plague. Hippocrates was also so represented when he delivered Athens from the plague. Hermes and Hygeia, daughter of Asclepios, are also associated with the serpent of healing, which was portrayed by the **Caduceus**. But the serpent typifies darkness in connection with Apollo, for he slew the Python which came from the mud of the deluge of Deucalion; Apollo at Delphi is light overcoming darkness. As associated with the underworld of Pluto serpents are coiled on the chariot wheels of Persephone and Hermes/Mercury's caduceus has underworld connections in his aspect as a psychopomp. The vital principle, the soul, was said to leave the body in the form of a snake. Zeus, Father of the Gods and Men, has the serpent as a phallic symbol and it appears with him in his many different aspects as Zeus/Ammon, Zeus/Chthonios and Zeus/Meilichios; in these aspects he could appear in snake form.

The serpent symbol was paramount in agricultural societies, denoting the fertility of the earth, and as it sheds its skin, the renewal of life. Triptolemus, fabled to have taught the people agriculture, is represented with a winged car drawn by serpents. The serpent was sacred to Athene as wisdom and a caged serpent was the Guardian Spirit of her temple at Athens. Women with hair of serpents, such as Medusa, Graia and the Erinyes, typify the powers of enchantment and magic connected with the wisdom and guile of the serpent.

In the same way Rome associated the serpent with saviour deities, healing and fertility, Hygeia being identified with Salus and Minerva as Athene and wisdom. Snakes were kept or encouraged in the household as the protective spirits, the Lares. The Cretan Mother Goddess, also a protector of the household, holds snakes in both hands, and on coins she is shown as caressing a snake. The serpent could be an ancestor or incarnation of the dead and was often depicted on burial places as symbolizing resurrection and immortality.

Numerous myths are recorded by the ancient writers. Plutarch says the serpent is a symbol of the deity, as it feeds on its own body, and as all springs from God, so all will be returned to God. Aristotle and Herodotus write of flying serpents. Ovid and Pliny record the ancient belief that snakes were born from the spinal marrow of a human corpse, but Aelian adds that they generate only from the bodies of bad men. It was believed that the snake injected venom with its tongue, though another view was that it struck with its tail. Pliny and others maintain that the reptile is dim-sighted. Snakes have certain antipathies – they will not go near an oil tree, avoid trefoil and clover and dislike box wood for its hardness and cypress for its bitterness. Striking a serpent with a reed will kill it. Eating snakes causes rejuvenation.

For the Hebrew the snake was an unclean food and its symbolism is generally evil; it represents the souls of the damned in Sheol. But the brazen serpent of Moses is homoeopathic, 'like heals like', and was also his magic rod. The serpent is frequently mentioned in the Old Testament, first as the Tempter at the Fall, then as an object of general dread, danger, subtlety and deceit, also as a symbol of the sharp-tongued and those deaf to the truth, as it was believed the adder was totally deaf. The serpent was cursed by god 'above every beast of the field' and was put at enmity with mankind. Leviathan is a serpent of the deep and lightning is the 'crooked serpent'.

The snake was an important Celtic cult creature, appearing with deities. The ram-headed serpent is the most frequent attribute of the Horned God, Cernunnos, as incarnating virility and fertility. The serpent again appears as an emblem of the Great Mother, the Celtic Bride, who had a festival at which the Snake Goddess was worshipped. She was later adopted by Christianity as St Bridgit.

In Norse mythology the serpent Nidhogg, the Dread Biter, lives at the foot of the Cosmic Tree, the Yggdrasil, continually gnawing at it and representing the evil powers of the universe. The Midgard serpent envelops the world with the endless coils of the abyss of the oceans. At Ragnarok, or Doomsday, the malevolent serpent Midhgardh floods the world with its venom but dies in the flood it causes.

The Vile (singular *Vila*) of the Serbs were shape-shifters and could transform themselves into serpents or swans.

Christian symbolism is ambivalent where the serpent is concerned: it can represent Christ as wisdom and, as raised on the Cross (the Tree of Life) it is Christ's sacrifice for the healing and salvation of the world. The serpent at the foot of the Cross, however, is evil, it is the Tempter, the agent of the Fall, the Devil; it is overcome by the Cross. The serpent is often depicted entwining the Cross or a tree, if with the Tree of Life it represents wisdom and is beneficent, with the Tree of Knowledge it is Lucifer and malefic. Dante equates the serpent with the damned, but Tertullian says that Christians called Christ 'The Good Serpent'. The Virgin Mary is portrayed crushing the head of the serpent, in marked contrast to Eve's yielding to it.

The *Physiologus* says that the serpent has four characteristics:

1. Growing old it fasts forty days, goes into a crevice and casts its skin to renew its youth. So must man put off the old Adam and pass through the strait gate.
2. Going to drink it leaves its venom in its hole; so he who would refresh his soul at the waters of life must leave behind all carnal sins.
3. The serpent fears a naked man and flees from him, but will attack him if clothed. When Adam was naked in the Garden the serpent could do him no harm; so if we put off the vanities of the world the serpent can do us no harm and we need not fear the assaults of the wily serpent, the Devil.
4. When one seeks to kill a serpent it exposes its whole body in order to save its head; so must the Christian endure every trial and affliction for the sake of Christ, the head. The serpent also stops its ears to the music of the charmer; so must we close our ears to Satanic suggestions.

Nature – the cosmic power, the shakti, the non-manifest – is symbolized by the serpent in Hinduism. As the cosmic ocean

Vishnu sleeps on the coiled serpent of the primordial waters, the unpolarized state before creation; his two serpents, or nagas – whose bodies intertwine – depict the fertilization of the waters; from their union rises the Earth Goddess. The dark serpent, the potentiality of fire, is a manifestation of the Vedic Fire God Agni. It is lightning, the divine spear and warlike power. As Kaliya, the serpent king slain by Krishna, the serpent is evil and Krishna is often portrayed dancing on its head or with it underfoot. Bala-Rama, brother of Krishna, was an incarnation of the serpent Sasha, chief of the nagas. Ananta, the thousand-headed ruler of the serpents, represents the 'endless', infinite fertility; Vritra, the imprisoner of the waters, is the underworld darkness which swallows the waters and causes drought; while Ahi, 'the throttler', is a three-headed snake slain by Indra, who releases the waters again with his thunderbolt. Two serpents moving upward and downward symbolize the Sleep and Awakening of the cyclic nights and days of Brahma (see also **Naga**).

Nagas also appear in Buddhism. The Buddha changed himself into one to heal the people at a time of disease and famine. He tamed the nagas and became their king and thus a controller of the rain and waters. Nagas were present at his birth and he is depicted as seated on or protected by them. But the snake in Buddhism can represent anger; it appears at the centre of the Round of Existence with the pig as greed and the cock as carnal passion; the three representing the sins which bind humanity to the world of illusion.

The **Dragon** largely takes the place of the snake in China, but when the two are distinguished the snake becomes malevolent, destructive, deceitful and cunning; it is a symbol of sycophancy and is one of the five poisonous creatures. In *yin-yang* representation the brother and sister Fo-hi and Niu-kua can be portrayed as two intertwined snakes with human heads; they have affinities with caduceus symbolism. She-Wang, the King of Serpents, is depicted in various forms but mostly as a snake. The Snake is the sixth of the animals of the Twelve Terrestrial Branches.

In Japan Susanoo, God of Thunder and Storms, is personified by a serpent. For the Ainu of Japan the first serpent came down with such force that it made a hole in the ground, but this hole led to the underworld and the original snake now has its abode there as King of the Serpents. Snakes are feared; having established themselves on earth they dislike mankind and do it harm. A phallic symbolism is shown in that the snake came down from heaven accompanied by the Goddess of Fire, with whom he was in love; it is considered dangerous for a woman to have a snake cross her path, as it will possess her.

In Polynesia the serpent can be a world creator and in some parts it is said to live underground and will ultimately become the destroyer of the world. It is also usually associated with pregnancy. For the Australian Aboriginal the snake is the masculine principle and lightning; again it is connected with pregnancy. The Rainbow Serpent, also called the Celestial Serpent, is of great importance in the myths. It is the Water Spirit who gave the people the first water by urinating, otherwise all would have died of drought and thirst. She also showed them how to dig for food and how to breathe; she shapes babies inside their mothers. Also the Old Woman came from the sea in the form of a serpent and gave birth to the Ancestors. The Rainbow Serpent is a creator, a sky hero, associated with the Dream Journey and Dream Time ceremonies. It varies in different parts of Australia, being either bi-sexual, masculine or the Old Woman. The name Ungad is sometimes used. In Maori lore the serpent represents earthly wisdom, it is a swamp worker connected with irrigation and growth. Cambodia was founded by the marriage of a prince to a serpent and snakes feature prominently at Ankor.

The Plumed or Feathered Serpent, attribute of Quetzalcoatl, Aztec and Toltec God of wisdom, fertility and the wind, was a combination of the Quetzal bird and the snake and represents the sun, the spirit, the power of ascension and the elements. It also accompanies all rain and wind gods and is an intermediary between gods and men; it is unending time and is also phallic and solar. It is the White God from whose black bowels the rain falls; but it becomes lunar when the serpent depicts the Earth Mother, the Snake Woman, Coatlicue. She wears a skirt of woven snakes and was the mother of the War God, Huitzilopochtli, who is portrayed as encircled by snakes and as having a great drum of serpent skins and a sceptre of snakes. The Feathered Serpent also signifies the Evening Star which dies but is born again as the Morning Star. The snake can be a mythical ancestor or culture hero. The Serpent God can be depicted as held in the grip of a bird of prey; from the serpent's blood humanity was born, symbolizing the dismemberment of original unity and the coming of multiplicity in the world. The serpent grasping its own tail is the 'great century', the cyclic.

In North Amerindian tradition snakes are ambivalent: they can be both intermediaries between men and gods, also harbingers of death and symbols of eternity. They are associated with thunder and lightning and are rain-bearers. The horned serpent lives in the sky and is at enmity with the **Thunderbird**; it is also a water spirit, the fertilizing power of the waters. Among the Creek Indians it is invoked in hunting and unites the hunter and the hunted. The serpent with horns is also the Great Manitou which transfixes the evil Toad or Dark Manitou. There is also a Celestial Snake, with a head but no body, which lives on dew; it combines the powers of nature. The Horned and Feathered Serpent of the South-west Tribes is a powerful water deity, controlling floods and earthquakes. The double-headed serpent of the Kwakiutl has the same significance but also controls all liquids, such as blood and tears. For the South-east Woodlands the Rattle Snake is the head of the vermin category of animals. The Hopi associate the serpent with the moon, as it sheds its shadow to be reborn. The Snake Dance shows affinities with the Hindu Kundalini, having a serpent energy coiled in the lower pelvic region. It is roused by the marriage of the Serpent Maiden to the Antelope Youth. The snake is the power of the waters and the generative organs.

Many African tribes regard the snake as immortal and some have sacred serpents, especially the python, which must not be killed; they can also be associated with the living dead. In an African myth the snake stole the skins which God had provided for the people, so the snake can renew its life by shedding its old skin, whereas man dies. This accounts for the enmity between Man and Snake. In Zulu lore the snake can be an ancestor returned to the family and should be addressed as such; it is also believed that souls of the dead can enter serpents. Many tribes of East Africa revere the snake as either an ancestor or as a soul-animal. It is of good omen.

In Heraldry the snake is most frequently represented *nowed* – that is, in a knot – sometimes erect, and occasionally gliding or *glissant*. Alternatively it can be depicted as the Ouroboros, with its tail in its mouth. As associated with medicine it occurs frequently in grants and arms made to physicians, usually appearing as a rod of Aesculapius.

See also **Basilisk**

Serra. According to the Bestiaries the Serra is a winged creature which tries to out-fly ships but gets bored with being out of the water and so dives back. It symbolizes 'people who start off trying to devote themselves to good works but afterwards get vanquished by nasty habits, and, undependable as the to-fro waves of the sea, they dive down to Hell.'

Shark. Revered in Polynesia, the shark represents the Milky Way as the 'Long-blue-cloud-eater', and is one of the creatures embodying sacred beings and powers, as are the **Octopus**, **Lizard** or **Turtle**, all of which can be regarded as individual incarnations of important people such as chiefs. In the Solomon Islands the shark is sacred and addressed as 'grandfather'. Hawaii's shark gods were worshipped and were believed to be ancestral spirits appearing in shark form. Sharks could also be sorcerers' familiars, helping them in time of need. The gods could change into either human or shark form.

The shark is also held sacred in some West African cults. If accidentally killed rites of propitiation must be performed for three days; the flesh may not be eaten before this rite of atonement.

In Greece shark flesh was a forbidden food at the women's festival
of the Haloa.

Bones or hair cast into the sea can become sharks serving the
Ocean Spirit.

In the West a shark following a ship foretells a death.

Shearwater. The restless habits and dark plumage of this bird
make it evil for Moslems, who say it incarnates the souls of the
damned.

Sheep. Generally symbolizing silliness, timidity, helplessness and
unintelligent conformity, the sheep needs a shepherd to lead it; it
also signifies placidity.

Sheep were sacrificed to many deities; held sacred at Hieropolis
they were sacrificed by pilgrims who, having eaten the flesh, clothed
themselves in the skins. The Egyptian Ament, female counterpart
of Amon, was sometimes represented as sheep-headed; she is also
equated with Mut. The Greeks and Romans sacrificed sheep to
Zeus/Jupiter, Hera/Juno, Mars, Silvanus, Terminus, Aphrodite (in
Cyprus) and others and sheep appear frequently in Roman and
Roman-Christian art, with Christ as the Good Shepherd. The Good
Shepherd is itself an ancient tradition and symbol, appearing also
in Sumerian, Persian, Orphic, Pythagorean, Hebrew and Tibetan
lore. Christianity symbolizes the sheep as the saved and **Goats** as
the damned.

The sheep is evil for Hindus, but holy for Muslims, while for the
Hebrews it is one of the most important animals, the greatest source
of wealth in the days of the patriarchs and the most valued
possessions. Kept for their flesh, milk and wool – clothing being
almost exclusively made from wool – the fat was also highly valued.
Job possessed 7,000 sheep originally and 14,000 after his recovery.
The sheep was pre-eminently the animal of the sacrifice of the **Lamb**,
as it denoted purity and innocence. No other animal was acceptable
for the Passover. It is the first named animal in the Old Testament
(Genesis 4: 2).

Chinese shepherds worshipped the God of Sheep, Huang Ch'u-
Ping, who could grant them large flocks. The sheep symbolizes the
retired life and is the eighth of the animals of the Twelve Terrestrial
Branches; it is a lucky animal.

In Madagascar sheep incarnate the souls of ancestors and such
families may not eat them. Among West African cults the eyelashes
of sheep, combined with lizards, are used to concoct 'evil medicine'.

Blade bones of sheep are used in divination.

Sheldrake or Brahminy Duck. Also called the Ruddy Sheldrake,
this bird is a Buddhist emblem of devotion and fidelity, depicted on
Asoka's pillars as a tutelary deity in Tibet.

Shrew. The shrew is sacred in ancient Egypt but unlucky in Europe, where it has a bad reputation as causing paralysis and putrefaction if it runs over a limb and is credited with a poisonous bite. Anything it runs over becomes unlucky. It causes cramp in people, horses, cows and sheep. Topsell says: 'It is a ravenous beast feighning itself gentle and tame, but being touched biteth dogs and poysoneth deadly. It beareth a cruel minde desining to hurt anything, neither is there any creature that it loveth.'

Simurgh. Also called Samurv, Semmurv and later Simurg or Sinmru. A Persian fabulous creature, half-bird, half-mammal (it suckles its young) 'like a bat'. It symbolizes the union of heaven and earth and lives in the land of the sacred Haoma plant, whose seeds cure all evil. The Simurgh is a beneficent creature. Similar birds, the Simargal, Sima and Sinam, occur in Russian and Caucasian lore. It is prophetic and has magic powers and its feathers have healing qualities. It is the bird of the Persian Tree of Life, where all seeds were gathered – it scattered these seeds when it alighted. One tradition said it combined the peacock, gryphon, lion and dog and that it lived 1,700 years and then, like the **Phoenix**, immolated itself. It has certain qualities of the Indian **Garuda** and some affinities with the **Roc**. It is at enmity with all snakes.

Siren. In Greek art sirens are depicted as birds with the heads of maidens. There are three types: half-woman, half-bird; half-woman, half-fish and half-woman, half-ass, the first being the most

Crowned Siren

usual. Bird sirens in Egypt were souls separated from the body, but in Greek mythology they represented temptation, feminine seduction and blandishments, distracting man from his true goal. The Ulysses legend was used by Christians to represent the ship of the Church keeping the faithful safe from the temptations of the world; the mast was the cross to which they must cling.

Sometimes the siren in its fish aspect is confused with the **Mermaid**. A siren can be depicted with a fish in one hand to represent a soul caught in the grip of passions.

Sirrush or Mushrush. A Babylonian serpent-like composite creature depicted with Ishtar. It has a scaly skin, snake's head and tongue, cat's forefeet and bird's claws for hind feet.

Skaffin. An Icelandic **Basilisk** which can kill with a glance.

Skins. Skins of sacrificial animals are probably the oldest form of ritual clothing. Wearing skins of animals, as in Shamanistic rites, identifies the wearer with the powers and energies of the creature; they are more than a disguise, they help the shamen achieve an actual metamorphosis, a transformation, conferring qualities such as strength, swiftness, flight, cunning or courage. This is a recurrent theme in myth and fairy tale, as in stories where the animal can shed its skin and become human, and someone getting hold of its original skin prevents the animal or bird (usually a seal or swan) resuming its previous shape.

Skins of animals killed ritually were worn by priests and shamans or were placed on images – these were often those of sacred or totem creatures. Sabazius wore the skin of a fawn, Dionysos that of a leopard, the priests of Atargatis wore the fish head and skin and shamans have feathered robes. Pilgrims sacrificed sheep at Hieropolis and after eating the flesh they wore the skins.

The skin can represent the fat of an animal, which is especially important since it is the animal's life-sustaining produce.

Wearing the skin of an animal sacred to some deity puts the wearer in touch with that divinity.

In Roman times, on the other hand, leather, as the skin of a dead animal and therefore in touch with death, was unlucky and avoided, especially by women and children. Only the skins of sacrificed animals could be used.

See also **Sacrifice**

Skunk. In Northern Amerindian myth the skunk represents self-esteem, respect and reputation, as it has the ability to attract or repel at will. It is used as a symbol in the rites of the Snakes and Two Horn Hopi clans as 'a carrier of hot embers', signifying the sun sending out hot rays.

In Europe 'skunk' is a term for a contemptible person and it also symbolizes complete defeat.

Skylark. A solar bird as it ascends to the heavens and is associated with the dawn. In Ainu myth the skylark was sent down from heaven with a message and told to return the same day, but he liked the earth so much that he stayed to play, spending a night on earth and returning to heaven next day, but God was annoyed and told him he could not be admitted but should live on earth and that though he would soar heavenwards he would always return to earth; thus he tries each summer to get up to heaven to argue with God, but must return to earth where he plays 'sky larks'.

Sloth. A symbol of laziness and slow movement.

The sloth is a totem animal among South American Indians and is venerated and has significance in ritual dances.

Slug. Laziness, slow movement. 'Slug' was an old English term for complete lethargy and inertia.

Snail. As it emerges from a shell, the snail symbolizes birth, or it can be taken as dawn issuing from the cavern of darkness. It has lunar associations in many countries and can be a symbol of parturition. It is usually regarded as lucky and can be used in divination; if placed on a slate it will inscribe the name of a woman's future husband. It was believed to wear itself away as it moved leaving its slimy track; this is suggested in Psalms 58: 8.

Hesiod says that it indicates the time of the harvest; when it climbs stalks it is time to stop digging in the vineyards and to sharpen the sickles.

Snails appear on Mayan stelae and the Mexican Moon god, Tecciztecatl, is portrayed as enclosed in a snail's shell. The appearing and disappearing characteristics of the snail are lunar qualities and thus symbolize rebirth; as such it is depicted on the head of Aztec gods. There is a Snail Clan among Zuni Indians.

Snake. See **Serpent**

Snipe. A totem of the Snipe Clan of the Seneca Iroquois tribe. The Ainu say that the snipe was sent down from heaven as a bringer of good health; he is a sort of physician and heals headaches and ears while his feet cure deafness.

Snowshoe Hare. See **Hare**

Sparrow. A strong erotic symbolism is attached to the sparrow; this caused it to be used as an aphrodisiac. It represents wantonness, lust and fecundity. In Greece it was an attribute of Aphrodite and was identified with Lesbia.

In the Old Testament the sparrow is used as a symbol of loneliness – 'alone upon the house top' (Psalms 102: 7) – but it is suggested that this refers to the Blue Rock **Thrush**, as sparrows are not lonely, but flock. There are frequent references to sparrows in the Old Testament, but these references probably denote all small passerines. In the New Testament the sparrow depicts the humble and worthless, as in the quotation 'two sparrows sold for a farthing' (Matthew 10: 29). Christianity depicts the sparrow as lowliness and insignificance, but also as lewdness and lechery.

Sphinx or Sphynx.   There are both male and female sphinxes. The Egyptian sphinx is male, while the Babylonian sphinx, representing Astarte, is female, as is the Greek form. Sphinxes with the bodies of lions and human heads were carved on Hittite rocks under Egyptian influence; one was depicted with a double-eagle carved on its side.

The Egyptian sphinx symbolized royalty, wisdom, physical power and the pharaohs; it also signified the enigmatic. It was associated with Osiris, Amon, Neph (the Greek god Jupiter) and Phreh (Helios) and was depicted as a man-sphinx, ram-sphinx or hawk-sphinx according to the deity worshipped. It has been suggested that the sphinx symbolized the Nile floods when the sun was in Leo and Virgo, but the Egyptian sphinx was always male. It is also suggested as symbolizing theological mystery, appearing as it does in association with temples.

The female sphinx can be a combination of virgin, lion, dog, bird and serpent. The Greek version had the head and bust of a woman and had wings, unlike the Egyptian sphinx. The Greek sphinx was a monster sent by Hera/Juno to devastate Thebes; it put the 'riddle of the sphinx' to passers-by. Oedipus answered it and so rid the country of the monster.

Both male and female sphinxes appear in the Mayan ruins of Yucatan.

Spider.   For all its weakness the spider is one of the most powerful creatures in myth and symbolism. It depicts the Great Mother in her terrible aspect as weaver of fate. She is often shown as a huge spider and called the Great Spider, the Cosmic Spider, or the Great Weaver and is the attribute of all lunar goddesses. She is also a creator who spins the thread of life from her own body and attaches all men to herself by the umbilical cord, binding them and weaving them into the web of the world. At the core of her web she is the Cosmic Centre and the rays of her web can be solar (the rays of the sun), lunar or the life-and-death cycle and the web of time.

In Egypt the spider was an emblem of Neith as weaver of the world, in Babylon of Ishtar and Atargatis, and in Greece as an attribute of Athene in her aspect as world-weaver. For the Moirai she represented the Fates, spinners of destiny. The same symbolism also occurs in Norse mythology, with Holda and the Norns as Fates.

The symbolism of the spider is world-wide. In Hinduism and

Buddhism it is the weaver of the web of illusion, *maya*, and is also a creator, weaving the thread of life from its own substance. Buddhism adds that as the spider catches flies in its web, so must the devotee capture and destroy the lust of the senses.

In Japan the Spider Woman can lure and ensnare unwary travellers and there is also a Goblin Spider who is a shape-shifter, changing form in order to harm people. The Tsuchi-Gumo was a huge spider which caused trouble; steel could not kill it, but it was eventually trapped in a cave and asphyxiated with smoke.

The Old Spider is an Oceanic Creator Goddess of the South People; she made the earth and sky when she opened the giant clam with the help of two snails and a worm. Her son, the Young Spider, created fire. The Andanamese *Biliku* (the north-west monsoon) can be represented as a spider: temperamental, unreliable and perilous but at the same time beneficent. The Australian Aboriginal Great Spider is a mythical Sky Hero.

Among the Ashanti, in Africa, the Great Spider is God, the Wise One. The spider is also an African **Trickster** and this myth travelled with the slave trade to Jamaica and the spider became Anansi, the Great Spider of Jamaican folklore, taking with it the legends of his feats against tigers and lions, which do not exist in the Caribbean; he takes on gods, humans and animals and even sometimes outwits the gods.

In Amerindian myth Spider wove the first alphabet, after weaving the stream of the manifest world, and symbolizes the power of creation. The eight legs are the four directions and the four winds of change. Spider is a feminine creative power and also weaves the web of Fate. Spider Woman, Kokyangwuti, was herself created to bring life to the earth; she generated the original twins from the earth and then created all plant life and animals, giving them all names, after which she created humans. There is a Trickster Spider, Inktomi, of the Plains Indians, who is also a shape-shifter; he brought culture to the people. The south-west tribes have a Spider Grandmother as a cosmic creator. For the Hopi the spider represents the 'medicine' power of the earth; it can be a demiurge. Elsewhere myth has it that Old Spider escaped the Flood and helped to found the human race. Spider was a member, with **Hare** and **Otter**, of the Council of Animals, which enabled the people to Recover the Light.

The spider is generally regarded as lucky, a money-spinner and it is unlucky to kill one; but it can also symbolize wiliness. In early times it was believed to be poisonous. Pliny says that powdered spider skins are an antidote to snake bite. It was also said to feed on herbs and to suck out poison. Swallowing a spider in butter cured jaundice and wearing a spider in a nutshell cured fever.

In the Old Testament the flimsy and perishable nature of the spider's web symbolizes the destruction of the designs of the wicked or the hypocrite in spite of all cunning. Christianity equates the spider with the Devil's ensnaring of sinners. It also represents the miser bleeding the poor.

Springbok. In Bushman myth springbok were changed into humans by **Mantis**. In totemistic rites there are springbok dances; dancing and miming being a usual preliminary to hunting.

Squirrel.   The Irish goddess Medb has the squirrel and bird as her emblems. In Norse mythology the 'Ratatosk' is a bringer of rain, water and snow. The squirrel, which lives in the branches of the Yggdrasil, the Scandinavian Tree of Life, represents spitefulness and mischief-making and creates strife between the **Eagle** and the **Serpent**. Christianity attributes avarice and greed to the squirrel. In Buddhism it is a symbol of warding off spiritual attack, as it uses its tail as a cudgel to fend off assault, so the devotee should ward off carnal thoughts and spiritual foes with the staff of meditation.

The squirrel was a sacrifice to Mayan gods. Among the Indians of the Amazonian forests it is a fire animal and is one of the manifestations of Desana, Master of Animals. Southern Amerindian women, planting crops of groundnuts, must not eat the flesh of the squirrel or howler monkey as this would cause the crops to dry up and take on a burnt-sun colour. The Tunguses Indian reckoned the coming of winter from the catching of the first good squirrel, the coming of summer by the spawning of the **Grayling**. In general the squirrel depicted gathering, planning, saving and being prepared.

In Ainu lore, squirrels came from the sandals of the god Aioina, who shed worn out sandals which, being in contact with the divine, could not rot and so turned into squirrels. The animal can be a form of dangerous witches who like to cast spells on people and it is perilous to pass under a branch with a squirrel on it.

Stag. The stag is pre-eminently a solar symbol, at war with the chthonic serpent. The stag trampling on the **Serpent**, like the eagle with the snake in its talons, depicts the conflicting opposites, positive and negative, the final triumph of good over evil, of light against darkness and the spirit over matter. The stag often appears with the Tree of Life and is a sacred animal from early times, appearing in the Black Sea and Anatolian area and on Hittite monuments. It was sacred to the Hittite God of the Countryside and was important as the mount of the masculine protective gods. The god of animals stands on a stag and small figures of the animal were found in tombs. In Sumero-Semitic rites an image of the fertility god was sometimes dressed as a stag for sacrifice.

Pausanias writes of a procession in Greece in which a virgin priestess of Artemis rides in a chariot drawn by stags, which were an attribute of Artemis/Diana. Dionysos/Bacchus also has a stag-drawn chariot. Actaeon was turned into a stag by Artemis.

The stag is an important cult animal in Europe, especially in Celtic tradition where it is associated with the Horned god Cernunnos, Nurturer of Animals, with the Hunter God Cocidius and with Ossian. It is the attribute of the warrior and is virility, solar power and fertility; it is also therapeutic. In mythology stag hunts often lead to some supernatural meeting or situation. In solar cults it is often depicted with the **Bull**, **Horse** and **Swan**. In Norse tradition the four stags of the Yggdrasil represent the four winds.

In its war against the serpent the stag was said to draw the snake out of its hole with its nostrils. Pliny and Aelian state this, but the *Physiologus* says it swallows the snake. Christianity employs this enmity as representative of Christ or the Christian fighting against evil. The stag also represents piety, the soul thirsting after God, solitude and purity (Psalms 42: 1). The stag with a crucifix between its horns is an emblem of St Hubert.

Shou-Hsien, the Chinese God of Immortality, is represented as a white stag and the **Dragon** is called the Celestial Stag, as it is also called in Japan.

The stag is frequently used in Heraldry in every variety, as buck reindeer, antelope, roebuck, etc. It often appears as a crest.

See also **Wild Hunt**

Starling. Depicts pilfering. In Greek it is 'the farmer's curse'. In Ainu myth it was made on earth rather than in heaven as were most birds; it originally polluted a river by bathing in it while dirty, so may not now drink river-water but only rain-water.

Stork. There are various myths associated with the stork and its migrations; the most usual being that the old birds were fed by their grateful young, who also kept them warm and even supported them when tired in flight. Aristotle said this was a common story, and Pliny and Aelian corroborate it, though Pliny adds that when they gather to migrate on a set day the last to arrive is torn to pieces, after which the others leave. There was also a widespread belief that migrating birds could appear as humans in other lands and this applied particularly to storks and swans. Like the **Crane**, the stork was said to post sentries who stood with a stone in one claw so that if they fell asleep on duty the stone dropped and woke them. The idea of babies being 'brought by the stork' is an association between the bird and the creative waters of life, the womb of Mother Earth – the bird finding the embryonic life while it fishes.

The Egyptians used the belief in the storks' care for their elderly as a symbol of filial piety and the bird was also revered by them as a law-maker. In Greece, a law compelling children to care for their aged parents took its name from the stork. In the Greek Mysteries the stork goddess represented archetypal woman, the nourisher, the bringer of life. The bird was an attribute of Hera in Greece and of Juno in Rome, where it also depicted filial devotion, loyalty and piety and was a bird of good augury.

According to Aristotle the Thessalonians worshipped the stork because it rid them of the snakes which were so prolific that they threatened the existence of the people on the land.

The stork is an unclean bird for the Jews, as it was believed to be carnivorous; but for the Arabs it is the Prophet's or Marabout bird. Christianity uses it as a symbol of purity, piety and vigilance; as a harbinger of spring and new life, it is representative of Christ and his Annunciation. The Bestiaries say that it symbolizes brotherly love, comradeship and duty.

As a destroyer of reptiles the stork is associated with the **Eagle** and **Ibis** and is solar, but as a bird of the waters it is the creative feminine.

Heraldry makes little distinction between the stork, crane and **Heron**, except that the heron has a tuft on its head. The stork is often depicted with a snake in its beak.

Stormy Petrel.   Also known as Mother Carey's Chicken; the bird is said by sailors to embody the souls of dead mariners and is therefore sacrosanct, but it is also ill-omened, as it foretells bad weather.

Swallow.   Swallow mythology goes back to the Babylonian Deluge, when myth tells us that the swallow was sent out with the **Dove** and **Raven** and returned with the dove. It was an emblem form of Nina the Great Mother and the *Pyramid Text* says swallows are 'the imperishable northern stars' and depicts them flying above the Tree of Life.

In the Greek legend of Procne and Philomela the swallow is associated with the **Nightingale**. Procne was transformed into a swallow to escape from Tereus. In Greece the bird was sacred to Aphrodite, in Rome it was sacred to Venus. Ancient Greece seems to be the only place in which the swallow was deemed unlucky (because it appeared before the defeat of Pyrrhus and Anthony). It was regarded as lucky in Rome, and killing a swallow was unlucky as there was a belief that the spirits of dead children lived in swallows in order to visit their homes again.

Chinese symbolism sees the swallow as a bird of daring, unafraid of danger; it also represents coming success and fidelity, with two swallows symbolizing conjugal fidelity and happiness. On the contrary, in Japan the bird can signify unfaithfulness, but it is also domesticity and maternal care. Swallows are depicted with waves and willow trees in Japanese art.

The Old Testament calls the swallow a 'chatterer': 'like a swallow so did I chatter' (Isaiah 38: 14). In Christianity it typifies resurrection, new life returning in spring. The swallow is a holy bird for Moslems as it makes an annual pilgrimage to Mecca and makes its nest in mosques and holy buildings.

The Bestiaries call the bird the *Hirundo* and say: 'It is exalted by an uncommonly devout state of mind, builds wisely and is unique in its noble attention to duty.' It is also used to represent hope descending from heaven into the heart of the Christian. It was also reputed to be able to restore the sight of its young if they went blind. The *Physiologus* says that the swallow sleeps all winter and awakens to new life in spring, as it is written 'Awake thou that sleepest and arise from the dead and Christ shall give thee Light.'

In Sweden, the swallow was associated with the crucifixion; it was said to have cooled Christ with its wings and to have cried *Svala* – consolation (and hence its name, *Svalow*). It heralds sowing time.

Early beliefs were that the swallow, like the **Swift**, hibernated under water or in clefts and caves. It was said to have two stones inside, one red, which could affect an instant cure, the other black, which brought good fortune.

Coming in spring the bird is a natural symbol of hope, new life and good fortune, while the hope symbolism is stressed in that, descending from the sky, it took the form of an anchor. The ancient belief that the swallow had no feet is depicted in Heraldry, where its legs end in feathers. It is portrayed as the **Martlet**, Merlette or Merlot and typifies younger sons as they have no lands.

Swan. The myth of the beautiful dying song of the swan appears frequently in Greek and Latin literature and was believed by Socrates, Pluto, Ovid and many others, though Pliny expresses doubt about it. This myth gave rise to the swan's symbolism as bird of the muses. Socrates said that the swan's dying song was one of joy at the prospect of going to its divinity, whose messenger it is. The swan was also dedicated to Apollo as it came from the hyperboreal regions and as a lover of music it was associated with the Omphalos at Delphi; one legend said the soul of Apollo passed into a swan. Poets were also likened to swans for their sweet songs. Pindar and Virgil were examples of this, Zeno was called the 'learned swan' and Shakespeare the 'Swan of Avon'.

The swan also has amorous associations and is an emblem of Aphrodite/Venus and the form taken by Zeus to seduce Leda. Venus' chariot is sometimes drawn through the air by swans.

The swan and the **Goose** are often symbolically interchangeable, this being especially so in Hinduism. The Hamsa, which can be depicted by either bird, is 'that pair of birds who are Ham and Sa, dwelling in the mind of the Great'. They are often carved on temples and depict the perfect union towards which the celestial beings fly.

They also represent breath and spirit, inbreathing and outbreathing. Brahma rides on a swan, goose or peacock and has the swan or goose as his attribute as it is the divine bird which laid the Cosmic **Egg** on the waters, the golden egg from which he sprang. The Supreme Swan, the Paramahamsa, is the Self, the universal ground. The swan is also a mount of the goddess Sarasvati, wife of Brahma and goddess of wisdom, music and learning; she was an earlier Vedic river deity.

Celtic swan divinities are solar, benificent and sacred. They are prominent in Celtic symbolism and have magic powers of music, also the therapeutic powers of the sun and the waters; they also represent love and purity. Swans can be shape-shifters and can assume human form, a theme which appears frequently in myth and fairy tale; they can be recognized by having gold and silver chains round their necks. As a creature of the three elements – earth, air and water – the swan can command all three. This shape-shifting also appears in Scandinavian lore as an emblem and form of the Valkyrie and in Serbian tradition as the Vile (singular *Vila*), the nymphs of the wood who could change into swans or snakes. There was a widespread belief that migrating birds could take human form, but if the bird's skin could be stolen the bird could not resume its original form. There are endless swan-knights and swan-maidens in European mythology.

In Amerindian tradition the swan represents trust, a state of grace and surrender to the will of the Great Spirit. The Navajos have a great white swan which conjures up the winds from the four quarters.

The Black Swan of Australia represents the two sister-wives of the All Father of the Lake Victoria region.

The Ainu's swan was created in heaven and kept there as an angel until the time when the Ainu became degraded and wicked and tried to kill each other until only one child was left. The swan descended to earth, changed into a woman, saved and reared the boy and married him to re-establish the race.

The swan brings good luck to sailors, and was used as a figurehead, as it does not plunge itself below the waves.

The stellar Swan, Cygnus, lives in the Milky Way, the River of Heaven.

In Heraldry the swan is a favourite charge and is also used as a crest, usually found 'close', but on a crest 'rising'.

Swift. Swifts have a sinister reputation and are known as 'devil birds', Skeer, devils or devilings and birds of Satan, which are sometimes called lost souls. It was believed in earlier times that swifts and **Swallows** hibernated under water or in clefts and caves. Swifts are a natural symbol of speed and rapidity. The Arabs call them the 'chatterers'. For the Ainu all migratory birds have their home in heaven and return there every autumn.

Swine. Swine were found universally except in Australia and New Zealand. They have a varied symbolism, representing extreme fertility and hence prosperity but also the height of greed, gluttony, lust, obstinacy, passion and the unclean. As fertility the sow is associated with the Great Mother goddesses and so has lunar connections. The pig is an unclean animal in many traditions and can be the home of evil souls, but it is also important in agriculture and was frequently a sacrificial animal. In Rome swine were sacrificed to Mars in his aspect of God of Agriculture and also to Ceres and Tellus at harvest festivals, in Greece swine were sacrificed to Demeter as a fertility goddess. Romans also sacrificed swine when making treaties and alliances. Pigs were sacrificed at the Eleusinia, and at the Thesmophoria pigs which had been thrown into chasms at the summer festival were recovered, placed on altars, then spread on the fields as fertilizers; to complete the fertility aspect phallic symbols were thrown into the chasm, the chasm representing Persephone's descent into the underworld. The sow was sacred to the Dictean Zeus, who was suckled by a sow. As a sacrificial animal the pig was the cheapest of all and within the purse of poorer people. Swine's blood was used as a purifier.

While sacred to Isis as a Great Mother in Egypt, the pig was also the typhonic aspect of Set when, in the form of a black pig, he became the ruler of the land of damned souls. He swallowed the left Eye of Horus, symbolizing the waning of the moon (the right eye being the sun), so that 'the pig is an abomination to Horus'. The pig was unclean for Egyptians and Phoenicians. It was taboo for food, but its symbolism varied between the evil and the sacred.

It is the most unclean of all animals for the Hebrews and the parable of the Prodigal Son being sent to feed the swine represented the acme of degradation for the Jew; any contact with the animal ritually defiles. The same applies in Islam. Christianity equates the pig with Satan and uses it to signify gluttony and sensuality.

Swine played an important part in the life of the Celts. Its flesh was regarded as food for the gods at otherworld feasts. The pig was the attribute of Manannan, whose pigs provided supernatural food since when they were killed and eaten they returned daily to supply more. The Celtic sow goddess Keridwen, the 'Old White One', is a Great Mother and Phaea, the 'Shining One', represents the moon and fertility. Maccus was a swine-god and the worship of the pig was widespread. Some tribes abstained from swine flesh and it was not eaten by the Galatian Celts and little eaten in the Highlands of Scotland, although it was eaten in Ireland. The boar was ceremoniously hunted and killed by the Celts and was of great

Osiris seated in judgement. The swine or pig in the boat represents Set. (*From a sarcophagus in the Louvre*)

importance in Scandinavia (see also **Boar**). The black sow is death, cold and evil.

For the Chinese the pig signified untamed nature, naturally greedy and dirty but useful and fertilizing when tamed. Chu Pa-chieh, the Pig Fairy, was banished to earth and reborn by mistake as half-man, half-pig. A gross character who was later reformed and became a Buddhist monk, he accompanied T'ang Seng on his journey to India, recounted in the Chinese classic *Monkey*, and was rewarded by being taken to the Western Paradise to become head Altar-washer. In Buddhism the pig at the centre of the Round of Existence represents ignorance and greed and is one of the three senseless creatures (with the **Snake** and the **Cock**). In Tibetan Buddhism the Diamond or Adamantine Sow is Vajnavrahi, Great Mother and Queen of Heaven. In Buddhist teaching as the pig cools itself in a pond in hot weather, so the devotee should cool evil passions and use the cooling exercise of compassion.

The pig is important in Oceania. In Hawaii the Hog-child features as a shape-shifter and is mated to the volcanic Fire Goddess. Pigs, with humans, were the chief sacrifices. In Melanesia the Tusked Boar was the most sacred and important object in the men's secret societies; the Spirit of the boar passing into the sacrifice and protecting him in death, it is also closely associated with the labyrinthine journey to the after-world. The tusks are particularly prized and venerated; they have a lunar significance. The ritual boar hunt is prominent in Oceanic myth and legend.

The pig is a lunar and thunder animal among the Amerindians and is a rain-bearer.

There is an heraldic Wonderful Pig of the Ocean, a sea-pig with horns that have eyes, or with an eye in its belly. It has a fish tail, dragon's feet and a quarter moon behind its head.

Swordfish. There is a swordfish divinity among the Ainu. The swordfish, together with whales, sea-lions and sea-tortoises, must have divine honours paid to it.

T

Tadpole. The Creek Amerindians have a ritual dance in which four men and four women, known as Tadpoles, perform at the New Fire Festival.

Takujui. A Japanese composite creature, similar to a **Bull** but with a man's head and with horns on its back; it has three eyes on each flank. Like the Chinese **Ky-lin** it was auspicious and appeared to virtuous mortals.

Taniwha. A Maori monster of the deep, said to be a man-eater but also to have rescued people from shipwrecks or escorted canoes to safety. The type of monster varied, they were either of whale, shark, reptile or crocodile form and embodied the faces of sickness and death. They could inhabit the sea, fresh water, or even the air and could be ill- or well-disposed towards humans.

Tanuki. The Japanese **Badger** or wind-badger Tanuki promotes the growth of the rice crops.

Tapir. The totem animal of a South American Indian tribe; it can be the animal from which the tribe descended, or the medicine man can incarnate in the form of a tapir. The Mayas associated the animal with the Rain and Thunder God Chac, who is depicted with a truncated nose and tusks.

Tarantula. The belief that this **Spider's** bite caused a form of hysterical madness was prevalent in Southern Europe, but music played to make the victim dance until exhausted effected a cure through intense perspiration.

Tench. This **Fish** is immune from all diseases and can cure other fish, or humans, by rubbing them with its slime.

Tengu. A Japanese monster demon man-bird. It is a trouble-maker, a lover of war and conflict and is particularly anti-Buddhist, resenting the homage to the Buddha which it feels should be given to it. The Tengu haunts woodlands, mountains and valleys and can possess people. A lapsed priest becomes a Tengu. It has a long red nose, enormous, glaring eyes, bird claws and feathered wings.

Three-legged Animals. Animals or birds depicted with three legs can be solar, depicting the rising, noon and setting sun, or lunar, the three phases of the moon. Another symbolism is that of having power on the earth, in the air or in the sea.

Thrush. The thrush is mentioned with the **Blackbird** in Greek literature, and Homer is said to have received a present of one for reciting a poem. The bird was said to build its nest on a sprig of myrtle or to place myrtle leaves in the nest as a charm. Pliny writes of a talking thrush.
  See also **Ouzel**

Thunder Animal. The Japanese Raju, called the Thunder Animal, is more closely associated with lightning than thunder. It can take the form of a weasel, badger or monkey. During fine weather it is tame and gentle, but before or during a storm it is savage and unmanageable, it leaps from tree to tree and has dangerous claws and it likes navels, so it is wise to lie on one's stomach during a storm.

Amerindian Thunderbird

Thunderbird. A mythological creature of the Amerindian spirit world, the Great Spirit; a wind and cloud spirit and an association between thunder and birds, it is usually depicted as eagle-like and appears all over North Amerindian culture. Pacific Indians portray it as a huge bird having a lake on its back from which the rains come. It can eat whales.
  The thunderbird of Japan resembles a rook. It has fleshy spurs which when struck together produce a horrible sound; it flies about during storms and feeds on the tree frog. It is connected with the great destructive powers in nature – lightning and thunder – and is also a guardian of the approaches to the Sky-heaven, home of the Earthmaker who confers the power to become incarnated.

The thunderbird is often equated with the whirlwind and has a counterpart in the Siberian Giant Eagle, whose flashing eyes make lightning and flapping wings thunder. There is also a Sky Bird of the North Asian tribes which has many of the properties of the thunderbird.

Tiamat. Depicted as a **Dragon**, Tiamat represented the primaeval ocean, chaos and darkness. She and her counterpart Apsu were responsible for the birth of the gods of the world. In a war between Apsu and Ea Tiamat sent her hoard of monsters, which included eleven dragons, against Marduk, God of Light. She was defeated by Marduk and from her severed body the heavens and earth were created.

Tien Kou. The Chinese Celestial Dog.
 See **Dog**

Tiger. In the East the Tiger takes the place of the **Lion** as the King of Beasts; it represents royalty, fearlessness, ferocity and wrath – Tigers of Wrath'. It is always a power symbol. In India it is an emblem of the Kshatriyas, the royal warrior caste, and there is a legend of descent from tigers among the Rajputs. Siva and Durga, as destroyers, are associated with the tiger. Durga rides a tiger and Siva wears a tiger skin when depicted in his destructive aspect. The Tiger-god Kalachakra can represent Padha-Sambhava when he appears in his fierce demon-destroying guise. It is appropriate to use a tiger or deer skin to sit on during yogic meditation.

The tiger is of great importance in Chinese myth and symbolism as King of the Beasts and Lord of the Land Animals. In this *yang* aspect it takes the place of the lion as authority, courage, prowess, military might and the ferocity necessary for protection. It was originally one of the **Four Auspicious Creatures** but was later replaced by the **Ky-lin**. The tiger is frequently depicted with wings to indicate its supernatural nature. It is the third of the animals of the Twelve Terrestrial Branches, the mark of military officers of the Fourth Class and the personification of war. The God of Wealth rides a tiger as guardian of the money chests and in this aspect the tiger is an emblem of gamblers. Chang Tao-ling, the first Pope of popular Taoism, rides a tiger as authority. But the symbolism of the tiger is ambivalent, for when it is in conflict with the Celestial Dragon it becomes *yin* as representing the earth and the two together denote the opposing forces of spirit and matter. In its *yin* aspect the tiger is lunar and chthonic, as it is able to see in the dark, and depicts the growing power of the new moon, a symbolism which is sometimes portrayed as a child escaping from the tiger's jaws; the child is 'the ancestor of the people', humanity, while the tiger is the power of darkness from which the new moon, light, escapes. As *yin* the White Tiger represents the West, autumn and the element of metal and is guardian of the graves, frightening away evil spirits; it must always be depicted with its head to the South and its tail to the North. The Blue Tiger is plant life, the East and spring; the Red tiger is fire, the South and summer; the Black Tiger is water, the North and winter; the Yellow Tiger is the centre, the Sun, the Ruler. The Goddess of Wind rides a tiger and the animal represents Orion in Chinese astrology. For an ordinary person to 'ride a tiger' is to encounter and confront dangerous elemental forces. In any context the tiger is power and energy.

In Malaysia the tiger must not be mentioned in case it responds to its name; it is 'hairy face', 'the striped one', 'grandfather' or 'lord'. There is a particularly dangerous were-tiger and the soul of a wizard can enter the body of a tiger. In Sumatra were-tigers are powerful but friendly and the souls of the dead can incarnate in tigers. As a were-animal the tiger is associated with shamans, as is the jaguar of South America. Java has friendly were-tigers.

Although mythical In Japan the tiger is credited with a fabulous age of a thousand years. It is used to symbolize courage and the qualities of warrior heroes.

In Buddhism the tiger is one of the Three Senseless Creatures, depicting anger while the **Monkey** represents greed and the **Deer** love-sickness.

Greek iconography sometimes substitutes the **Leopard** for the tiger in drawings of the chariot of Dionysos in his Indian triumph, or he can be shown riding a tiger; the skin on which the new-born Dionysos was placed by Hermes/Mercury is variously referred to as that of a tiger, leopard or fawn.

Heraldry has two kinds of tiger, the heraldic Tigre and the ordinary Royal or Bengal Tiger; the former being the only one used in heraldry until recent date in Europe. The animal, being unknown in Europe, was therefore stylized. It has a body similar to that of a wolf but with more powerful, massive jaws and canine tusks and has a short curved horn at the end of its nose. There are tufts of hair on the back of its neck and its tail is that of a lion. It symbolizes fierceness, strength, cruelty and destructiveness; it is often indistinguishable from the leopard, panther or ounce.

Tigre. See **Tiger**

Tit. In the mythology of the Ainu of Japan these birds were made on earth, not in heaven. God made them for his amusement to talk to, as he was lonely on earth.

Titans. The twelve children of Gaea and Uranus were personifications of violence in nature; they were in conflict with the Olympian deities and were sometimes portrayed as half-human, half-serpent. In Buddhism they are depicted as supermen who suffer from the failings of ambition and warlikeness, which ultimately cause their destruction.

Toad.   As an animal of the humid principle and one that appears and disappears, the toad is lunar in its symbolism but also represents resurrection. It can also depict evil, the loathsome and death. In the West it was assumed to be venomous, spitting out poison. Pliny and Aelian maintain this, but Aristotle does not mention it. Like the serpent, the toad carried a 'precious jewel' in its head, the Borax stone, which had the power of detecting and acting as an antidote to its poison. The toad represents the dark side of nature in Alchemy; it is the lower, but fertile, dregs of earthly matter.

In Zoroastrianism the toad belongs to Ahriman, the power of evil, and is greed, envy and avarice, but it is also fertility. Christianity maintains the same symbolism when the toad is the Devil and enters into those possessed by him. It is also a witches' familiar and an ingredient of a witch's brew and is used in magic. In Celtic symbolism it can take the place of the serpent as evil power.

The toad is one of the emblems of the Greek Sabazios.

The lunar symbolism of the toad is prominent in Chinese myth, where it represents the *yin* principle, also longevity, wealth and money-making, also the unattainable. It is an attribute of the Taoist Hon Hsien-hsing. The three-legged toad lives in the moon; its three legs representing the three lunar phases. It is an emblem of the Immortal Liu-hai. The toad can swallow the moon at a lunar eclipse.

Some Japanese Sennin, similar to the Taoist Immortals, are associated with animals: Gama is a wizard toad. In Polynesia the toad is a symbol of death.

In Amerindian lore the Dark Manitou is represented by the toad as the moon-waters, the powers of darkness and evil overcome by the Great Manitou, but in Mexico the toad depicts the earth and the toadstool is equated with the sacred mushroom which gives enlightenment. The Toad God, sitting under a toadstool, portrays the Mushroom God: the two poisons together, those of the toad and the mushroom as an hallucinogen, provide power for the shaman. In this connection the toad is also associated with the **Jaguar**.

Torpedo or Cramp Fish.   Called the *Narke* in Greek, this fish was said to be the origin of the word 'narcotic'; it is the Electric Ray. Aristotle says that 'It narcoticizes the creatures it wants to catch, overpowering them by the shock that is resident in its body.' Socrates uses it as a simile for benumbing an opponent in debate. It is frequently referred to in literature.

Tortoise, Turtle.   The land- and sea-tortoises and turtles were not

distinguished until the 16th century. As a creature of the waters the
tortoise is lunar in its symbolism and typifies the creative powers,
fecundity, regeneration, time. As the beginning of creation it
frequently is depicted supporting the world.

In Hindu mythology the tortoise supports the **Elephant** on whose
back the world rests. The elephant being solar-male and the tortoise
lunar-female the two together portray the two great creative powers.
The lower shell of the tortoise represents the earth and the upper
shell the heavens. In the Vedas the mythological tortoise is equated
with Prajapati, Lord of Creatures, the Creator; he changed himself
into a tortoise when creating other creatures. This later became
the Tortoise incarnation of Vishnu as the power of the waters, the
Preserver. The tortoise also represents Kasyapa, the North Star, the
first living creature, the progenitor. In Buddhism the tortoise was
also one of the early incarnations of the Buddha.

Chinese mythology also has the tortoise as a supporter of the
world, its four feet being the four corners of the earth. P'an Ku,
architect of the world, gave it this task and it is his attendant. It is
one of the Four Spiritually Endowed, or Auspicious, Creatures,
representing the watery element, the *yin* principle, the North and
the colour black as it symbolizes primordial chaos. The tortoise is
also called the Black Warrior and then depicts strength, endurance
and longevity. The Dragon and Tortoise Banner was carried by the
imperial army as a symbol of indestructibility, since both creatures
survive a fight, neither being able to destroy the other; the **Dragon**
cannot crush the tortoise and the tortoise cannot reach the dragon.
The tortoise and **Crane** often appear together to portray longevity.
The mate of the tortoise was said to be the snake and they are
depicted together. Hsi Wang-Mu, Queen of the Western paradise,
is sometimes called the Golden Mother of the Tortoise; Wu Hsien
is the Transcendent Tortoise. In Taoism the shape of the tortoise
symbolizes the Great Triad, the entire cosmos, with its dome-
shaped back as the sky, the body in the middle as either the earth
or the people, the mediators between heaven and earth, and the
lower shell as the waters. The creature was said to have oracular
powers and its shell was used in divination. In both Chinese and
Japanese myth the tortoise attains a fabulous age of 1000 years or
more.

In Japan the abode of the Sennin and the Cosmic Mountain are
supported by a tortoise, and various Sennin are associated with
animals: Roko balances himself on a flying tortoise.

Among the Ainu of Japan the tortoise is a servant of the chief God
of the Sea; it must be venerated and honoured as a messenger
between people and gods, taking prayers to the God of the Sea.

Tartars and Sioux Indians both have a myth of the world being
a huge tortoise floating on the waters; in another myth four tortoises

Chinese Female Tortoise with Male Snake

support the earth. The Hurons say that a giant tortoise supports the earth and that it was from him that Ioskela, the White One, learned the secret of making fire. For the Delaware the earth is symbolized as a giant tortoise who saved the people from the Flood and now carries the new earth on his back. The Winnebago turtle represents both the earth and the waters and is a primordial deity associated with the life-giving powers of the waters. It is also the Mother Earth, the feminine power of the earth and waters and hence protection and compassion. Among Pueblos there is a Spring Land Turtle Dance and an Autumn Water Turtle Dance. The tortoise or turtle can also appear as a **Trickster** who leads the company of animals on the War Path and creates trouble. The people decide to punish him and he pleads not to be drowned – then, when they throw him in, he surfaces and laughs at them. This theme is found world-wide. There are various Turtle Clans among the Mohawks, the Iroquois and Algonquins, and the animal is the central figure in Passamaquoddy myth. Turtles appear on Mayan stelae.

As one of the oldest of the mythical animals of West Africa the tortoise represents the feminine power, with the snake as the masculine. The tortoise was the origin of all ju-ju and symbolizes fertility: it is impaled in fertility rites. In folklore Tortoise is something of a Trickster-joker and is always outwitted by others. He also appears in Caribbean lore, having been introduced there from Africa.

In Polynesia the turtle can be the embodiment of beings of special power and is the incarnate power of the Gods of the Ocean. It could be used as a substitute for a human victim in sacrifice and, as food, was restricted to chiefs and priests.

In ancient Egypt two tortoises are depicted with the sign of the scales as the measure of the flood waters of the Nile. In Sumeria the tortoise was sacred to Ea-Oannes as Lord of the Deep.

In Graeco-Roman myth the tortoise represented the feminine power of the waters and was an emblem of Aphrodite/Venus, who rose from the sea. It was also an attribute of Hermes/Mercury. Pausanias said that the Arcadians would not kill tortoises, or let any one else do so, as they were sacred to Pan. The tortoise was said to swallow vipers then immediately eat oregano or marjoram as an antidote. Aristotle maintained that this had actually been observed. It was also believed that, like the **Ostrich**, the tortoise 'hatches its eggs with looks only'.

The turtle is referred to as unclean food for the Jews in the Authorized Version of the Bible (Leviticus 11: 29) but not in the Revised; it is eaten by Arabs and in Africa.

The Aztecs used the turtle as a symbol of lubricity, treachery, of someone boastful but cowardly (in retiring into its shell), of something hard on the outside but feeble within.

Christianity employed the tortoise as a symbol of modesty in marriage, with women being retired in their homes like the tortoise into its shell; but it was also depicted in early Christian art as evil as contrasted with the **Cock** of vigilance. Early Celtic art also portrayed the cock and tortoise together, but in this case as an attribute of the Celtic Mercury.

In general symbolism the tortoise represents steady persistence and there are the well-known fables of the **Hare** and the tortoise and of Zeno's paradox of the race between Achilles and the tortoise.

Totemism. Totemism has been defined in various ways. Karsten says it is 'A special class of animals or plants to which a certain group of people pay reverence, assuming a mysterious affinity between themselves and the animal or plant.' Frazer calls it 'a class of material objects which people regard with superstitious respect, believing that there exists an intimate and altogether special relation with every member of the class.' E. O. James defines it as establishing a bond between man and his bewildering environment with 'the community resolved into a co-operative fellowship . . . [the totem] acquires a spiritual quality which does not belong to its own nature'. Elkin considers totemism as 'a philosophy which regards man and nature as one corporate whole.' He divides it into three classes: individual, social and cultic, though the cultic also involves the social and individual; he also says that it 'provides a tangible, visible expression of man's relationship to his deities'. Reinach maintains it is 'a religious compact . . . between certain classes of men and certain species of animals' which are associated with the environment and natural phenomena. Karsten criticizes many of the definitions as being applied too loosely and says that an affinity between a tribe or person and an animal is not necessarily totemistic and that true totemism is found only among Amerindians, Australian Aboriginals, in New Guinea and parts of India and Africa but not among Indo-Europeans or the majority of Mongolians or Finno-Ugarians. Nor does it apply to the Egyptian or Semitic religious associations between men and animals.

In early times in Europe, however, there were nations and clans associated with certain animals and which claimed animal descent. There were the Cynadae of Athens and the Porcii of Rome; the Myrmidons were ants, the Mysians mice, the Lycians wolves and the Arcadians bears. How far this is totemism may be a moot point, but what does seem evident is that totemism proper is practised mainly by hunting peoples such as the Amerindians, Australian Aboriginals and some African tribes, and that it disappears when an agricultural way of life takes over; nor does it occur in societies which keep domestic pets.

In Australian Aboriginal totemism, as Burndt points out, the totem and Dreaming were inseparable. Totems 'linked people with the non-empirical world and they established a firm foundation for belief in the essential unity between people and their natural environment'. In the Dreaming the people and Nature are one.

A totem animal is usually a direct ancestor or is connected with a human ancestor and the totem is not merely a representation of that particular animal, nor only symbolic, but is the actual spirit of that creature, related to the tribe as a whole and to each individual member. The relationship is ritualistic and rites connected with totem animals usually include dancing accompanied by miming of the animals' movements, cries and characteristics. The members of a tribe can identify with the animal to the extent that they regard themselves as one with the creature; for example the Jaguar people of Central America are feared by other clans as jaguars.

In many cases a dying person is wrapped in the skin of the totem animal and told 'you came hither from the animals and are going back to them.' The souls of the group, being closely bound up with the totem, would naturally reincarnate in that animal. Children were named after the animal from which the tribe descended. Most totemistic cultures are exogamus and lineage often traced in the female line. Among Australian Aboriginals there are complicated stipulations as to intermarriage between tribes and moieties: for example a Crow marries a Cicada, an Emu a Rat, a Dingo a Water-hen. In their totemism, called *Kobong*, the animal or plant is always revered as a friend who shares the same life as the people.

It has been suggested that Heraldry originated in people's having animals or birds as totems.

Toucan.   In Central or South America the toucan is associated with evil spirits and can be the incarnation of a demon. Where couvade is practised the father must not eat toucan flesh as it might bewitch the new-born child and cause it to fade away. But the toucan can also be a tribal totem and the medicine-man can use it as an incarnation to fly to the spirit world.

Tree-creeper.   In the Bestiaries this bird's sharp pecking on a tree, which frees the tree from worms and larvae, symbolizes the ordeals to be suffered by the repentant sinner before his prayers are heard.

Trickster.   Joseph Campbell writes: 'this ambiguous, curiously fascinating figure of the trickster appears to have been the chief mythological character of the paleolithic world of story. A fool, a cruel lecherous cheat, an epitome of the principle of disorder, he is nevertheless the culture bringer also and he appears under many guises, both animal and human.' Human forms appear in the Sumerian god Enki, the Greek Hermes and Cronos – who was, according to Homer and Hesiod, 'of crooked council' but who was also a God of culture – and the Scandinavian Loki, but more frequently the trickster is zoomorphic. He appears in all parts of the world – from early times in Greek, Chinese, Japanese, African and Amerindian lore. In this last he plays an important cultural part. Among the North American plains and Western mountain regions his usual form is **Coyote**; in Woodland forests tribes of the North and East he is the Great **Hare**, or White Hare or **Rabbit**. In the Northern Pacific regions he is **Raven**, while Blue **Jay** is another of his guises. As Rabbit he is clearly connected with African trickster myth, being imported to North America, via the Caribbean, and becoming Brer Rabbit with his well-known trickster stories. **Mantis** is another African trickster-hero. In Europe the trickster-character becomes Reynard the Fox; in China the **Fox** is also the arch shape-shifter and in Japan Badger plays this same role.

The Trickster is also a creator-destroyer figure, a demiurge, and is often the cause of bringing conflict and death into a once-happy world. But he is also a Culture-Hero, bringing fire and light to humanity and founding its culture. He restores the world after the Flood, organizing the once-shapeless cosmos and slaying the monsters of chaos. In this role he can symbolize the evolution and development of the Hero from the chaos of the unconscious to the integrated person. But he also typifies the life of the body. As Kerényi says, he is 'the personification of the life of the body; never wholly subdued, ruled by lust and hunger for ever running into pain and injury, cunning and stupid action'. He is totally amoral, the archetypal disorder which survived in the mediaeval Fool and Jester and is the 'Buffoon-Hero' of carnival character, providing laughter to expose weakness; breaking conventional taboos and holding them up to ridicule. Kerényi adds that 'the mythological Trickster is immediately recognizable in whatever cultural costume he assumes . . . disorder belongs to the totality of life and the function of his mythology is to add disorder to order and so make a whole.' In the Blackfoot Lodge Tales 'he is a combination of strength, weakness, wisdom, folly, childishness and malice,' also 'a blend of innocence, greed and stupidity but he may be creatively helpful as well as negatively influential'. The Trickster also represents nimble mind outwitting brute force; the weak versus the strong, the triumph of the underdog. Often he is used as the villain to throw the Hero and the good into relief and his laughter at weaknesses leads to the discovery that much that is taken seriously is, in fact, ridiculous, both in society and oneself.

Triton.   Born of Poseidon and Amphitrite, Triton was depicted as having a human body and the tail of a fish or dolphin; he attended Poseidon/Neptune and blew a conch-shell horn to control the seas; alternatively he can be depicted holding Poseidon's trident. He is the personification of wantonness and mischief. Sometimes Tritons appear in the plural in literature.

Trout.   In Europe the trout is a symbol of health and fertility. The Celts celebrated the return of the sun after the winter months with fertility-rite dancing of 'the springing of the trout': the dancers imitated the rising of the fish, associating it with the rising of the sun.

Turkey.   The sacred bird of the Toltecs and Mayas; a form of the Aztec Tezcatlipoca; the 'Jewelled Fowl', the 'Great Xolotl'. The turkey and the **Dog** were domesticated early in Central and South America and were also sacrificed to Mayan gods. The Turkey Dance is part of the Creek Indians New Fire Festival. In Amerindian lore the bird is called 'give-away', representing the spirit of self-sacrifice, giving, sharing, sustenance and caring for others. The turkey later

Triton (*from a 16th-century engraving*)

became the food for Thanksgiving Day in the United States, commemorating the Pilgrims' harvest in 1621, which was celebrated with a feast of four wild turkeys. Later the bird was introduced into England and eaten at Christmas in place of the traditional goose or beef.

Turtle. See **Tortoise**

Typhon. Born of Gaea by Tartarus, Typhon is represented as a snake-headed giant in Greek mythology. With **Echidna** he fathered the monsters **Cerberus**, the **Hydra** and the Nemean **Lion**. He was a man-beast with a hundred dragon heads, a human torso, wings, feathers and a serpent's tail. He was taller than any mountain and could stretch from East to West. He was slain by Zeus and buried beneath Mount Etna.

U

Unicorn. The mythology and symbolism of the unicorn is complex in the extreme, dating from early times and appearing world-wide. The belief in its existence survived longer than belief in any other legendary animal, into the 18th and 19th centuries. One tradition said that it lived in early days but perished in the Flood. It has been reported and depicted from East to West, in China, Mongolia, Tartary, Persia, the Carpathians, Babylon, Assyria, Chaldea, Elam, the Holy Land, Egypt, Africa, Poland, Scandinavia, Florida and the Canadian Border. It was represented in Buddhist temple paintings and sculptures.

Herodotus mentions the unicorn as living in Lybia. Aelian says it lives in India and that the Brahmins call it the Cartazonon and say that it reaches the size of a large horse when mature, that it frequents desert regions and wanders alone and solitary. Cresias also places it in India. Pliny calls it the Indian ox. Ethiopia was said to have unicorns – ferocious beasts, impossible to capture. Virgil and later writers of the Middle Ages confuse India and Ethiopia as the home of the unicorn and the Hereford *Mappa Mundi* depicts it in the upper Nile region. The Arabs had a well-developed unicorn tradition and unicorns were said to be seen 'in the Temple of Mecca which are not seen in any other place', according to Vertomannus, travelling in 1503. Egypt has versions of the animal, as had Abyssinia, and missionaries and travellers testified to its existence there and in Central Africa. Caesar said it dwelt in the Great Hercynian Forest and was the size of a bull and shaped like a stag. A Chinese traveller of the 11th–12th centuries said that unicorns occurred in great numbers in Tibet and that Genghis Khan met one on Mount Djadanaring.

In the 19th century the Abbé Huc said, 'The unicorn really exists in Tibet and is known by the name of Serou, or Kere in Mongolia,' and in 1820 a British Major Latta said that beyond doubt he had found one in Tibet and that it was called the one-horned Tso'Po. A priest visiting the Holy Land in 1389 saw a unicorn water-conning. The unicorn is mentioned as a distinct creature in the *Septuagint*:

the 'monoceros', later translated as 'unicorn'. In the New World the unicorn is referred to by the Conquistadors, by Sir John Hawkins in 1564 in Florida and by a Dr Dappe in 1673 as 'on the Canadian Border', he describes exactly the conventional unicorn.

The size and shape of the unicorn varies from those of a kid to those of a gazelle or even an elephant. Aelian says that in India it is the size of a mature horse and 'possesses a mane and reddish-yellow hair . . . it excells in swiftness. Like an elephant it has inarticulate feet and has a boar's tail and one black horn projecting between the eye-brows, not awkwardly, but with a certain natural twist and terminating in a sharp point. It has, of all animals, the harshest and most contentious voice.' Caesar says it is 'a bull, shaped like a stag, with one horn projecting from the middle of the forehead between the ears.' The mediaeval Vertomannus wrote: 'these unicorns have feet divided in two much like the feet of a goat.' Accounts of the shape of the feet differ: according to Aristotle, Pliny, Aelian and Solinus they were solid, but are said to be cloven by Strabo, Albertus Magnus and others. The horn varies greatly in length and colour and can be either straight or twisted (see **Horns**).

The conventional unicorn of Heraldry has the head and body of a horse, the tail of a lion and the legs of a stag, with a single horn on its forehead. The *Physiologus* says 'it is a small animal, but exceedingly strong and fleet, with a single horn in the centre of its forehead.'

Accounts of the unicorn's temperament vary as much as do accounts of its size. In some cases it is said to be fierce and of great strength, in others to be gentle and playful. Pliny writes of 'a fierce animal called the monoceros'. Aelian says the unicorn of India is gentle with other beasts but fights its own kind. The Bestiaries make it a symbol of the violent and cruel person, only subdued and made gentle by the grace of God.

The unicorn is a water-conner, its horn, called the Alicorn, is able to detect and counteract poison and was therefore greatly sought after and prized and was used especially by kings and princes who had drinking vessels made from it to detect poisoned wine. To test the horn as genuine a circle is inscribed in the earth and a scorpion, spider or lizard placed in it; if genuine the creature will not be able to escape. It has been suggested that the horns so traded and valued were probably those of the narwhal or narwal. The belief in the medicinal value of the horn can be traced back to the 4th century BC.

It was said that the unicorn could never be captured by the hunter, only by stratagem. The *Physiologus* gives an account of the Holy Hunt or the Virgin Capture – 'namely by decking a chaste virgin with beautiful ornaments and seating her in a solitary place in the forest frequented by the unicorn, which it no sooner perceives her than it runs to her and laying its head gently in her lap, falls asleep. Then the hunters come and take it captive to the King's palace and receive for it much treasure.' The Virgin with a unicorn resting on her lap was a common feature in ecclesiastical architecture, particularly in stained glass windows; it symbolized the triumph of chastity. Other traditions say that the virgin had to be naked and in some cases she was depicted as tied to a tree. Mediaeval poets used the virgin-capture theme to represent the lover being lured to his capture or destruction. Christianity also used it to depict the Devil, who can only be overcome by purity and innocence.

As Odell Shepard wrote: 'There has never been any lack of allegorical possibilities in the unicorn legend; the difficulty is in avoiding them.' Christianity extended the symbolism of purity and the Virgin Capture to associate the unicorn with the Virgin Mary, but its chief association was with Christ, who, according to St Ambrose, 'is this unicorn the only-begotten Son of God'. It is also Christ who 'raised up the horn of salvation', or, again, 'I and the Father are One.' The horn as an antidote to poison represents Christ's power of destroying sin. The unicorn as a solitary animal, derived from Pliny and Aelian, was used as an emblem of monastic life. As chastity it is associated with the two Saints Justinia, of Antioch and Padua respectively.

In translating the Old Testament into Greek the Hebrew *Re'em* is the monoceros – 'one-horned' (later taken and translated as the unicorn or wild-oxen) and is a symbol of fierceness, but the Re'em was the rhinoceros in the Vulgate. In Hebrew it represents royalty, power and strength. In Egypt the unicorn depicted all normal virtues. In Graeco-Roman lore the unicorn is an attribute of all virgin moon goddesses, especially Artemis/Diana whose triumphal chariot is drawn by eight unicorns. The unicorn had the same lunar significance in Sumero-Semitic tradition and was also depicted with the Tree of Life.

Probably the oldest form of the unicorn is the Chinese **Ky-lin**. A one-horned animal, it appeared to Fu Hsi about 3000 BC, coming up out of the Yellow River. It appeared again at the death of Huang Ti and at the birth and death of Confucius. It is one of the Four Spiritually Endowed or Auspicious Creatures and is the essence of the five elements; it is also the union of the *yin* and *yang*, with the Ky as masculine and the Lin feminine, but if it is depicted as white it is lunar and *yin*. It symbolizes gentleness – never striking with its horn – also good will, felicity, benevolence, longevity, wise administration and famous offspring. The horn is a happy augury for the Emperor.

In the West the white unicorn is lunar and is associated with the golden **Lion** (solar); the conflict between the lion and the unicorn represents solar and lunar powers and the pair of opposites, but the two horns joined in one depicts their union. The unicorn is gentleness, chastity, purity, virginity, the good, and strength of mind. It is also closely associated with royalty, the single horn being symbolic of unlimited and individual power. This is prominent in Heraldry, in which the unicorn appears frequently with the lion as representative of the solar-lunar powers.

See also **Rhinoceros** and **Horns**

Unnati. In Nepal the Unnati is the wife of the **Garuda** Bird.

V

Vegetable Lamb. Like the **Barnacle Goose**, the Vegetable Lamb or Tartary was a combination of animal and vegetable. Mandeville says that there were plants which bore fruit from which a 'lytylle Lamb' emerged live. A Hebrew account said that certain lambs grow from the earth on a short stem, but die of starvation once they have eaten all the vegetation within reach. The flesh was said to taste of fish and the blood of honey, while the bones were used ritually and conferred the powers of prophecy and divination.

Vicuna. The sacred royal animal of the Incas, rarer than and superior to the **Llama** but having the same symbols and uses.

Young vipers eating their way through their mother's body

Viper. It was believed that the birth of the young vipers caused the death of both parents, the female eating through the neck of the male at mating and the young eating their way out of the mother's body and so killing her. This was maintained by Herodotus and Pliny, but was doubted by Aelian. The myth appeared in the *Physiologus* and so passed into literature. According to St Ambrose the Viper or Vipera is the most villainous of creatures, the most lustful and the most cunning; it has 'a bastard union with the sea-eel'.

The general symbolism is one of treachery.

See also **Serpent**

Virtues and Vices. In Christian art certain virtues and vices are often depicted by people riding on, or accompanied by, a symbolic animal.

Humility – the **Panther**
Chastity – the **Unicorn**
Patience has a helmet adorned with a **Swan**
Love has a **Pelican** on her shield
Devotion rides an **Ibex**
Pride has an **Eagle** on her shoulder
Avarice bestrides an **Ape**
Ovis, the **Sheep**, signifies a simpleton or ninny
Liberality is mounted on a **Cock** and pours out gold coins
    from a vessel.

Vishap. An Armenian **Dragon** living on Mount Ararat; it has poisonous blood.

Vishnu. The Hindu God Vishnu, the Preserver, appeared in various incarnations, the first four being animals.

1. The **Fish**, *Matsya*, which rose from the waters of the Flood and towed the ship containing Manu, the seven Holy Men and the seeds of all living things to a peak where it rested until the Flood subsided.
2. The **Tortoise**, *Kurma*, which brought forth from the bottom of the sea of milk many valuable things such as the elixir of immortality, the moon, the Tree of Wishes, the Cow of Plenty and the beautiful wife Lakshmi.
3. The **Boar**, *Varahi*, in which form Vishnu fought a terrible demon and lifted the earth from the chasm into which it had been thrown, returning it to the surface.
4. The man-**Lion**, *Nara-Sinha*, combining man and animal to destroy the Demon King, who could not be killed by a god, man or animal alone.

Vishnu's tenth and final avatar as *Kalki*, the White **Horse**, will come at the end of the present age, the Kali Yuga, when evil has reached its peak and the cosmic revolution takes place before the coming of the new age of peace and righteousness.

Volkh. A Slav shape-shifter, guardian of Kiev, appearing as either animal, bird or insect and having magic powers.

Vulture. In early times all vultures were believed to be either female, with the **Hawk** as the male, or parthenogenetic; they thus symbolized the female principle and maternal solicitude and were supposed to be dedicated mothers, feeding their young on their own blood in times of need – a legend later transferred to the **Pelican**. The Egyptian priest Horapollo says: 'The Vulture is the type of merciful man, because if food cannot be obtained for its young it opens its own thigh and permits them to partake of its blood, so that they do not perish for want.' It represented the Mother Goddess, maternal love and care; Isis once took the form of a vulture. It is also sacred to Mat as Goddess of Maternity and Mistress of the Sky and she is often depicted with the head of a vulture or as wearing a vulture head-dress. Hathor can also be vulture-headed. Nekhebet of southern Egypt, sister to Uatcaat of northern Egypt, sometimes takes the form of a vulture. Vulture plumes were used in the funeral rites of Osiris, fixed four to each corner of the coffin. As a symbol of power the vulture appeared on the breastplates of the Pharaohs and was known as 'Pharaoh's Hen'. The vulture was also associated with the **Scarab**, the former representing the female principle and the latter the male.

The Griffon Vulture was a royal bird and appeared on the royal standards of Assyrian and Persian armies.

Among Arabian deities there was a Vulture God, Nasr. In West Africa the vulture Fene-Ma-So, the Bird of the Sky, the Vulture Spirit, is king of the birds.

The Hebrew word for vulture – *Racham*, meaning a compassionate creature – follows other beliefs. The Zoroastrians called it 'the Compassionate Purifier' as it cleans up corpses, performing this office in the Parsee Towers of Silence.

In Graeco-Roman myth the bird is associated with Pallas, Ares, Mars and Apollo and is the mount of Cronos/Saturn. It is also sacred to Hercules, who slew the vulture which tore out the liver of Prometheus. The **Harpies** have the heads and breasts of women and the bodies of vultures.

The symbolism is thus ambivalent, being both compassionate and protective on the one hand and destructive and voracious on the other. There are also various myths associated with the bird. It was said by both Pliny and the *Physiologus* that the vulture and eagle did not lay eggs but gave birth to live young which emerged fully

feathered. Aelian says that sweet perfumes cause death to vultures;
pomegranates and myrrh are also fatal. Vultures' feathers, if burnt,
drive snakes from their holes and Pliny and Galen say that the heart
and liver were used medicinally. The claw of the vulture, like the
horn of the **Unicorn**, detects poisons in food and drink. Vultures
are prophetic and can divine beforehand any place of battle.

W

Wagtail. In India the wagtail is a bird of divination and bears a holy caste mark. It is looked for and the situation in which it appears is an omen: if near a lotus flower or in the neighbourhood of elephants, cows, snakes or horses it is propitious, if near bones, ashes or refuse it presages evil and the gods should be placated.

Japanese legend has wagtails sacred to Izanagi and Izanami, who were taught love by them. In Ainu myth the wagtail was sent by the **Cuckoo** to the earth, which was then a sterile quagmire. It beat the earth down, flattening the rough places with its wings and tail until it hardened and became elevated in places so that the water drained away, leaving the land fit for the people. The water-wagtail is the Ainu Cupid and its feathers and bones are love charms.

Walrus. Palaeo-Siberian people have a marine divinity, the Walrus Mother, who watches over and protects the sea animals.

Wasp. In ancient Egypt, Rome and Greece and in Europe in the Middle Ages there was a belief that wasps were generated from the decaying bodies of dead donkeys. Socrates classes wasps with **Ants** and **Bees** as creatures that live harmoniously in communities.

Zoroastrianism connects wasps with Ahriman as evil. A Polish myth says that God created bees but that when the Devil tried to imitate them they turned into wasps.

There is a Wasp Tribe among the Comanche Plains Indians and the medicine-man can incarnate in this form. Among the Buriats a shaman in the form of a wasp stung the High God to make him release the soul of the people, which the shaman then took back with him.

Water-hen. An Australian Aboriginal totem animal; among moieties a Water-hen must marry a Dingo.

Water-horse. The Manx Water-horse Glashtin or Cobbyl Ushtey can take the form of a real horse, except for its back-to-front hooves; it tempts people to mount it and then careers off to the nearest water to drown its rider. The Gaelic Kelpie is also a shape-shifter horse of the waters.

Water-snake. See Hydra

Weasel. Almost universally associated with evil, the weasel was often feared and given fancy names for fear of attracting it. It was sacred in Egypt, however, and Aelian tells us that the Thebans worshipped it. In China it was one of the **Five Animals**. For the Amerindians it symbolizes stealth, energy and ingenuity. It is reputed to hear everything that is said and to see below the surface of situations. It was the weasel who foretold the coming of the white men and the disaster they would bring. Among the Washo the short-tailed weasel is a sibling of the long-tailed weasel. The Hopi call it the 'tobacco-odour carrier'.

The weasel is the only animal other than the **Cock** that can kill the **Basilisk**, who is afraid of it.

The Bestiaries say it is an example of dissimulation, hearing God's word but being bound by the love of earthly things.

The flesh of the weasel salted and drunk in wine was a cure for snake-bite.

Were-wolf. See Lycanthropy

Whale. Also called the Whinlepoole, the whale symbolizes the power of the waters and hence regeneration, but it is also the engulfing grave. The jaws of the whale are used to represent the entry to hell and the belly of the whale is the place of death and rebirth, a dark place of initiation from which the initiate emerges after the three days of the dark of the moon to be reborn to a new life, resurrection. This is the 'great fish' of the Bible myth of Jonah, sometimes portrayed as a whale, sea-monster or dolphin (Jonah 1: 17 and Matthew 12: 40). The belly-of-the-whale is a widespread myth.

There was a legend that whales could be mistaken for an island in the sea and that sailors would land on one and cook their food, but that then, feeling the heat, the whale would plunge under the waves and the sailors would be drowned. This legend occurs in the Arabian Nights and an Arctic tradition says that the earth rests on the back of a whale and that earthquakes are the result of its movement. Russia had the same tradition and the Slavs said the world was supported by four whales. The same myth occurs with the **Tortoise** or Turtle in India and elsewhere.

The *Physiologus* uses the whale-as-island story to illustrate the Devil luring people to destruction and the Bestiaries say this is the fate of unbelievers who fall into the wiles of the Devil and 'place their hopes in him and his works'. They also say that the whale was the fish that swallowed Jonah and that its great belly is Hell. It feeds by emitting a pleasant-scented breath which attracts the fish it devours – 'so are people who pander to the senses swallowed by the

Devil and the Gates of Hell.' This symbolism is general in Christianity and Origen says that great whales represent violent passions and criminal impulses.

In Norse lore whales can carry witches and have magic powers in themselves.

Among the Ainu of Japan the whale can be a mount of the chief God of the Sea, like the sword-fish, sea-lion and sea-tortoise, and thus has divine honours paid to it. The whale is also venerated in parts of Polynesia, where it can be a manifestation of the Gods of the Oceans.

The 'belly-of-the-whale' theme occurs among the Innuits (Eskimos) in the legends of Raven as **Trickster** and these tribes have whaling festivals. There is a Killer Whale tribe of the Kwakiutls of North America and a Killer Whale clan of the Tsimshian tribe of the North West coast.

The Whale in Heraldry has a boar's head, tusks, spikes on its body and four claws for feet.

Whip-poor-will. The incarnation of the Amerindian God of the Night, who made the moon by magic, changing a **Frog** into the moon. The bones of the bird are used in charm-making. The Indians of Pennsylvania say the coming of the whip-poor-will announces the time to plant maize. It is a prophetic bird.

Wild Cat. See **Cat**

Wild Duck. An Australian Aboriginal totem animal. Among moieties a Wild Duck, *Matturi*, must marry a Snake, *Kikarawa*.

Wildebeest. An African Bushman cult animal. There are ritual wildebeest dances.

Wild Hunt. The Wild Hunt, or Ride of Death, appears in various forms in Europe. In Norse and Teutonic myth a pack of phantom hounds is led by Odin/Woden, the original Wild Huntsman, or the Erl King, in stormy weather; they hunt lost souls and to hear the hunt is an omen of death. Desolation and destruction follow in the wake of the hunt. The hounds, with their leader, are doomed to hunt forever through the air, though another Norse version said they rode on the night of New Year's Eve. The object of the hunt varies from lost souls (the most common quarry) to a visionary boar, a white horse, white-breasted maidens or wood nymphs.

There are many other hunts: that of the Teutonic Dietrich of Berne, the French Grand Huntsman of Fontainebleau, the Irish Hounds of Hell, the Celtic *Annwr*, the Dogs of Hell who hunt the souls of the damned, and the Norse *Lusse*, an evil spirit or witch who can take the form of a bird of prey during the longest night of December 12–13 and lead the Wild Hunt, the *Lussiferd* or *Lussireidi*.

There are also Gabriel Hounds, Yeth Hounds (or Whistlers), the Dartmoor pack of hounds and the North of England Wisht Hounds who hunt high in the air on wild nights; they presage death and are said to incarnate the souls of unbaptized children. Other sinister characters such as Herod or Cain can lead the Hunt, but King Arthur was also said to ride with a pack. One tradition in England was that a small black dog could be left behind; it cowered and whined on a hearth and had to be kept and fed for a year unless exorcized.

Winged Animals. The symbolic use of wings for deities, supernatural beings or animals occurs more frequently in the West and Middle East than in the East, though the latter has the **Garuda** Bird, the Winged Cosmic **Horse** and Winged **Dragon** and the *Rig Veda* equates wings with knowledge – 'he who knows has wings.'

Wings are a natural symbol of the element of air, of flying, the spirit soaring heavenward, power, speed, volition, freedom, victory and transcendence. They are often added to animals held in veneration, for example the solar Cosmic Horse, which is often ridden by heroes, and the Chinese Celestial Dragon. Proclus says that the First God, who bore the heads of many animals, was winged.

The winged **Serpent** is probably the most ancient and frequently cited winged animal. Two- and four-winged serpents are depicted on Egyptian sculptures. Josephus speaks of flying serpents that infested the lands bordering the Nile; Cicero tells of the **Ibis** devouring the flying serpents of Lybia; Aristotle states that there were winged serpents found in India and that they were nocturnal and noxious; Virgil writes of 'snakes with strident wings' and Lucan, Ovid and other poets allude to winged serpents, although Herodotus said they were found only in Arabia. In Egyptian iconography winged serpents guard the trees which produce frankincense. The wings are not feathered but bat-like. The feathered or plumed serpent of the Aztecs was a combination of bird and snake and an attribute of Quetzalcoatl (see **Serpent**). The Algonquin Rain God had the form of a winged snake with a man's face and tiger's beard. In China the Celestial Dragon has wings, the serpent and dragon being interchangeable there.

Witch Animals. It is a widespread theme in mythology that witches can change themselves into certain animals or are accompanied by them as 'familiars' – especially if the variety is black or a bird of prey – or that they can use these animals to carry them to the Sabbat. Care must be taken in speaking about any of these creatures, as to name them is to attract them; nor may they be killed in any but a ritual manner as part of the rites of sorcery, lest they take vengeance.

The chief animals concerned are **Hares**, **Horses**, **Cats**, **Dogs**, **Wolves**, **Toads**, **Cocks**, **Rats**, **Mice**, **Newts**, **Ferrets**, **Hedgehogs**, **Lizards**, **Frogs**, **Owls**, **Geese** and **Bats**. The **Cuckoo**, **Quail** and **Magpie** were also associated with sorcery, as were snakes; other animals could be witch forms, such as the **Squirrel** among the Ainu and the Norse *Lusse*, an evil spirit or witch which could take the form of a bird of prey for the **Wild Hunt**. In Cherokee myth witches can change into any person, animal or bird. The **Hedgehog** in Ireland could be a transformed witch, taking that form to suck cows dry. All witch animals are shape-shifters, especially the **Hare**; when occupied by a witch the hare can only be killed by a silver bullet.

Witchetty Grub. The totem of the Australian Aboriginal people of the Alice Springs district.

Wolf. Although the general symbolism of the wolf is one of evil, destructiveness and devouring, its fierce qualities can also be protective and therefore venerated. In its evil aspect it is associated with gods of death and can represent death itself; wolves and **Ravens** are frequently familiars of primitive gods of the dead. As incarnating all the powers of the dark, destructive side of nature the wolf becomes, when worshipped, one of the terrible deities.

The Egyptian god Upuat or Ap-Uat can be depicted as a wolf or wolf- or jackal-headed; he is also Khenti Amenti, the Opener of the Way, and was a psychopomp, conducting souls through the Gates which had to be passed and ruling the souls of the dead. He also guided the barque of the sun and his standard went before the king in victory.

In Zoroastrianism the wolf is a legionary of Ahriman and is frequently a symbol of evil in human nature – 'the wicked two-legged one' and is himself 'the flattering, the deadly wolf'. Hinduism also holds the animal as evil, as the Asvins rescue the Quail of day from the Wolf of night.

Both Plato and Pausanias write of the cult of Zeus Lycaeus in Arcadia; the rites followed the original totemistic wolf-cult in which the animal was sacrificed and eaten and its essence thus absorbed by the devotees, who became one with the sacred wolf, calling themselves *Lukoi*. Aelian says that the Delphinians worshipped the wolf, which was associated with Apollo, and there was a bronze image of a wolf at Delphi. The wolf was also sacred to Ares and Silvanus and to the Roman Mars. The wolf, suckling the twins Romulus and Remus at the founding of Rome, is a symbol of that city and is prominent in Roman art and gave its name to the Lupercalia, the festival of Mars.

The Old Testament represents the wolf as destructive and associated with the evening (Jeremiah 5: 6); it also symbolizes dishonest gain, bloodshed and destruction (Ezekiel 22: 27,

Zephaniah 3: 3). The wolf and the **Lamb**, traditionally enemies, represent when depicted lying down together the coming Messianic rule (Isaiah 65: 25). In the New Testament 'ravening wolves' typify false prophets leading the faithful astray. Christianity equates the wolf with the Devil, the spoiler of the flocks, and with cruelty, craftiness, heresy and stiff-necked people – it was believed that the wolf could not turn its neck. It is an emblem of St Francis of Assisi, who tamed the wolf Gubbio.

Plato and Pliny recount the belief that if a wolf is seen by a man with its mouth shut it loses the power of opening it again, but if the wolf sees the man first and the man's mouth is shut it is the man who loses his voice. This myth was carried over into the *Physiologus* and the Bestiaries and on to mediaeval literature. The wolf is Satan, fierce and insatiable in contrast with the meekness of the lamb, the Saviour. In the Bestiaries the word 'wolf' means 'the ravisher', and symbolizes rapacity; it is used as a name for a prostitute. In Latin *lupa*, the she-wolf, represents a lewd woman and the *lupanar*, a wolf's lair, a brothel. The wolf also resembles the Devil in regarding people with an evil eye and its eyes shine in the night since it works for the Devil. When suffering pangs of hunger the wolf fills its stomach with clay which it later, when it finds prey, vomits up by putting its paws into its gullet. This trick depicts the Devil in his dealings with mankind. 'A wolf in sheep's clothing' typifies hypocrisy and deceit.

The wolf appears in a generally favourable light in Celtic and Irish myth. An Irish tribe claimed descent from a wolf and Cormac, King of Ireland, was, like Romulus and Remus, suckled by wolves and was always accompanied by them. They frequently appear as **Helpful Animals** and have much in common with the **Dog** in Irish legend; both have affinities with Celtic deities, and heroes and deities could manifest as wolves as well as **Horses**, **Bulls** or **Salmon**. In Celtic art Cernunnos, as Lord of Animals, is depicted as accompanied by a wolf, **Bear** and **Otter**.

The Scandinavian and Teutonic wolf is ambivalent: a bringer of victory and ridden by Odin/Woden but also the Fenris wolf or Fenrir, the incarnation of evil, one of the monsters created by Loki. Fenrir was captured but will return at Ragnarok, the Norse Doomsday, although he will be vanquished ultimately by Vidhair; he symbolizes the death which results from evil. Two wolves, with two **Ravens**, were companions of Odin, and the two wolves (Sköll and Hati – repulsion and hatred) incessantly pursued the sun and moon to swallow them so that the world might be lost in primordial darkness; they achieve partial success at eclipses and will succeed at Ragnarok. Wolves are ridden by the Valkyries across the sky. Wolf-headed men appear in Norse art. 'War with the wolf' symbolizes the gods versus evil at the end of a cosmic cycle.

The wolf is admired by the Ainus of Japan for its ferocity, tenacity and swift attack. It is from heaven and to be venerated. Wolves can help people against evil bears and may be invoked for that purpose. Tartars take the name of the wolf but do not necessarily make the animal a cult object. Paleo-Siberian people had a wolf festival at which a wolf was killed and a man dressed in its skin to walk round the hearth.

Numerous Amerindian tribes or clans are associated with the wolf. It is a teacher, the pathfinder, loyalty. It represents Sirius, the Dog Star, the home of the gods, and the moon is its ally, symbolizing psychic powers. The Kwakiutls say that when a land-hunter dies he goes to the realm of the wolves and the Shoshoni say the soul goes to the land of the wolf or **Coyote**. Tribes also claim descent from wolves, who are also brothers of the Culture Hero or the actual Hero. The Innuits (Eskimos) have a Great Wolf hero, Amarok.

In Armenia wolves are evil and charms are employed against them. In witchcraft the wolf can be the mount of witches and warlocks, who can assume the form of the were-wolf (see **Lycanthropy**).

Wolverine or Glutton. In Amerindian lore the wolverine represents vigour, perseverance and hardihood. It accompanied and helped the Fisher in the healing of a hole in the sky, which gave the people entry into the Heavenly Plane of Perpetual Spring, but returned through the hole to the Mountain Top. The name is taken by Tartars but the animal is not necessarily a cult object. Used as a symbol of greed or gluttony.

Woodcock. Signifies a simpleton, being easily snared. 'Woodcock hay' was a symbol of uselessness as it would have to be stored before the migrating woodcock arrived in England. The Ainu of Japan say that the woodcock was made on earth, not in heaven as were most birds, and that they always live in pairs and spend the whole time in the mountains in idleness.

Woodlouse. A universal panacea when swallowed as a pill and particularly said to cure teething troubles when hung as a necklace round children's throats.

Woodpecker. In Indo-European myth the woodpecker is a bird of fire and lightning, symbolized by its red mark and by the fact that the sound of its tapping resembles that of striking wood to make fire. It is a prophetic bird with magic powers and is a guardian of kings and trees. It is the Aryan bird of the storm clouds and can typify war, sudden attack and destruction. It can be a form of Zeus/Jupiter and in Greece and Rome was sacred to Ares/Mars as war, to Silvanus and Triptolemus. A woodpecker watched over and fed the infants Romulus and Remus while the **Wolf** suckled them.

Woodpecker

Called the *Picus* in the Bestiaries, the bird represents augury as used by Picus, son of Saturn, in soothsaying. Christianity equates the woodpecker with the Devil as heresy and the undermining of belief and human nature. In England the 'yaffle' foretells rain.

War symbolism occurred among proto-historic Amerindians and the woodpecker is a totem of the Omaha tribe. The Ainu say that the woodpecker is a friend of the **Snake** and so is disliked; it lives in holes in trees with the snake and is a depraved creature, but it is also the boat-maker's bird as it hollows out wood and was sent by God to show the people how to make boats.

The woodpecker is supposed to be at enmity with the **Quail**.

Worm. In general symbolism the worm represents the earth, death, dissolution, cringing, cowardice and misery, but in earlier times the term was also applied to the **Serpent**, 'that great worm', or to **Dragons**. This occurred particularly in Teutonic and Scandinavian myth, where the Midgard Worm, the offspring of the evil Loki, is coiled round the world. The worm or serpent gnaws at the root of the Yggdrasil (Tree of Life). In England there was the great Lambton Worm of Durham.

In the Bible the worm is a figure of humiliation and degradation (Isaiah 41: 14 and Job 25: 6), of decay (Exodus 16: 20) and of hell (Mark 9: 48).

There was a mediaeval belief that worms aided conception (five were to be swallowed in a drink). They were also a specific against jaundice, gallstones, baldness and impotence and, according to Angelius (a monk of the 13th century), they 'helpe agaynst the crampe and agaynst shrinking of the sinewes and also agaynst the biting of serpents'.

The Aztec Hero-God, originator of agriculture and the calendar, was helped by worms and **Bees** on his journeys, which he made in the form of a dog, to the Land of the Dead.

Wren. Known as The Little King in the West, it is also called the King of the Birds, though a German myth says it won the title by deceit in a contest against the **Eagle**. The wren can take the place of the **Dove** as symbolizing Spirit, but it also appears as a witch bird and is then unlucky and malefic, although its feathers are a charm against witchcraft. It was the Druid King of the Birds and auguries were drawn from its chirping; in Celtic lore the wren is prophetic and the direction from which it calls is highly significant. The bird was sacred to the Celtic Taliesen, as it was to the Greek Triptolemus. In Scotland it was the Lady of Heaven's Hen and killing it was considered extremely unlucky; but in England and France there was a Hunting of the Wren on St Stephen's Day, December 26, a ceremony which rose from an ancient pre-Christian rite. Hunters, dressed ritually, killed a wren, hung it on a pole and took it in procession, demanding money; they then buried it in the churchyard. It was associated with the underworld and these hunting rituals were connected with the winter solstice and the death of vegetation. Another origin of this ceremony at Yule was the myth that a Norse **Siren** responsible for luring men into the sea had been hunted but had escaped in the form of a wren; this wren reappeared once a year and was then hunted and killed. At other times of the year, however, the wren was protected, as it was ill-luck to kill it.

In Brittany if the young birds are touched while in the nest the person is stricken with the Fire of St Laurence – a rash on the face and legs. Also if a person kills a wren he and his flocks will be either struck by lightning or his fingers will shrivel and drop off.

The wren is a lucky bird in Japan and is highly thought of by the Ainus; it brings good fortune to hunters and should be saluted when seen. It was a tiny god who came down from heaven and brought fire. The wren is a totem animal of an Australian Aboriginal tribe.

Wryneck. Sacred among Persians and Babylonians, the wryneck was also sacred to Adonis and Aphrodite in Greece and appeared in art as associated with Dionysos. It had a phallic symbolism and was used as a charm to bring back an errant lover. The witch who caused Zeus/Jupiter to fall in love with Io was transformed into a wryneck by the jealous Hera/Juno. The bird was used as a love-charm in lunar rites, during which it was tied to a wheel and spun round.

Heraldic Wyvern

Wyvern. As a serpent-like dragon with wings but with only two legs (which resembled an eagle's talons) and a barbed tail, the wyvern appears frequently in Heraldry. It betokens war, pestilence, envy and viciousness. It is the Saxon *Wivere*, a serpent. The wyvern without wings is the **Lindworm**.

X

Xochipilli. The Aztec God of the Flower Feast, the xochipilli wears a helmet-mask of the Quetzalcoxcoxtli bird with its blue plumage, and is associated with abundant maize.

Xolotl. An Aztec God of Magicians and invoked by them, the xolotl was a shape-shifter, taking on the forms of various animals. He was said to be the twin of Quetzalcoatl, the feathered **Serpent**.

Y

Yak. In Tibet the Yak takes on the function and symbolism of the **Ox**.

Yale. One of the Queen's Beasts in Heraldry, the yale is antelope- or horse-like with a spotted body, boar's tusks and an elephant's tail. Its horns are unique as branching in opposite directions and reputed to be movable. The yale appeared on the arms of John, Duke of Bedford and were later adopted by Lady Margaret Beaufort, mother of King Henry VII. The arms may be seen on the Great Gate of Christ's College, Cambridge.

Yata Garasu. The Japanese three-legged crow of the Sun Goddess Amaterasu and a messenger of the gods. It is similar to the Chinese three-legged 'crow in the sun', which causes sun spots.

Yellowhammer. A bird of the Devil, who inoculates it with his blood on May 1st; it was therefore persecuted.

Ypotryll. The heraldic form of the **Camel** or dromedary.

Z

Zebra. A dual-purpose animal, used both for work and as food in India and Indonesia. The Zebra was said to be held sacred to Helios in the regions of the Red Sea and was also known as the Tiger-horse.

Zeus. Among his numerous intrigues Zeus either changed himself or his lovers into animal form. As a **Cuckoo** he wooed Hera; in the shape of a white **Bull** he abducted Europa; as a **Swan** he seduced Leda. In one tradition he turned Callisto into a **Bear** to deceive Hera and he changed Io into a white heifer to protect her from Hera. Zeus fled from Typhon in the form of a **Ram**. Zeus Meilichios appeared, and was worshipped, in the form of a **Snake**.

Ziz. A huge bird of Hebrew mythology personifying the power of the air, associated with **Behemoth** as the power of the land and **Leviathan** as the sea. It is similar to the Arabian **Roc** and Persian **Simurgh**.

Zodiac. The Zodiac, which is symbolic of relationships in the universe and seasonal changes, is based on animal imagery (from the Greek *zoon*, an animal), and many of the signs and constellations are directly represented by animals – the Ram, Bull, Crab, Lion, Scorpion or Eagle, the Centaur, Goat and Fishes. The Chinese Zodiac, or the Twelve Terrestrial Branches, is depicted entirely by animals – the Rat, Ox, Tiger, Hare, Dragon, Snake, Horse, Goat, Monkey, Cock, Dog and Boar – known as the Beasts of the constellations, which are under the branches of the Year Tree. They represent six wild and six domestic animals, six being *yin* and six *yang*. In former Chinese marriage contracts the animal signs of the horoscopes of the bride and bridegroom had to be compatible. Animal symbolism appeared originally in the temples but was abandoned there, living on in astrology and the Zodiac.

Zu or Anzu. Zu is the Sumerian Storm God who appeared in the form of a bird or dragon and stole the Tablets of Fate which conferred omnipotence. They were recovered by Marduk, who is also known as Nimurta.

Authorities Quoted

Various authorities are introduced and quoted throughout this book, covering a period from 500 BC to comparatively modern times; they include naturalists, historians, philosophers, geographers and travellers, all of whom were concerned with, or interested in, the study of animals, their habits, myths and symbolism. These people greatly influenced the thought, beliefs and literature of their times and continue to be of importance to scholars today.

The following list gives a brief indication of the period, background and status of these authorities.

Aelian (–AD 220)
Claudius Aelianus. Italian historian who taught in Rome but perfected Greek to such an extent that he was called 'the honey-tongued'. Wrote a *Various History*, which was a collection of curious anecdotes, and the well-known *History of Animals*, *De Natura Animalium*.

Albertus Magnus (AD 1193–1280)
German Bishop of Regensburg. A philosopher so learned that he was called the Great and was accounted a magician. Wrote on many subjects including natural science. His *De Animalibus Historia* criticizes the *Physiologus* but accepts it as generally true.

Ambrose (AD 339–397)
Christian Saint and Italian Bishop of Milan. Famous for the breadth of his scholarship. Wrote the *Hexameron*.

Aristotle (384–322 BC)
Greek philosopher and scientist; a pupil of Plato and tutor to Alexander the Great who, in his conquests, supplied Aristotle with accounts of the animals of other lands; he studied them from a scientific point of view and corrected many previous fallacies with his *Historia Animalium*.

Augustine (AD 354–430)
Early Latin Christian Father and Saint. Lived in Carthage, was converted to Christianity and became Bishop of Hippo. A prolific writer and commentator.

Basil (AD 326–379)
Early Greek Christian Father and Saint. Bishop of Caesarea, and called 'the Great'. His extensive works were published by the Benedictines of St Maur.

Bede (AD 673–735)
'The Venerable'. Christian Saint and historian, as a monk he devoted his life to writing and teaching. Wrote many historical and scientific treatises.

Cassian (AD 360–435)
Celebrated Christian recluse in Bethlehem and the Nile desert; he became a priest in Rome and wrote *Collationes Patrum Sceticorum* on the kinds of knowledge derived from Biblical study.

Celsus (c. AD 178)
Platonist philosopher also having a wide interest in national religions and mythologies. Opposed to and wrote against Christianity. Little is known of his life.

Cicero (AD 106–143)
Roman statesman, orator and philosopher. Travelled in Greece and Asia before returning to Rome. His writings are of great importance.

Ctesias (c. 398 BC)
Greek physician of Cnidus, of the priestly caste of Asclepiadai, he went to Persia to the court of Darius II where he remained for seventeen years serving Darius and Artaxerxes. He returned to Greece and wrote a history of Persia and *Indica*, written largely from travellers' tales as he himself had not been to India. He was influenced by a love of the marvellous.

Diodorus (c. 44 BC)
A Sicilian historian who wrote a *Universal History* or *Historical Library*, a work of forty volumes covering the period from the Creation to 60 BC.

Epiphanius Christian Bishop of Salamis, born in Palestine. He wrote treatises in Greek against heresies. His writings are more valuable for the fragments of others which he preserved rather than for their own worth.

Herodotus (c. 484 BC)
Greek historian, called the Father of History. He travelled in Greece, Europe, Africa and Asia, from which he gathered material for his

history. He recorded many tales of marvels told in Egypt and wrote *Nights and Days*, but was accused of inaccuracy that stemmed from his love of the marvellous.

Horapollo (4th century AD)
Egyptian priest, Greek grammarian, he wrote commentaries on Greek poets and a history of Alexandria.

Huc (AD 1813–1860)
The Abbé Huc – French missionary priest. He travelled to Macao then through China and Tartary and lived in a Buddhist monastery. In 1852 he left for France, travelling through Egypt, Palestine, Ceylon and India. Among other works he wrote *Travels in Tartary, Thibet and China*.

Isadore (*c.* AD 570)
Christian Saint, Bishop of Seville in 601. One of the most learned men of his time, he wrote several books on 'Etymology' and on classical and biblical subjects.

Jerome (*c.* AD 340–420)
Early Latin Christian Father and Saint. He travelled in Gaul, Asia Minor, and Syria and collected a Library in Rome. He later settled in Bethlehem.

Josephus (*c.* AD 37–100)
Jewish historian, he became a Pharisee. Lived in Rome for a time then later returned to his own country. Translated the Old Testament into Latin, which became the basis of the Vulgate, and wrote *Antiquities of the Jews*.

Lucian (*c.* AD 200)
Celebrated Greek philosophical and satirical writer, noted also for his eloquence. Appointed Registrar of Egypt by Marcus Aurelius.

Macrobius (AD 395–423)
Latin writer, philosopher and grammarian, supposed to have been a Greek. Wrote commentaries; the value of his work is largely in quotations from earlier writers.

Mandeville, Sir John (*c.* AD 1300–1372)
English traveller who spent thirty-four years travelling through the Middle East, Egypt, Palestine and China. Wrote a narrative of his voyages and the marvels seen, although many of these are regarded as greatly exaggerated or even fictitious.

Martial (*c.* AD 103)
Latin poet from Bilbilis in Spain, he lived in Rome most of his life and is said to have visited Athens.

Nicander (*c.* 135 BC)
Greek poet, grammarian and physician from a family of the hereditary priesthood of Apollo at Colophon. A voluminous writer, but only two of his works survive. His long poem *Theriala* had as its subject the nature of venomous animals and the wounds they inflict.

Oppian (2nd century AD)
The name of two Greek poets, formerly thought to be one poet but now accepted as the work of two different people of Cilicia. There were poems on fishing, hunting and bird-catching.

Origen (*c.* AD 185–254)
Early Greek Father of the Christian Church. He lived in Alexandria but made journeys to Rome, Antioch and Arabia. A prolific writer; among other works he wrote *Commentaries on the Scriptures.*

Ovid (43 BC–AD 17)
Roman poet. Among other books his *Metamorphoses* gave mythical accounts of miraculous transformations. Lived in Rome but was banished by Augustus to Tomi on the Euxine in AD 8; he died there.

Pausanias (2nd century AD)
Asiatic Greek, probably from Lydia. Historian and traveller. He lived at a time when the ancient cults still survived. In later works he gave accounts of the natives of the countries he had visited, detailing their rites and superstitions, and made notes of the native animals. His observations were regarded as accurate.

Pliny the Elder (*c.* AD 23–79)
Italian famous for his works on geography, mineralogy, astronomy and zoology. A keen observer of nature, his *Natural History* of 37 volumes is regarded as 'one of the most precious monuments left us by antiquity' (Cuvier); it is an encyclopaedia of ancient history and a record of popular superstitions and beliefs rather than of scientific observation. He died in the eruption of Vesuvius, being there to study that phenomenon.

Plutarch (*c.* AD 46–120)
Greek biographer, he lectured on philosophy in Rome and travelled through Greece and Egypt. Friendly with Lucan, Martial and Pliny the Younger. Wrote *Lives of Illustrious Men* and, from his observations in Egypt, *De Iside et Osiride.*

Polo, Marco (*c.* AD 1250–1323)
Venetian traveller to Central Asia, India and China, he lived at the court of Kubla-Khan for many years. On returning to Venice he was taken prisoner in the war with Genoa and while in prison wrote the first narrative of his adventures. On regaining his freedom he revised

and published the manuscript, which was one of the most interesting works on geography and customs.

Proclus (AD 410–485)
Philosopher of the Neo-Platonist school at Lycia. He wrote against Christianity, defending the ancient beliefs and customs, also wrote commentaries, including one on Hesiod's *Works and Days*. He died in Athens.

Solinus (3rd century AD)
Roman writer, compiled historical, geographical, natural history and religious commentaries. Followed Pliny slavishly. Wrote *Polyhistor*.

Statius (AD 45–96)
Roman poet. A native of Naples and favourite and court poet of Domitian.

Strabo (*c.* 63 BC–AD 24)
Greek geographer. He travelled widely in Egypt, Syria, Palestine and Greece. Wrote *Geography*, the only work of his to survive.

Suidas Greek lexicographer of whom little is known. Wrote historical and geographical works in about the 10th or 11th century.

Varro (116–27 BC)
Roman writer, antiquarian, historian, poet and naturalist. Supervised the Greek and Latin libraries in Rome. Wrote *De Rustica*. He is regarded as the most learned and voluminous of Roman writers.

Virgil (70–19 BC)
Celebrated Roman poet, born near Mantua but settled in Rome. He was later thought to have been a magician and his works were used in divination; the greatest of these was the *Aeneid*.

Xenophon (*c.* 430–359 BC)
Celebrated Athenian general, historian, philosopher and essayist. Follower of Socrates. Among other works and memorabilia he wrote essays on hunting and on various animals.
For Bestiaries and *Physiologus* see text.

Bibliography

Abbot, J., *The Keys of Power*, New Jersey, 1974.

Aelian, *De Natura Animalium*.

Ashe, Geoffrey, *The Ancient Wisdom*, MacMillan, 1977.

Aristotle, (D'Arcy Thompson, trans.), *Historia Animalium*, Oxford, 1910.

Barber, Richard, and Riches, Anne, *A Dictionary of Fabulous Beasts*, Baydell Press, 1971.

Barrett, Leonard, *The Sun and the Drum*, Sangsters, Jamaica, 1976.

Batchelor, John, *The Ainu and their Folklore*, London, 1901.

Beals, Carlton, *Land of the Mayas*, Abelard-Schuman, 1966.

Benson, Elizabeth P. (ed.), *The Cult of the Feline*, Dumbarton Oaks, 1970.

Berndt, R. M. (ed.), *Australian Aboriginal Anthropology*, Australia Institute, 1970.

Berridge, W. S., *Marvels of the Animal World*, London, 1921.

Bleakley, Alan, *Fruits of the Moon Tree*, Gateway, 1984.

Briggs, K. M., *The Anatomy of Puck*, R K P, 1959.

Bromwich, Rachael, *The Welsh Triads*, Cardiff, 1961.

Brown, Joseph Epes, *The Sacred Pipe*, University of Oklahoma, 1957.

Buck, C. H., *Faith, Fairs and Festivals of India*, Asian Publications, 1979.

Budge, A. E. Wallis, *Osiris and the Egyptian Resurrection*, London, 1911.

Burland, Cottie Arthur, *North American Indian Mythology*, Hamlyn, 1968.

Campbell, Joseph, *The Hero with a Thousand Faces*, Princeton University Press, 1949; Paladin, 1988.

--, *Oriental Mythology*, Penguin, 1962.

--, *The Mythic Image*, New York, 1975.

--, *Occidental Mythology*, Penguin, 1983.

--, *Historical Atlas of World Mythology*, Harper & Row, 1984.

Campbell, J. F., *The Celtic Dragon Myth*, 1911.

Canisdale, G. S., *Animals of the Bible*, Paternoster Press, 1970.

Carey, Margaret, *Myths & Legends of Africa*, Hamlyn, 1970.

Carpenter, Edward, *Pagan and Christian Creeds: their Origin and Meaning*, Allen & Unwin, 1920.

Cesaresco, Evelyn Martinengo, *The Place of Animals in Human Thought*, Fisher Unwin, 1909.

Charbonneau-Lassay, L., *Le Bestiaire du Christ*, Paris, 1940.

Clark, Rundle R. T. *Myth and Symbol in Ancient Egypt*, 1966.

Clodd, E., *Magic in Names and Other Things*, London, 1920.

Collins, A. H., *Symbolism of Animals and Birds in English Church Architecture*, 1915.

Cooper, J. C., *An Illustrated Encyclopaedia of Traditional Symbols*, Thames & Hudson, 1978.

--, *Symbolism, The Universal Language*, Aquarian, 1982.

--, *The Aquarian Dictionary of Festivals*, Aquarian, 1990.

Cottrell, Leonard, *Lost Worlds*, London, 1962.

Cowan, James, *The Dream Journey*, Temenos 7, London, 1984.

Creuzer, F. G., *Symbolik und Mythologie der Alten Völker*, Leipzig 1836–42

Cumont, Franz, *Les Religions Orientales dans le Paganisme Romains*, Paris, 1906.

Cushing, F. H., *Zuni Fetishes*, K C Publications, 1883.

Dale-Green, Patricia, *The Dog*, Hart Davis, 1966.

Davidson, H. R. E., *Pagan Scandinavia*, Thames & Hudson, 1967.

Davis, F. Hadland, *Myths & Legends of Japan*, Harrap, 1919.

Deane, J. B., *The Worship of the Serpent*, London, 1830.

Deren, Maya, *The Divine Horseman*, Thames & Hudson, 1953.

Diodorus Siculus, *Historical Library*.

Doré, Henri, *Researches into Chinese Superstitions*, Shanghai, 1914.

Douglas, Norman, *Birds & Beasts of the Greek Anthology*, London, 1928.

Eliade, Mircea, *Shamanism*, R K P, 1964.

Elkin, A. P., *Studies in Australian Totemism*, Sydney, 1938.

Elworthy, F. T., *Horns of Honour*, John Murray, 1900.

Evans, G. P., *Animal Symbolism in Ecclesiastical Architecture*, Heinemann, 1896.

Farbridge, M. H., *Studies in Biblical and Semitic Symbolism*, New York, 1927.

Ferguson, G. W., *Signs and Symbols in Christian Art*, New York, 1954.

Fox-Davies, Arthur C., *The Art of Heraldry: An Encyclopaedia of Armory*, London, 1904.

Frankland, Edward, *The Bear in Britain*, London, 1944.

Frazer, J. G., *Totemism and Exogamy*, MacMillan, 1910.

Gardner, James (ed.), *Faiths of the World*, Edinburgh.

Gibson, Frank, *Superstitions About Animals*, London, 1904.

Glueck, N., *Deities and Dolphins*, Cassell, 1966.

Goldsmith, Elizabeth, *Ancient Pagan Symbols*, London, 1929.

Goodenough, Edwin R., *Jewish Symbolism of the Graeco-Roman*

Period, vols. I–IV, New York, 1953–4.

Gould, Charles, *Mythical Monsters*, Allen & Co, 1886.

Guénon, René, *Symbols Fondamentaux de la Science Sacrée*, Gallimard, 1962.

Guerber, H. A., *Myths and Legends of the Middle Ages*, Harrap, 1909.

––, *Myths of the Norsemen*, Harrap, 1919.

Gurney, O. R., *The Hittites*, Allen Lane, 1975.

Hall, James, *Dictionary of Subjects and Symbols in Art*, Murray, 1974.

Handy, E. S. C., *Polynesian Religion*, Honolulu, 1927.

Hausman, Gerard, *Meditations with Animals: A Native American Bestiary*, Bear and Co., 1986.

Henderson, J. L., *The Wisdom of the Serpent*, Ambassador, 1963.

Hentze, Carl, *Mythes et Symboles Lunaires*, Antwerp, 1932.

Herodotus, (J. A. Evans, ed.), *The Penguin Herodotus*, 1941.

Hesiod, *Works and Days*.

Highbarger, E. L., *The Gates of Dreams*, Baltimore, 1940. (Archaeological Examination of Virgil's *Aeneid*, VI).

Hocart, A. M., *The Progress of Man*, Methuen, 1933.

Hood, Sinclair, *The Minoans*, Thames & Hudson, 1977.

Hooke, S. H., *Babylonian and Assyrian Religion*, Hutchinson, 1953.

Howey, M. Oldfield, *The Cat in the Mystery Religions and Magic*, New York, 1956.

Hultkrantz, Ake, *Attitudes to Animals in Soshoni Indian Religion*, Studies in Comparative Religion, 1970.

Hunt, R., *Popular Romances of the West of England*, London, 1930.

Ingersoll, *Birds in Legend, Fable and Folklore*, London, 1923.

James, E. O., *Prehistoric Religion*, Thames & Hudson, 1957.

James, T. G. H., *Myths and Legends of Ancient Egypt*, Hamlyn, 1970.

Julius Caesar, *De Bello Gallico*.

Karsten, Rafael, *The Civilizations of the South American Indians*, London, 1926.

––, *The Origins of Religion*, London, 1935.

Kerényi, Karl, *Essays on the Science of Mythology*, London, 1950.

Kramer, S. (ed.), *Mythologies of the Ancient World*, New York, 1961.

Krappe, A. H., *The Sources of Folklore*, Methuen, 1930.

Lang, Andrew, *Custom and Myth*, London, 1884.

Langdon, S. H., *Semitic Mythology*, Boston, 1931.

Lawson, J. C., *Modern Greek Folklore and Ancient Greek Religion*, Cambridge University Press, 1910.

Leitch, Barbara A., *The Concise Dictionary of Indian Tribes of North America*, Reference Publications, 1979.

Levy-Bruhl, L., *Primitives and the Supernatural*, New York, 1936 (reprinted 1973).

Lissner, Ivar, *Man, God and Magic*, Cape, 1961.

Lum, Peter, *Fabulous Beasts*, Thames & Hudson, 1952.

MacCulloch, J. A., *The Religion of the Ancient Celts*, Edinburgh, 1911.

MacKenzie, D. A., *Teutonic Myth and Legend*, London, 1912.

MacQueen, J. G., *The Hittites*, Thames & Hudson, 1975.

Markdale, J., *Celtic Civilization*, Paris, 1976.

Mbiti, John S., *African Religions and Philosophy*, Heinemann, 1969.

McKay, J. G., *The Deer Cult and the Deer Goddess of the Ancient Caledonians*, Transactions of the Folklore Society, vol. XLIII, 1932.

Mead, G. R. S., *Orpheus*, Madras, 1896.

Nilsson, M. P., *Greek Popular Religion*, New York, 1946.

Oesterley, W. O. E., *The Sacred Dance*, Oxford University Press, 1923.

Ovid, *Metamorphosis*.

Petrucci, R., *La Philosophie de la Nature dans l'Art d'Extrême Orient*, Paris, 1910.

Piggott, Stuart, *The Druids: Ancient People and Places*, Thames & Hudson, 1968.

Pliny, *Natural History*.

Plutarch, *De Iside et Osiride*.

Post, Laurens van de, *Testament to the Bushmen*, Viking, 1984.

Powell, T. G. E., *The Celts*, Thames & Hudson, 1958.

Radcliffe-Brown, A. R., *Structures and Function in Primitive Society*, London, 1952.

Radin, Paul, *The Story of the North American Indians*, John Murray, 1928.

--*The Trickster*, R K P, 1956.

Ransome, Hilda M., *The Sacred Bee in Ancient Times and Folklore*, Allen & Unwin, 1927.

Reed, A. W., *Maori Myth and Legend*, Reed, NZ, 1972.

Reinach, S., *Cultes, Mythes et Religions*, Paris, 1908.

Ringgren, H., and Ström, A. V., *Religions of Mankind*, Fortress Press, 1967

Roberts, Melva J., *Dreamtime Heritage*, Rigby, 1975.

Robin, P. Ansell, *Animal Lore in English Literature*, John Murray, 1932.

Ross, Anne, *Pagan Celtic Britain*, Cardinal, 1974.

Rout, E. A., *Maori Symbolism*, Kegan Paul, 1926.

Sams, Jamie, and Carson, David, *Medicine Cards*, Bear and Co., New Mexico, 1988.

Sejourné, Laurette, *Burning Water*, New York, 1958.

Shepard, Odell, *The Lore of the Unicorn*, Allen & Unwin, 1930.

Sillar, F. C., and Myler, R. M., *The Symbolic Pig*, London and Edinburgh, 1961.

Smith, Elliot G., *The Evolution of the Dragon*, Manchester, 1919.

Spence, Lewis, *The Myths and Legends of the North American Indians*, Harrap, 1917.

--, *The Gods of Mexico*, Allen & Unwin, 1923.

--, *Myths and Legends of Ancient Egypt*, Harrap, 1930.

Spence, Lewis, and Edwardes, M., *A Dictionary of Non-Classical Mythology*, Dent, 1923.

Stretlow, T. G. H., *Australia, Religions of the Present*, vol. II, Leiden, 1971.

Sullivan, L. E. (ed.), *Native American Religions*, MacMillan, 1989.

Talbot, P. Amoury, *Tribes of the Niger Delta*, Sheldon Press, 1972.

Thompson, D'Arcy W., *Greek Birds*, Oxford University Press, 1936.

Topsell, E., *The History of Four-footed Beasts and Serpents*, London, E. Cotes, 1658.

Toynbee, J. M. C., *Animals in Roman Life and Art*, Thames & Hudson, 1973.

Tristram, H. B., *The Natural History of the Bible*, London, 1867.

Van Marle, Raimond, *Iconographie de l'Art Profane au Moyen Age et de la Renaissance*, Hague, 1931.

Vinycomb, John, *Fictitious and Symbolic Creatures in Art*, London, 1906.

Vissner, M. W., *The Dragon in China and Japan*, Amsterdam, 1913.

Vries, A. de, *Dictionary of Symbols and Images*, Amsterdam, 1974.

Waters, Frank, *Book of the Hopi*, Ballantine, 1963.

Werner, E. T. C., *A Dictionary of Chinese Mythology*, New York, 1961.

White, T. H., *The Book of Beasts*, Cape, 1954.

Whitlock, Ralph, *In Search of Lost Gods*, Phaidon, 1979.

Wilder, Joseph, *Psychic Pets*, Dent, 1980.

Willetts, R. G., *Everyday Life in Ancient Crete*, Batsford, 1969.

Willetts, William, *Foundations of Chinese Art*, Thames & Hudson, 1963.

Zimmer, Heinrich, *Myths and Symbols in Indian Art and Civilization*, London and New York, 1946.

Also available . . .

The Aquarian Dictionary of
Festivals

J. C. Cooper

Despite the great divides of continents and oceans, early civilizations were remarkably similar in their beliefs, inspired by common themes – birth and death, moon and sun, gods and heroes. Around the world man devised different ways of demonstrating corporate delight and thanks, hope and grief – through rituals, carnivals, fêtes, even sacrifice. This new book brings together ceremonies and customs from both the oldest civilizations, including Babylonian, Chinese, Greek and Inca, and the major religions of today, including Hindu, Sikh, Hebrew and Christian.

The Aquarian Dictionary of Festivals is a highly informative and accessible guide which takes us on a fascinating journey to every corner of the globe, describing in detail festivals ancient and modern, together with a variety of subjects associated with them and their performances. Placing emphasis on myth, religion and custom, J. C. Cooper's enlightening entries demonstrate how many of today's fairs, fêtes and holidays, so often taken for granted and associated with quite different occasions, are in fact direct descendants of rites and celebrations based on the primitive urges and instincts of ancient tribes and religions. Furthermore, this illustrated sourcebook will open up a world of forgotten feast days which people today can preserve for future generations.

The Aquarian Guide to
African Mythology

Jan Knappert

Africa: the most distinctive land mass on the surface of the earth. Yet for all its majesty it is a country whose historical and religious wealth remains a mystery to all but a very few of Western observers. How many people know anything at all about pre-Colonial Africa?

The Aquarian Guide to African Mythology is the first comprehensive overview of the beliefs, myths and cosmology of African peoples. It deals not only with traditional stories woven around a pantheon of gods and mythical figures but also with legends, fables and more general subjects that played a part in African mythology and African life. The wide range of entries include religious concepts, prophets, the best-known tribes, mystical phenomena, spirits and demons, and the many animals that played such a large part in African mythology.

Dr Jan Knappert's alphabetical guide is founded on his many years of personal experience in Africa. Its very accessible style makes it ideal not only as a reference work for students of anthropology but as a sample for general readers wishing to dip in and be informed on any subject that appeals to them. The book is fully cross-referenced and is illustrated with examples of African art. Wherever the reader opens it, he or she will be informed, stimulated to further thought and study, and entertained.

Greek Mythology

Richard Stoneman

Zeus and Athena, Heracles and Achilles, Delphi and Olympia, Medusa and the Minotaur . . . the stuff of the oldest and most powerful mythological tradition in Europe. As familiar to most people as the characters and events in the Bible, the great legendary heroes and stories of classical Greece are a unique legacy, their traditions having influenced the art, literature and culture of Western Europe like no other. Yet for all the colourful sources that exist – from Homer downwards – it is still difficult for the enthusiast to piece together a coherent picture of the genuine uncorrupted traditions of Greek mythology.

Greek Mythology is the key to the jigsaw. Including in dictionary form all the major figures of Greek mythology, the book provides a handy but comprehensive guide for newcomers and offers further help to those who want to learn more. Deliberately excluding the Roman myths which can blur the true image of the Greek heritage, Richard Stoneman covers the gods, heroes and men, places, mythical creatures and religious terminology that make up the whole gamut of Greek mythology. Complete with illustrations based on contemporary Greek art, the book is also the first to encompass both classical and post-classical folklore and legend, bringing in Alexander the Great, vampires and the terrible kallikantzaroi, which will broaden the vocabulary of all who are interested in the wealth that is Greek mythology.

Chinese Mythology

Derek Walters

China is a vast and geographically varied country, and one that has been subject to many cultural influences, from Hindu and Buddhist India to the Mongol hordes. In addition, it is made up of many different peoples, and its legends and myths are consequently highly diverse.

Thanks to a long literary tradition kept alive by record-keepers and poets, the myths and legends of ancient China have been preserved, often in several different versions. In many cases, too, they have survived in popular custom and belief right up to the present day. Here, factual history blends with legend and a pantheon of gods: actual emperors become immortals; immortals disguise themselves and mingle with mankind; richly conceived concepts of Heaven and Hell blend with Buddhist, Taoist and Confucian doctrine and with the older beliefs of shamanism.

Derek Walters is an expert on several aspects of Chinese culture and has written widely on subjects ranging from Chinese astrology to Feng Shui. His alphabetical guide will be invaluable to the student and historian, whether looking up a particular subject or just dipping in, and will stimulate and entertain the general reader.

DICTIONARY OF FESTIVALS	0 85030 848 8	£7.99	☐
AFRICAN MYTHOLOGY	0 85030 885 2	£7.99	☐
GREEK MYTHOLOGY	0 85030 934 4	£7.99	☐
CHINESE MYTHOLOGY	1 85538 080 3	£7.99	☐
NATIVE AMERICAN MYTHOLOGY	1 85538 028 5	£7.99	☐
BRITISH & IRISH MYTHOLOGY	1 85030 605 1	£7.99	☐
INDIAN MYTHOLOGY	1 85538 040 4	£8.99	☐
PACIFIC MYTHOLOGY	1 85538 133 8	£8.99	☐

All these books are available from your local bookseller or can be ordered direct from the publishers.

To order direct just tick the titles you want and fill in the form below:

Name: _____

Address: _____

_____

_____ Postcode: _____

Send to: Thorsons Mail Order, Dept 31T, HarperCollins*Publishers*, Westerhill Road, Bishopbriggs, Glasgow G64 2QT.

Please enclose a cheque or postal order or your authority to debit your Visa/Access account —

Credit card no: _____

Expiry date: _____

Signature: _____

— to the value of the cover price plus:

UK & BFPO: Add £1.00 for the first book and 25p for each additional book ordered.

Overseas orders including Eire: Please add £2.95 service charge. Books will be sent by surface mail but quotes for airmail despatches will be given on request.

24 HOUR TELEPHONE ORDERING SERVICE FOR ACCESS/VISA CARDHOLDERS — TEL: **041 772 2281**.